Surfing Britain

Chris Nelson and Demi Taylor

The forever changing coastline and scenery, from beach to reef to point break; a backdrop of cliffs, sandy beaches or a bird's-eye view of the industrial steel business that hugs part of the coastline. Also getting perfect waves with just your friends sharing it with you. That's what makes our surf scene special.

Former British Champion, Brad Hockridge

Star breaks...

⭐1 **Lynmouth**
▸▸ p42.

⭐2 **Fistral Beach**
▸▸ p58.

⭐3 **Porthleven**
▸▸ p76.

⭐4 **Thurso East**
▸▸ p166.

⭐5 **Crab Island**
▸▸ p227.

Atlantic Ocean

North Sea

Lewis
Stornoway
North Harris
South Harris
Ullapool
North Uist
Skye
Inverness
South Uist
Rum
Aberdeen
Mull
Oban
Perth
Dundee
Jura
Islay
Glasgow
Arran
Edinburgh
SCOTLAND
North Channel

Shetland
Lerwick
Orkney
Kirkwall
John O'Groats
Thurso

A9
A835
A96
A9
A82
M8
M74

Carlisle
Kendal
Isle of Man
Lancaster
Blackpool
Liverpool
Bradford
Leeds
Manchester
Sheffield
Lincoln
Derby
Nottingham
Newcastle upon Tyne
Gateshead
Darlington
York
Kingston upon Hull

A1
A19 A171
M62
M6
M1

Anglesey
Caernarfon
Snowdon
Aberystwyth
Fishguard
WALES
Swansea
Cardiff

Birmingham
Coventry
Leicester
Peterborough
Northampton
Cambridge
Milton Keynes
Luton
ENGLAND
Cheltenham
Gloucester
Oxford
Bristol
Bath
Reading
London
Ipswich
Norwich

A5
M40
M11
M5
M4
M25
M3

Taunton
Newquay
Exeter
Plymouth
Penzance
Isles of Scilly
Southampton
Bournemouth
Isle of Wight
Portsmouth
Brighton & Hove
Dover

A40
A30

English Channel

N
50 km
50 miles

Motorway
A Rd
B Rd
Minor Rd
Airports

Sometimes it's hard to dispel the myth that there is no surf in Britain. When people see British surfers entering the water, they assume we're making the most of a bad lot, putting up with our paltry rollers between trips to tropical locations and serious waves, killing time before another fix of the real thing. Yet Britain is a great place to be a surfer. No British city is more than two hours away from the nearest stretch of a 11,075-mile coastline and, with waves breaking on all four shores, our island is one of the most flexible surf destinations in Europe. So you see, British surfers don't have to venture overseas to find a real wave; we have our very own peaks to ride, peaks that challenge the world's best: Scotland's Thurso East, The Cove in Yorkshire, The Pole in Wales, Cornwall's Leven. Oh yeah, and some of the world's best surfers just happen to be British, too.

Best time to visit: **Autumn** Pumping swells, warm weather and warm water.

Britain rating

Surf
★★★

Cost of living
★★★★★

Nightlife
★★★

Accommodation
★★

Places to visit
★★★

Contents

Essentials

England

Scotland

Cover image
Josh Ward at his home break, North Cornwall by *Kirstin Prisk*
Title page image
Compton Bay, Isle of Wight by *Roger Powley*

Wales

Map symbols

Motorway		City/town (extent)	
A road		Ferry route	
B road		▲ Mountain	
Minor road		♦ National park/	
A882 Road number		wildlife reserve	
✈ Airport		○ Place of interest	
⁂ Archaeological site		★ Star surf break	
○ City/town		❶ Surf break	

① RNLI Beach Lifeguard seasonally patrolled beaches. For full, up-to-date listings including patrol dates check out www.rnli.org.uk/beachlifeguards

Beach Lifeguards

Sleeping

L	over £70/€100	**C**	£40-49/€60-74	**F**	£15–19/€20-29
A	£60-70/€90-100	**D**	£30-39/€45-59	**G**	less than £15/€20
B	£50-59/€75-89	**E**	£20-29/€30-44		

Prices are based on the cost for a double room in high season

Wetsuits

Winter
December - February

Spring
March - May

Summer
June - August

Autumn
September - November

Contents

CHRIS GRIFFITHS

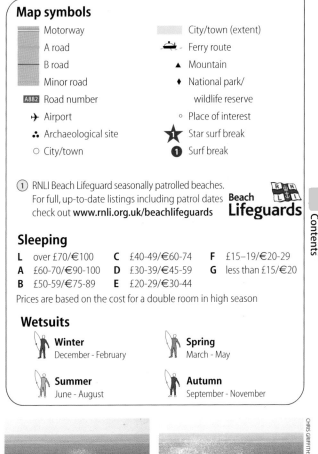

About the book

In the past 20 years the surfing lifestyle has changed unbelievably. Surfers were once a virtually unknown cult that lurked in semi-secret pockets around Britain's coast. Boards were ordered in an almost clandestine manner from foam-covered magicians like Nigel Semmens in Newquay, John Purton in South Wales and Andrew Harrison in the Northeast. Most surf shops were tiny Tardises run by grizzled sea dogs who would bail for the beach at the first sniff of surf. Back then a trip to Newquay was like stepping into a candy store. All those boards and wetsuits, ranges of neon 'surfwear', more stickers than you could cover your board with and new-fangled accessories like deck grip. A trip to Britain's 'surf-city' was an inspiring event. Today there are surf outlets on every high street in every town, the length and breadth of Britain. Being a surfer used to set you apart. Today surfing is seen as a mainstream 'sport'. At contests surfers no longer smoke between rounds – they have become well-paid, professional athletes. Our lifestyle has taken on a new identity.

There are many well-articulated arguments about the drawbacks to this surf boom; increased numbers in the line-ups is probably the most commonly voiced. We see this down side every day. Crowded peaks. Beach car parks full whenever there's a swell. A loss of etiquette as people try to gorge themselves on waves during their weekend at the coast. There are always going to be those who want to go back to the good ol' days of empty breaks and leaky wetsuits

– most of us have those thoughts every time we look at our favourite spot, crowded again.

There is however an upside to this boom that isn't aired very often. The tools of our trade are improving. We now ride better boards than ever – shapers get more feedback from the increased number of consumers but also there is more competition in the market place. That same competition has kept board prices at a ridiculously low level, almost unchanged in 20 years. There are skilled shapers across the whole of Britain, crafting boards specifically designed with local conditions and breaks in mind, many of whom have taken the time to contribute to this guide. More consumers in the market place have also resulted in wetsuit companies investing in better technology so you can stay in the water for longer, and women finally have suits designed with women in mind. There are more surfers making a living from the lifestyle, providing services for other surfers. There are magazines to read, books to inspire us, films to watch and camps to visit. Travel is easier to more and more exotic destinations. Airlines actually have surfboard policies. Some even specifically cater to surfers. Perhaps most importantly of all, with increased competition in the line-up, we now surf better than ever. And in our desire to escape the crowds, we are going that extra mile and striking out to discover new breaks.

From the earliest days of waveriding, the social element and the storytelling have been a central part of surf culture. The reliving of great sessions, epic waves or hideous wipe-outs are the central theme of every post surf drinks session which is where the idea for the Surfers' tales came in. Surfing in Britain is as varied as the people who surf in Britain

Porthtowan ▸▸p61

– one man's disappointingly mellow roller is another man's idea of longboarding perfection; one woman's busy city beach is another's thriving urban surf scene. By spending time talking to surfers in every destination – from local rippers to national surf stars – we have tried to reflect the unique characteristics of every destination and every break, giving you an honest insight into surfing Britain. Just as each region has its advantages and drawbacks, so every surfer is unique, striving for something a little different from every session and trip. We have more than our fair share of grinding reefs, mellow peaks, peeling points and urban breaks. Although we have covered the length of the coastline in detail, anyone with knowledge of their local secret spots will be able to judge this guide not just by the breaks we have included but also by the secrets we have kept. Secret spots are the Holy Grail of surfing – once they've been blown, you cannot make them secret again and, like the Grail, it's often more about the quest than the discovery. These are not the only breaks or places to eat, drink and sleep in Britain. We are a small island with a massive coastline of potential. Go. Explore.

Acknowledgements

There are many people we would like to thank for contributing their thoughts, tales, wisdom, images and time to this project. A big thank you, as always, to **The Gill** for his invaluable input, enthusiasm and ability to sniff out a swell days before it arrives. Thanks also goes to Albert Harris whose excellent **ODD** boards have taken us through years of surf exploration. A special thank you to Roger Powley for his Isle of Wight insight and images. Our appreciation also goes out to Sam Lamiroy, Lee Bartlett and Alan Stokes who made the time to contribute despite their tight schedules, as well as to Dominique Kent-Munroe and Antonia Atha who've been flying the flag for the ladies. Thanks also goes to Chris Griffiths of **Guts Surfboards**, Chops of **Beach Beat**, Jools at **Gufstream**, Pete and Mark at **Lindsell**, Martin McQueenie at **MCQ** and John Isaac at **Revolver** for their insight into board design. We would also like to acknowledge the contributions of Isaac Kibblewhite, Simon Tucker, Chris French, Colm Garrett, Brad Hockridge, Dan Harris, George Sohl, Spout, Alf Alderson, Carwyn Williams, Greg Owen, Turtle, Robyn Davies, Claire King, Richie Hopson, Craig Gledhill, Sarah Thorowgood,

Joe Moran at **PitPilot**, Mark at **Eastcoastsurf**, Mike at **Surfriders.co.uk**, Ester Spears, Scott Wicking, Stu Norton, James Stentiford, Alex Williams, Gary Rogers and Nick Noble of **Saltburn Surfshop**, Sam Boex, James Hendy, Adam Tarry, James at **Sharkbait**, Joe Truman, Nick Whittle, Gail Sheath, Jez at **Small Planet**, Andrew Harrison and Ben Pepler at Zero Gravity, Roger and Tommo of **Secret Spot**, Emily Caulfield, Eloise Taylor, Helen Gilchrist of **Stranger Magazine**, Gary Knight, Al McKinnon, Minzie, John Craze, Steve Wills and Philippa Thompson of the **RNLI**, JB and Tom at **Ocean Sports**, Drustan Ward, Robin Kent, Damian Prisk, Turnip Ward, Steve Bunt of **Best Ever Surfboards**, Sean Lascelles, Nick at **Animal**, Andy Hill of **Troggs Surf Shop**, Mark Lumsden of **Cold Rush**, Chris Noble, Andy Bain, Sam Christopherson at **C2C**, George Noble of **Broch Surf Club**, Mark Cox, Ian Masson, Jamie Blair at **Clan**, Derek McCloud of **Hebridean Surf**, Mike Fordham, Chris Gregory, Pat Kieran, Suds of **Wild Diamond Surf**, Tony Marsh and Damon Hewlett. Thanks to Josh Ward for his front cover aerial and to Kirstin Prisk for capturing it on film.

Special thanks go to Damien Tate and Joe Traynor for technical support and Sarah, Maisie, Bryony and Bron for moral support.

We would like to say a big thank you to the whole Footprint team. Footprint epitomizes the true spirit of travel. They are honest, have a wealth of knowledge and are always excited about new projects. We would especially like to thank Laura Dixon, Pat Dawson, Alan Murphy, Debbie Wylde, Rob Lunn, Tim Jollands, Liz Taylor, Angus Dawson, Sarah Sorensen and the rest of the Footprint crew.

About the authors

When they're not exploring, **Chris Nelson** and **Demi Taylor** check the Cornish surf from their bedroom window every morning. Chris grew up surfing the frigid reefs of northeast England. He founded and edited two of the UK's most influential boardsports magazines – *Asylum* and *Freeride*, spending almost a decade interviewing surfing's heroes and anti-heroes. He is a freelance writer, but more importantly he's a sucker for a right-hand point break. Demi has travel in her blood – her childhood spanned four continents. She caught her first wave in '92 and has been hooked on surfing ever since. After handling the UK communications for the world's largest surf brand, she left to become a freelance writer and photographer and to spend more time surfing those left-hand beach breaks she loves so much. Together they have written *How to be a Surfer* and Footprint's *Surfing Europe*.

quiksilver

nathan phillips

quiksilver.com

Dave Young, St Agnes
▸▸ *p 59*

Essentials

Surfing Britain

"The UK surf scene is unique because of many factors. The chill, the regular North Atlantic storms, the continental shelf, the fact that there are so many A-grade waves hidden around its coasts and world-class days on offer to those who seek. Small winding roads, hot pasties and fish and chips. Warm beer helps, too." Alex Dick-Read, Editor, The Surfer's Path

In the early days of European surfing, the British took to the water with typical enthusiasm and determination. They watched visiting Aussie lifeguards on their Malibu boards and were soon building their own. With an amateur gusto and huge determination, Britain produced the continent's pioneering surf brands and dominated the competition scene. Brands like Bilbo, Tiki, and Gul sprang up in the Southwest, and surfers like Rodney Sumpter, Nigel Semmens and Ted Deerhurst were the best in Europe. In the Northeast Nigel Veitch charged the cold North Sea breaks and headed onto the world tour, before returning home to inspire a new generation of local surfers. While it was inevitable that the rest of Europe, with their warmer climates, better organization and 'youth infrastructure' would catch up, the British have managed to build on these strong foundations.

Despite the harsh winters, Britain has the second largest surfing community in Europe, with standards to match. A distinct lack of local WQS events has made it harder for British surfers to progress onto the upper levels of contest surfing, but that's not to say British riders don't compete on an international scale. Many riders, such as Alan Stokes, Sam Lamiroy, Nathan Phillips and Robyn Davies, are doing just that, with typically British grit and determination. Nowhere is this spirit better personified than in Russell Winter, the first European to make it on to the WCT. Without a big-money sponsor, Russell not only qualified for the WCT, he then managed to requalify against all the odds. It is this bulldog spirit that infuses the British surf scene. You can see it in those learning to surf, soldiering through their first winter without the luxury of a warm wetsuit; taking to the waters all around the British coastline on those bitterly cold winter's days in a 3/2

5 star breaks

① **Lynmouth** Long, long walling left-hand point in stunning north Devon. ➡p42.

② **Fistral Beach** Just because it's well known, doesn't mean it isn't a fantastic beach break. ➡p58.

③ **Porthleven** This is a world class reef that offers heavy, powerful barrels to only the best surfers. ➡p76.

④ **Thurso East** If you sat down and designed a perfect right-hand reef, you could do no better than this. Flat, slate reef, dry hair paddle out and long, hollow waves. ➡p166.

⑤ **Crab Island** Quality right-hand reef in the Welsh heartland. ➡p227.

or an ill-fitting 4/3, but kept warm by the sheer stoke of surfing. That spirit is the reason why British surfing is unique.

Climate

When it comes to climate and weather, Britain is world class. The British are a people obsessed with weather because they have so much of it – as an island off the coast of continental Europe, Britain is exposed to maritime, continental and Arctic weather systems, which roll across the country at regular intervals. Maritime systems ferry wet weather in off the oceans; continental weather systems filter in from mainland

MARK LUMSDEN

Chris Noble

Europe and can bring dry weather; while freezing Arctic systems can push down cold northerly winds bringing overnight snow and ice.

For the surfer, there are a mixture of benefits and drawbacks to this. Outside the summer season there is a fairly consistent stream of low pressures feeding swell to the Atlantic or North Sea coasts, but the accompanying wind and weather can be less than favourable. Cornwall picks up loads of swell but, with dominant trade winds from the southwest, can suffer from onshore winds. The Northeast is predominantly offshore, but is less consistent. Scotland has a wave-rich and undulating coastline that means that there is usually somewhere to surf, but in the winter the lack of daylight and cold temperatures make surfing a sport reserved for the seriously committed.

Don't get stuck in one place, see more and be rewarded. Check the Irish, Welsh and Scottish reefs and enjoy the Cornish beaches and party scene, go camping; save your cash and have more fun.

Joe Moran, Editor, Pit Pilot

Best seasons to visit

In the **summer**, Britain can be a surprisingly warm and pleasant country. Devon and Cornwall can have long sunny days with water temperatures high enough for shorties or 2 mm spring suits. There can even be years when a consistent stream of lows filter through a steady supply of small, summer waves. Summer also sees the WQS Rip Curl Pro roll into Newquay, and the beaches are jammed with beginners and holidaymakers. Scotland and Wales receive less swell in the summer, but can still have regular waves. The north coast of Scotland has the added bonus of virtually constant daylight in June, allowing maximum use of any summer swells on offer. Unfortunately for the east coast, the low pressures tend to dry up during the summer, and prolonged flat spells can drive the local surf community to near insanity. Luckily for them, autumn is always just around the corner.

For British surfers, **autumn** is a glorious time of year. The days are still long, the water is still relatively warm, the peak swell season kicks in and the tourists go home. In September

ANIMAL

Alan Stokes, British champion, tearing up summer waves

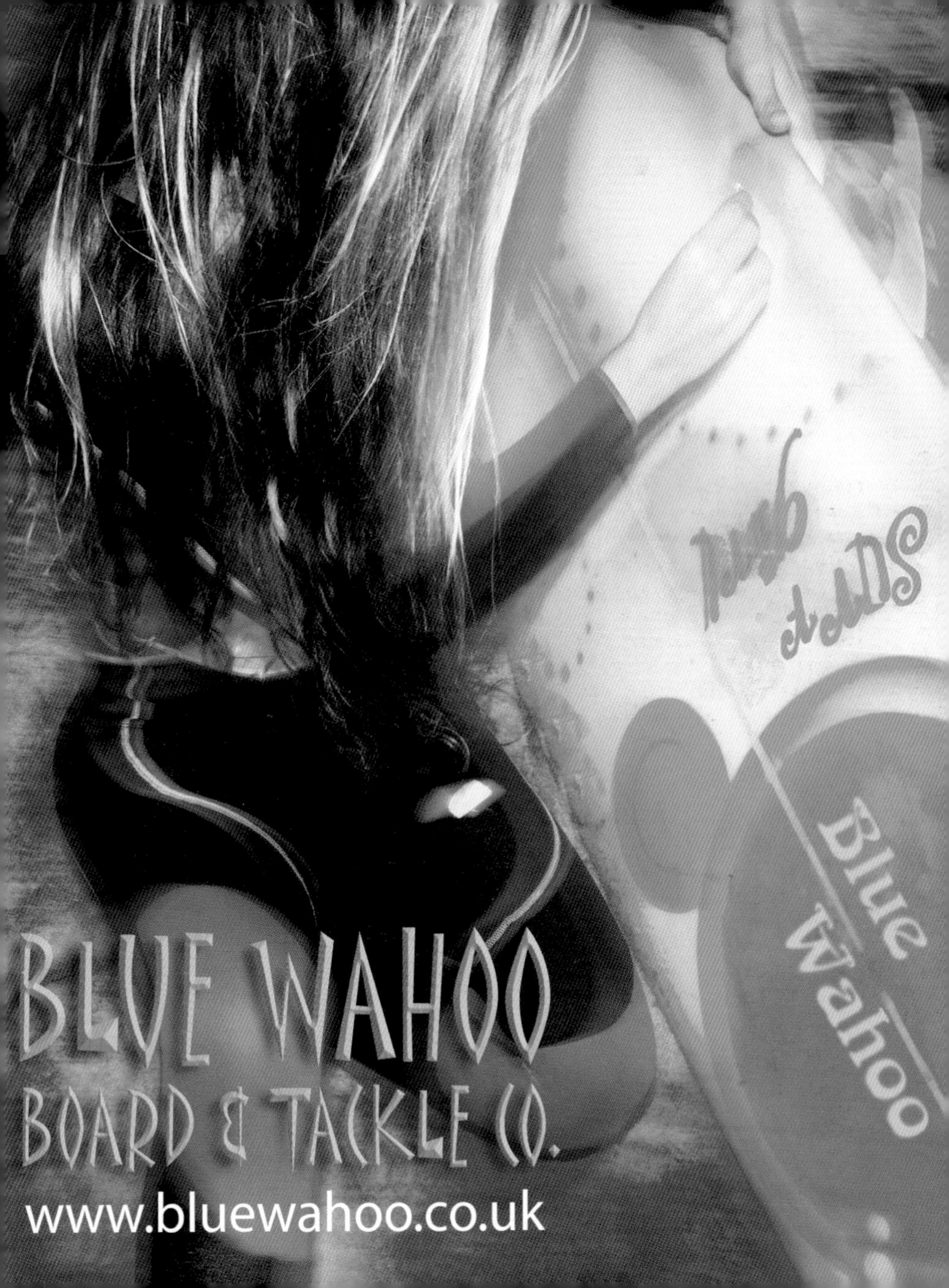
BLUE WAHOO
BOARD & TACKLE CO.
www.bluewahoo.co.uk
Blue Wahoo

Low Pressure Chart

Low pressures in the northern hemisphere spin in an anti-clockwise direction, with the wind pushing swell out from the centre.

A low in the slot (L1) will push swell down the North Sea, hitting Northern Scotland first, then the East Coast, Yorkshire, East Anglia and Joss Bay. (L2) is a classic North Atlantic low pressure. Swell will hit southern Wales, Devon and north and south Cornwall. (L3) will push southwesterly swell up towards north and west Wales, south Wales, Devon, Cornwall and along the Channel coast. A low that tracks to the south of Britain can sit in position (L4) in the southern reaches of the North Sea pushing a southeasterly or easterly swell all the way up the eastern seaboard of Britain. Check out the latest charts on www.bbc.co.uk/weather

and October, daytime temperatures can still be in the high teens or low twenties and the water is a mild 15-18ºC. The high pressures sitting over Europe force the low pressures to the north, funnelling well-travelled groundswells into the Atlantic coastlines. The lows tracking past Iceland send the north shore of Scotland into overdrive, and as soon as the depression passes across the top of the North Sea, the legendary reefs of the Northeast reawaken, as do the dormant beaches of the Norfolk coastline. In the autumn season, for many British surfers there is nowhere else they would rather be.

The **winter** and **spring** seasons can be a harsh time. Swells pump through the cold months, but water temperatures plummet, and air temperatures can regularly dip below freezing. It can be a time of 6-mm suits, hoods, gloves and booties. And although the surf may be classic,

few travelling surfers ever venture here to see it and many British surfers seek winter waves in warmer climes.

One thing the British climate has given to local surfers is a great sense of appreciation. During good swells, the British will cram in as many sessions as possible, and when travelling they appreciate any good waves they come across, never taking their next session for granted.

Good charts for surf

A classic chart for the Atlantic coasts of Cornwall, Devon and Wales would be a deep low pressure tracking slowly across the upper North Atlantic. This will pump swell into the westerly breaks for two or three days. As the low tracks above Scotland, the north shore should spring to life, and if the depression carries on tracking above the North Sea and sits over the Norwegian seaboard for a couple of days, the northeast of England will turn on. For the south coast a low sitting in the Bay of Biscay will pump swell into southern Cornwall. The breaks to the east – the Isle of Wight, Bournemouth and Brighton — need a good, solid westerly swell from a low sitting out in the mid Atlantic.

Geography and breaks

Cornwall is a jagged mix of cliff and sandy beaches. Exposed to the pounding of the Atlantic, the slate, granite, and sandstone has eroded in a disjointed way to produce a complex coastline dotted with tiny coves, open bays and hidden reefs. **Devon** has a less rugged coastline and, where forest-covered cliffs fall into the sea, some excellent points. The beaches are powerful and consistent but the reefs are few and always busy.

The **northeast** coastline of England is one of the most interesting in Europe for the surfer. Here fingers of flat slate produce some very high quality reef breaks and long, winding points. Its orientation is such that in northerly swells it produces predominantly left-hand breaks. The beaches can be powerful and punchy and the fine sediments ensure the water resembles anything from a weak cup of tea to a pint of Newcastle Brown Ale.

The **south coast of England** is home to probably the most committed and stoked surfers in Britain. The swells that hit spots like Kimmeridge, the Isle of Wight, Bournemouth and Brighton are a signal for locals to drop everything and head for their favourite spot. These beaches and reefs can be infuriatingly fickle, some work for two hours before becoming unsurfable – but those two hours may have to last days or weeks before the next fix arrives.

The coastline of **Wales** offers great diversity. The undulating shore encompasses polluted urban breaks, classic rocky points, huge open sandy beaches, and stunningly beautiful, deserted coves.

But for sheer surf potential, it is difficult to beat the north shore of **Scotland**. The sheltered harbours of Caithness once shipped the local slabstone around the world, paving streets as far away as Argentina and Australia. Today the same slate geography paves the way for quality reefs and points that the region is so famous for. Neighbouring Sutherland has a completely different coastal landscape, one where imposing cliffs give way to deserted bays with golden sand and crystal-clear waters. Seals wait to ambush the leaping salmon in the peaty brown rivermouths while puffins shuttle back and forth between the sea and their underground burrows.

Stands out a mile!

Surfed a place called 'Nash Point': super-fast, super-hollow right-hander. One Sunday many years ago my friend Giles called round the house midday in October, freaking. I had seen the surf earlier, it was big but with light onshores. He had just got back from the beach screaming that the wind had turned northerly, the hurricane swell was peaking, it was just about to get to low tide and Nash would be going off. Sure enough, going off was an understatement. Along with Giles and myself were Greg Owen and Chris Chip. The waves were a perfect 6 ft and bigger but had walls on them as far as you could see. The Point was peeling mechanically with gaping barrels firing off for 200 yds. It looked like a perfect day at Off The Wall (Hawaii) minus the clear blue warm water but also minus the crowds. It was super hollow and big enough to get your heart racing. When you caught one and got to the bottom and managed to line yourself up for the freight train, you just had to stand tall and weave your way through a faultless barrel. That is one of the best surfing experiences I have ever had – surfing a few miles from home with your friends in waves that would be hard to beat anywhere in the world. F***ING AWESOME!

Welshman Brad Hockridge is a super charger and former British champion.

THE GILL

Board guide

In Britain, the surf can be just about as varied as it can get, ranging from 2-ft slop to stand up barrels. So when it comes to boards, flexibility is the name of the game. As the majority of the surf falls into the 3 to 4 ft category, a good small-wave board is a must, either a fish or thruster with a bit of extra volume. A good second board would be a flexible performance thruster for when the swells kick in and the waves pick up. The boards you see in each regional section are recommended by respected shapers with knowledge of the waves in that region and of shaping boards that work in those conditions. Dimensions vary depending on many factors – experience, size and personal preference. A good shaper should be more than happy to sit down and talk through an order to ensure you get exactly what you are looking for in a new custom board. Don't be afraid to ask. And as Chops Lascelles of Beachbeat Surfboards says: "You just need to be honest about your ability and what you want from a board. Then the shaper can produce a board that suits you and your style of surfing."

Former British champion, shaper and surf explorer Lee Bartlett talks us through his quiver for British waves:

Lee Bartlett: 5'7" and 11 st (70 kg)
▸▸ 5'11" x 18¼" x 2¼"   My normal board, a very soft rounded pin. It's good from knee-high to just over head-high waves. Very flat rocker to cope with flat spots on the waves.
▸▸ 6'1" x 18¼" x 2¼"   This is for better surf, good sucky waves, rounded pin, good from head-high up. Bit more rocker in the nose and tail still quite flat through the middle.
▸▸ 6'4" x 18¼" x 2¼"   This is for well overhead surf, bigger reef breaks, the kind of place you don't want to get caught inside. As before, a rounded pin. Not quite a banana rocker but it gives me drive without being too tracky.

Average Joe: 6'0" and 13 st (83 kg)
▸▸ 6'4" x 19" x 2½"   For smaller waves you might want to try a small swallow tail; make sure it has more volume than your normal board. A swallow tail gives the board a very quick feel to a turn but you also lose speed faster.
▸▸ 6'4" x 18¾" x 2½"   Try this board when your local beach is firing. A little less volume than your small wave board, this will help you cope with the extra speed you get from good waves. A squash tail is the norm for this kind of board.
▸▸ 6'4" x 18⅝" x 2⅜"   This will get you going on those speeding reef walls. It's narrower so you won't spin out when turning – it will feel real drivey. Try a rounded pin to do cutbacks like Taylor Knox.

Lee rides boards shaped by **MMY**, Beach Rd, Newquay, Cornwall, T01637 852101, www.mmyworld.com

Lee's quiver

Lee Bartlett

Dominique's quiver

Dominique Kent-Munroe, British longboard champion, gives us the long and the short of a classic women's board quiver

Growing backwards in time – the trend for 'Retro' boards in the UK by John Isaac, Revolver Surfboards

Thankfully we are past the stage where every shaper would try to stick a novice female surfer on a mini-mal and send them off to the white water. This is my recommendation for a three board quiver that will be flexible, maximize your water time and the fun you have in the water.

A **fish** is an excellent board to have in your arsenal. As it is wider, it allows you to catch more waves. The extra float increases your wave time.

Fish – PF Flyer 6'4"x19¼"x2⁵⁄₁₆" double wing
▸▸ Good for 2-3 ft summer, or punchy 1-2 ft waves in the Badlands.
▸▸ Can handle bigger surf, but means a later drop – use bigger fins.
▸▸ Excellent wave catcher which is like riding a skateboard.

A lot of people go too short too soon with a **shortboard** – consider an extra couple of inches to increase your wave-catching ability. Although it takes more effort than a shorter board to manoeuvre, it means I don't struggle catching waves. It allows me to surf rail-to-rail, with drawn out turns and solid manoeuvres, using the whole face of the wave.

Shortboard – Thruster 6'2"x18½"x2¼" rounded square tail
▸▸ Good in 3-4 ft plus surf – I had an excellent session at 6-ft Godrevy.
▸▸ Easy to paddle out and duck dive when there's a lot of water to negotiate.
▸▸ Good wave-catcher due to the length giving you the upper hand in busy line-ups.

A **longboard** has loads of float, getting you into waves early, making it an excellent choice for the summer. A different type of surfing to that on a shortboard, it really allows you to work on your style as it gives you more time to think about how you are moving.

Longboard – Mal 9'1" x 21¼" x 2¾" narrow tail
▸▸ Good up to 4 ft beach break (depending on paddle out), bigger on a point.
▸▸ A progressive board with a narrow tail, allowing me to ride it off the tail like a shortboard. (Manoeuvres take more effort, turns are more drawn out.)
▸▸ Not a classic nose-rider – the tail must be in the pocket to nose ride.

ⓘ Dominique is sponsored by **Beachbeat Surfboards**, St Agnes, Cornwall, T01872 553918, www.beachbeatsurfboards.co.uk.

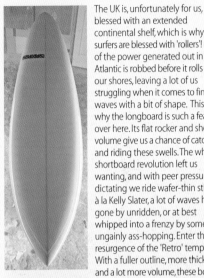

The UK is, unfortunately for us, blessed with an extended continental shelf, which is why UK surfers are blessed with 'rollers'! Most of the power generated out in the Atlantic is robbed before it rolls onto our shores, leaving a lot of us struggling when it comes to finding waves with a bit of shape. This is why the longboard is such a feature over here. Its flat rocker and sheer volume give us a chance of catching and riding these swells. The whole shortboard revolution left us wanting, and with peer pressure dictating we ride wafer-thin sticks à la Kelly Slater, a lot of waves have gone by unridden, or at best whipped into a frenzy by some ungainly ass-hopping. Enter the resurgence of the 'Retro' template. With a fuller outline, more thickness and a lot more volume, these boards catch a lot more waves, fly by those crumbly sections and put a lot more smiles on people's faces. Lets face it, isn't that why we do this?

6'8" Classic Pintail Single Fin
A good allround board for UK, it goes well in surf from 2-ft up to 6-ft plus. It draws such beautiful long lines & trims so well at speed.

Steve Lis /Skip Frye style fish 6'
And you thought Bonzers were fast!! The ultimate fun summer board, the classic fish is capable of generating warp speeds and beyond. You'll end up dreaming of a point break.

ⓘ John Isaac owns **Revolver**, T01637 873962, www.revolversurf.com, the Newquay outlet for some seriously beautiful retro and modern retro boards by the likes of Revolver, Fin, Harbour and Skip Frye.

Surfing and environment

The British coastline is a collection of very diverse coastal environments. It is a country where surfers have been at the forefront of the campaign to clean up the seas and protect areas under threat. Some of the most popular breaks sit in polluted waters. Areas of the Northeast, like the Gare in Teeside, and parts of South Wales around Aberavon suffer badly from industrial discharge. Other spots, such as St Agnes in Cornwall, suffer due to sewage infrastructure that is badly in need of updating. In northern Scotland, Dounreay nuclear facility casts a blight over the nearby surf spots like Sandside Bay, where radioactive particles have been found. There are still, however, vast areas of the coastline that enjoy pristine line-ups rich with wildlife, such as Northumbria, northern Scotland and southwest Wales.

In the UK, the non-profit organization **Surfers Against Sewage** (SAS) campaigns for cleaner seas and safer waters. "In 1990, surfers were getting sick of the state of the sea and sick *because* of the state of the sea," explains SAS campaigner Andy Cummins. "At the time the general attitude towards sewage disposal was pump it out to sea and dump it there untreated. Surfers and other water users were bearing the brunt of this outrageous dumping practice as raw sewage floated back to shore with the winds, waves and tide. The general public however remained unaware of the risk and the extent of the problem. SAS took on huge industries and government in order to get the changes everybody deserved. To do this successfully, SAS has always strived to present a solution-based argument of viable and sustainable alternatives. SAS highlights the inherent flaws in current practices, attitudes and legislation, challenging industry, legislators and politicians." Another key aspect of SAS is education and information, ensuring the public is aware of the real risks associated with the shortcomings of water companies, policy and legislation, ensuring we have a brighter future. SAS has regional offices, monitoring and campaigning right around the country. To find out more about SAS, to become a member and find out how you can make a difference, contact SAS today, T0845 4583001, www.sas.org.uk.

The **Marine Conservation Society** (MCS) is the UK's national charity, campaigning for the protection of the marine environment and wildlife. Since 1977, they have been highlighting concerns and issues regarding the marine environment, informing the government, EU and industry. They run several excellent campaigns including **Adopt-A-Beach** which was set up in 1999 to encourage local communities to care for their coastal environments, including quarterly beach clean-ups, litter surveys and data collation. They also run a useful resource, **The Good Beach Guide**, www.goodbeachguide.co.uk – an independent survey of the UK's bathing waters. To find out more about the Marine Conservation Society, how you can join, and how you can help improve the quality of our marine playground, go to www.mcsuk.org.

CHRIS GRIFFITHS

Fins out

Girls in the Curl
by Dominique Kent-Munroe

Twenty years ago, all I kept hearing day-in, day-out was how clean, how big, how hollow the waves were and of course I heard at length about the great wipeouts the boys were having. When your whole family is into surfing there is no getting away from it. But, hang on... where were all the girls? Surely some girls surfed!

I'd heard of one woman in Wales, Linda Sharp (19-time Welsh champion, 10-time British champion) and a couple in Cornwall – Eden Burberry (5-time British champion) and Deborah Watts who were surfing regularly but not many others. It was these few who really began to lead the way forward for women's surfing in the UK, who made everyone else see that it was possible.

Jump forward a few years. A young Robyn Davies bursts on the scene with a strong powerful style. It is her style and determination that sees her become one of the UK's greatest female surfers and the first British woman to compete at an international level.

These women, and the girls and women who have followed on behind them, have pushed for better wetsuits (yeah, finally they're making suits for us women too!). It's amazing to imagine now, but we've had to hassle to have women's categories included in competitions, to show that we are out there and want to be put on the map and taken seriously. Women's surfing in the UK is now at the next stage. It may have taken a while for us to gain the respect that is due, for us to have a place in British surfing, but now the ball is rolling – watch out!

We now see women-only surf comps, surf schools for women and holidays specifically designed with women in mind. Let's hope that with more coaching and training, some of the young, up-and-coming talent such as Taz Sheppard from St Ives, Gwen from Langland, Jadine from Porthtowan, Nicola Bunt from St Agnes and Lucy from Jersey, will achieve what they want, whether it's carving their names out on the international scene or just enjoying a great lifestyle.

Surfing has given me a passion, focus, a hunger for travel and a big smiley family, including two small surfer girls.

A lot of respect goes out to all the inspirational women who have got women's surfing to where it is today. Now, let's keep it moving forward.

Dominique Kent-Munroe is a British longboarding champion as well as a competition-level shortboarder. She is a strong advocate and champion for women's surfing in Britain. She recently established a girls' academy in St Agnes, Cornwall, to coach and encourage local surfing talent.

5 underground classics

① **The Cove** Cold water G-land in the heart of the Northeast, a secret spot.
② **The Pole** Heavy, fast, long, hollow – and no one will tell you where.
③ **Gills Bay** Classic and heavy Scottish point break ▸▸ p163.
④ **The Gare** Reeling, right-hand point in the mouth of the River Tees ▸▸ p130.
⑤ **Skaill Bay** Beautiful, walling right-hand point on the Orkney Isles ▸▸ p180.

THE GILL

The Cove

Just be respectful and don't drop litter. As the people at SAS say, leave nothing but footprints.

Sarah Bentley, former Cornish and Open Champion

Localism and surf communities

Surfing is founded on a set of unwritten rules. During the early years these were loosely interpreted and everyone got on with riding waves and having fun. Today with increased competition and more surfers in the water, it is important to make sure you travel and surf respectfully. Always follow the rules of wave priority, never drop in, never snake, don't bail your board and don't drop litter. Where there are localism issues, try to stay relaxed and friendly. Vibing out locals will gain few friends. If travelling surfers come to your break and are respectful, treat them the same. All surfers have one thing in common – we are all travellers.

Overall the British are polite to strangers. They can quickly warm to those with whom they have a common bond. This has traditionally been true of British surfers, who have always tended to give the benefit of the doubt to new arrivals in the line-up, and if no rules are broken and respect is shown, there have rarely been any problems.

There have been a few spots where the mere presence of a stranger in the line-up was enough to spark acts of localism. 'The Badlands' around St Agnes in Cornwall developed a reputation for heavy localism in the 1970s and 1980s, and the label has stuck. These beaches have very tight-knit, very competitive line-ups of high calibre surfers, but aggressive acts of localism are rare these days. Other breaks where tight-knit line-ups dominate include Crab Island on the Gower, Porthleven in south Cornwall, Fraserburgh in Scotland and the Cove in the Northeast.

Brief surf history

1770s → Captain Cook experienced Britain's first brush with surfing while exploring the South Pacific. 1920s → Surfing proves itself as the sport of kings – while in Hawaii, Edward Prince of Wales gives surfing a go. 1930s → Newquay's Pip Staffien builds and rides one of the first boards in Britain. 1937 → The Countess of Sutherland on a trip to Hawaii wins a trophy in a local surf contest. 1965 → Bilbo, the first British surf company, is established in Newquay by surfers and shapers Bob Head and Bill Bailey. 1969 → The UK's first surf magazine *British Surfer* is founded. 1978 → The British surf team are invited to tea at Buckingham Palace and Prince Charles becomes patron of the BSA. 1978 → British surfer Viscount Ted Deerhurst becomes Europe's first professional surfer. 1981 → *Wavelength* magazine launches. 1980s-1990s → The British surf scene continues to expand and Britain dominates in the European surfing stakes with top surfers including Carwyn Williams, Grishka Roberts, Spencer Hargreaves, Gabe Davies and Russell Winter. 1990 → Surfers Against Sewage formed in St Agnes, Cornwall. 1998 → Newquay surfer Russell Winter becomes the first European to take part in the prestigious WCT. 2004 → Britain's first dedicated Surfing Museum opens its doors in Brighton, attracting more than 15,000 visitors in a year. Present → Britain boasts four surf magazines, a booming surf industry and many of the continent's top riders.

Surf safe

The fundamental role of RNLI Beach Lifeguards is to prevent the loss of life through educating and informing the public of potential dangers. The RNLI, a charity supported by voluntary contributions, provides a lifeguard service to eight local authorities, currently covering 57 beaches in the southwest of England, with plans to extend cover in the future. The full lifeguarding season runs between 30 April and 30 September. Some beaches only have cover during the height of the summer season so surfers need to be mindful of their own safety for the rest of the year.

RNLI Beach Lifeguard **Antonia Atha** highlights a few dangers you many encounter at the beach:

Rip currents As water drains back out to sea via the easiest route, fast-moving 'rivers' of water, or RIP currents, are created. Depending on the nature of the beach, some will have a permanent rip while others will be affected at various states of tide. You can recognize a rip by a lack of breaking waves as well as discoloured water as debris floats out to sea. If you find yourself in a rip, and notice you are being pulled away from the beach or down the coast, DO NOT PANIC. A rip will eventually subside. You can paddle out of it at a 45° angle towards the breaking waves or let it carry you out to sea before then paddling across and back in. Don't try to paddle directly against it or get off your board and try to swim in. If you feel that you are in trouble, put your hand in the air and wave for assistance to alert a lifeguard or fellow surfer.

Drustan Ward, top Cornish surfer and RNLI Beach Supervisor, suggests: "Always seek advice from locals or lifeguards when surfing at an unfamiliar beach and check for rocks, groynes and rips etc. If no-one else is surfing, do not go in. Always know your limits."

Incoming tides Buy a tide timetable for the region and familiarize yourself with areas of the beach that may become cut off. The tide moves most quickly two hours either side of low and high tide and will be moving at its fastest on a big spring tide.

Other people

There is a code for surfing. The main rule is look before you go and don't drop in on others, even if you think you are Britain's version of Kelly Slater. It's not just irritating, it is dangerous when two boards, bodies and worlds collide. Generally be considerate and be aware of others sharing the sea.

Lifeguard, surfer and British bodyboarding champion Damien Prisk recommends: "Always surf with a friend so you can keep an eye on each other."

Advice and watch the flags Robin Kent, pro-surfer and long-suffering lifeguard asks: "Please don't surf in between the bathing (red and yellow) flags. The bathing and surfing areas are kept separate to ensure all beachgoers can maximize their fun and safety. Contrary to popular belief, lifeguards are not just there to ruin people's fun. The lifeguard motto is 'To save more lives', so the advice we give is for a reason." Black and white chequered flags designate a surfing area while a red flag means it is too dangerous to enter the sea.

The RNLI's Beach Safety team, working alongside Beach Lifeguards, aims to increase awareness and promote safety by educating all those who visit beaches in the United Kingdom and Republic of Ireland, not just those visiting the Beach Lifeguard-patrolled areas of the southwest. Through its pro-active approach, visiting schools to give educational talks, touring popular events with its beach safety road show and providing resources such as leaflets and fact cards, the Beach Safety team aims to provide the most effective means for reducing preventable incidents. The RNLI sees Beach Safety as an integral part of beach lifeguarding – reducing loss of life through prevention and education. For further information on beach safety, if you would like to make a donation to or are interested in becoming an RNLI Beach Lifeguard please visit www.rnli.org.uk/beachlifeguards.

Beach **Lifeguards**

Surfing Northern Ireland

Surfing in Northern Ireland has been somewhat overlooked for the past 10 years, with the surfing spotlight remaining focused on the western coastline of Eire. However, this stretch of northerly facing beaches and reefs is an excellent surf destination. A consistent swell catcher, it has powerful, high quality breaks. Low pressures track across the North Atlantic and past Iceland on a regular basis, pushing some heavy swells onto the exposed breaks. Combine this fact with the number of spots that work in winds from a southerly or southwesterly direction and you have one of the UK's most consistent surf regions. "Visitors tend to think west coast, west coast, west coast," says six-times Irish National Champion Andy Hill, "but our prevailing wind is offshore. We also have a relatively large swell window that also opens up to the west with Portballintrae."

"People have been surfing in the area since 1963, when my father, a customs officer based in Londonderry, first came over with a board," says Andy Hill of Troggs. "There was an underground interest during the seventies and eighties (maybe 20 locals), but it was with the advent of surf shops like ourselves, opening in the early nineties, that acted as a catalyst for the sport. It has really boomed in the last two years. All the beaches are busy on the weekends and holidays. But it's still very uncrowded during the week."

There has always been a high standard of surfing coming out of this area: **Alistair Mennie** was fifth on the British circuit in 2004 and is now concentrating on big waves, like Mavericks and Todos Santos. **Andy Hill** is a six-times Irish National Champion. Local legend **Stevie Burns** is the current National Longboard Champion and **Alan Duke** is a three-times Irish National Champ.

GERRARD MCAULEY

Blackrocks

Here are a few breaks suggested by Andy of **Troggs** to get you started. Check out www.troggs.com for more details.

Whiterocks
This beach break produces lefts and rights, and with a large swell window, is a consistent spot. Works best from mid to high tide, any wind from the south, southwest or west is offshore. Head 2 miles out of Portrush on the coast road to Bushmills and turn left just past the Royal Portrush golf course.

East Strand
Another beach working best from mid to high tide with peaks that fire if the swell is over 3 ft and the wind southwesterly. Found on the east side of the Portrush peninsula, turn into the car park on Causeway St. It is home to a very powerful, hollow beach break, famed for snapping boards. Consistent, good right bank at the end of the promenade with a peak in front of the stream. Watch for strong currents and rips. Advanced surfers only when big.

Blackrocks
At the western end of the beach lies an excellent, fast, left-hand boulder reef. Famed for its 'wedgy' take-off, barrels and long walls, it can be a fickle spot. Works best from mid-high tide with a south/southwesterly wind. Head for Portstewart, from the Metropole corner at the lower end of the Coleraine Rd, first left under the railway bridge. Advanced surfers only.

Portballintrae
Four miles from Portrush lies this swell magnet of a beach break, best from mid-high tide. A popular summer spot as it is often the only break working. Powerful, hollow waves, renowned as a board breaker.

Castlerock
Working through the tides, this beach can produce mellow or challenging peaks, depending on the swell. At the Barmouth end is a quality long right breaking off the rivermouth groyne. Across the river on the Portstewart side lies a mirror image set-up.

Getting there Northern Ireland is part of the United Kingdom and, as such, UK nationals do not need a passport to cross from the mainland into Northern Ireland. The most popular way of crossing the Irish Sea is by ferry. **Stena Line**, T08705 707070, run regular services from Stranraer-Belfast. **P&O Irish Sea**, T0870 2424777, www.poirishsea.com, run ferries from Cairnryan-Larne and Fleetwood-Larne. Flights are available with budget airline **Ryanair**, www.ryanair.com, who fly from London Stanstead to Derry, with easy access to the north shore. **Easyjet**, www.easyjet.com, offer a rival service into Belfast. Check with the airlines for their policies on ID as most require a photo ID such as a passport.

Stop off at **Troggs Surf Shop**, T028 70825476, on Portrush's Main St to stock up on hardware and to find out more about surfing in the area. If you're in the market for a new board or need to get a ding fixed contact Richard at **Westbay Surfboards** via Troggs Surf Shop or richard@westbaysurfboards.co.uk, www.westbaysurfboards.co.uk.

● **Sleeping** **MacCools Hostel**, Causeway St, Portrush, T028 70824845. They have internet access and beds in dorm rooms from £10 and twin rooms from £14. To the west, **Downhill Hostel**, T02870 849077, is in an excellent location overlooking the 10 km stretch of Benone Strand. It has a kitchen, lockers, a garden, beds from £8 and private rooms from £25.

☼ **Flat spells** Don't miss the geological phenomenon **The Giant's Causeway**. At the far end of East Strand Beach, perfect hexagonal columns comprise this 60 million year old rock formation leading from the cliff-side to the sea.

GERRARD McAULEY

Andy Hill surfing Whiterocks

Surf media and websites

Britain supports four main surf magazines: *Carve, Wavelength, PitPilot* and *The Surfer's Path*.

There are hundreds of online surf resources; here are just a few to get you started:

www.A1surf.com British site full of news, reviews and surf forecasting facilities for the entire British coastline including charts, webcams and tide tables.

www.britsurf.co.uk BSA website with a full list of BSA-approved surf schools, UK competitions, plus advice for beginners.

www.coldswell.com British site with good surf forecasting facilities including charts, reports and webcams.

www.magicseaweed.com British surf forecasting facilities.

www.mcsuk.org Marine Conservation Society site, campaigning for the protection of the marine environment and wildlife. Links to www.goodbeachguide.co.uk – independent survey of UK bathing waters.

www.rnli.org.uk/beachlifeguards A fun site with a serious purpose: lots of contact numbers as well as up-to-date information on which beaches are patrolled during the summer season.

www.sas.org.uk Surfers Against Sewage website, campaigning for clean seas and safe waters.

www.surfersvillage.com Excellent, up-to-date news from the entire world of surfing plus surf forecasting.

www.surfmagic.com British site, British surf news plus surf forecasting facilities.

ANIMAL

Josh Knowles

wavelength

surf mag since 1981   mail@wavelengthmag.co.uk

Britain Essentials

Where is it

Britain encompasses England, Wales and Scotland and as an island is surrounded entirely by water – good news for us surfers. To the west the force of the Atlantic Ocean is only softened by the presence of Ireland and the Irish Sea, but continues north through Scotland. To the east the North Sea dominates while the South Coast is hemmed in by the English Channel. Neither Northern Ireland nor the Channel Islands are part of Britain – they form part of the United Kingdom and British Isles respectively.

Locals and language

English, in a variety of guises, is the official language spoken nationwide. In Wales, road signs are written in both English and Welsh – keeping the national language alive. In Scotland 'Gaelic' is fairly uncommon except in the Hebrides where it is still used and features on road signs.

There is an amazing variation across the board in terms of attitude and style in the water. In the Southwest there is more hassling for waves, the focus is on style and finishing on a flourish; in the Northeast and Scotland, fewer numbers equals less hassle, style is generally less flashy – it's more about making the drop and tucking into solid sized waves; while the Welsh combine style with solid performances and never lose their sense of fun.

Costs

Britain is a relatively expensive place, especially in terms of petrol prices and public transport. Petrol in the north of Scotland is the most expensive on the mainland. In terms of general living costs, Wales is probably the least expensive.

Crime/safety

The UK is generally a safe place to travel. However, as with anywhere, don't leave valuables on display in cars and be more vigilant in urban/city environments. Cornwall and the South Coast have recently suffered a spate of summer car thefts resulting from surfers stashing their keys in wheel arches/exhausts – not a great idea. In terms of beach safety, **RNLI Beach Lifeguards** seasonally patrol selected beaches – highlighted on the maps throughout the book by a yellow circle with a red number. In an emergency, alert the **Coastguard, T999/112**.

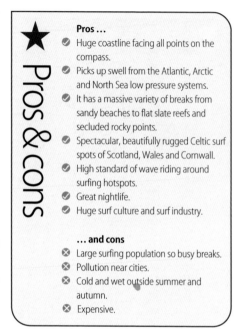

Pros ...
- Huge coastline facing all points on the compass.
- Picks up swell from the Atlantic, Arctic and North Sea low pressure systems.
- It has a massive variety of breaks from sandy beaches to flat slate reefs and secluded rocky points.
- Spectacular, beautifully rugged Celtic surf spots of Scotland, Wales and Cornwall.
- High standard of wave riding around surfing hotspots.
- Great nightlife.
- Huge surf culture and surf industry.

... and cons
- Large surfing population so busy breaks.
- Pollution near cities.
- Cold and wet outside summer and autumn.
- Expensive.

Health

EU residents need a stamped E-111 from their home country for free (or reduced cost) healthcare. Visitors from outside the EU/reciprocal agreement should invest in travel insurance. Free emergency treatment is available in most National Health Service hospital A&E departments. Recreational drugs are illegal in Britain.

Here are a few things to watch out for:

Diarrhoea Food poisoning, dirty drinking water, polluted seawater – it can happen anywhere.

Treatment Rest and rehydration are the key: keep your water levels topped up and keep out of the sunshine. Rehydration salts are also good as they replenish your body's mineral levels. Drugs such as Immodium help bung you up and can be useful if you really have to travel, but it's better out than in. If you have diarrhoea for more than three days, pass blood or are in any doubt, seek immediate medical attention.

Hypothermia The sea is cold in this part of the world! However much you want that last wave, be aware of

Surfers' tales

Variety is the spice of life...

I'm not sure who said variety is the spice of life, but it absolutely sums up the surfing experience in the UK. What a wonderful mix of surfing delights it has to offer. I grew up surfing in the cold waters of the northeast coast, with its thumping

northern Scotland with Thurso, the Nias of the north; the hidden treasures of the Welsh coastline; the world-class secrets of the east coast; and the abundant, virtually tropical to me, at least, beach breaks of Cornwall and Devon.

No pain, no gain ...
by Alan Stokes, British Champion

...that a rusty coat hanger had gone straight through my boot and into my foot. Ouch! I think Mitch said something real appropriate like "at least you won't have to take your wetsuit off to hang it out."

becoming confused or too cold and come in.
Treatment Prevention is better than cure – wear the right wetsuit and gloves/boots/hoods as applicable.

Jellyfish Jellyfish travel on the wind, tides and currents meaning they are more prevalent in the shallows following a prolonged period of onshores. Most jellyfish are relatively harmless and will only administer a small sting via their tentacles, but others can have more serious consequences. Don't touch any washed up jellies as they can still sting. If you begin to experience serious discomfort, feel dizzy, breathless or unwell, let someone – preferably a lifeguard – know as you may be experiencing an allergic reaction.
Treatment Pee is power! The natural solution and usually the most easily accessible is to wee on the affected body part, neutralizing the sting. If the area becomes swollen, antihistamine cream will help bring the swelling down and reduce the pain.

Sun Found everywhere, even in Scotland! The sun can cause sunburn, dehydration, heat stroke and even cancer.
Treatment Wear waterproof sunblock, and when you come out of the water, stick on a hat, drink plenty of water and try and avoid the intense midday sun.

Weaver fish Lurking in the shallows just beneath the sand on sunny, low tide days, these small fish are virtually impossible to spot and avoid. If you do tread on one, they'll administer a painful, protein-based injection through spines on their backs. Although painful, their sting is not usually fatal, although certain people may experience allergic reactions to the venom. If you feel dizzy or unwell, let someone – preferably a lifeguard – know.
Treatment Immerse your foot – or injured body part — into as hot water as can be tolerated, to break down the poison and stop the pain. Leave to soak for 10-15 mins.

Insurance
Joining the **BSA**, www.britsurf.co.uk, costs around £25 annually. Among other benefits you receive third-party public liability insurance worldwide for up to £2 million – handy if you injure someone else while surfing.

Sleeping
Accommodation in Britain is pricey when compared to the rest of Europe. **Bed & Breakfast (B&Bs)** do exactly what

Make sure you get a good wetsuit because it can get cold in Britain and a bad wetsuit will cut down your time in the water.

Sam Lamiroy, former British and BPSA Champion

→ Fact file

Currency Pound sterling (£)
Capital city London
Time zone GMT
Length of coastline 11,075 miles
Religion Christian
Emergency numbers
General emergency 999/112
International Operator 155
Electricity 240v 3 square pronged adaptor.
Opening hours 0900-1750 Monday-Saturday with some supermarkets opening on Sunday. Pubs generally serve food from 1200-1400 and 1700-2100 with last orders around 2300. In rural areas it can be hard to eat outside these hours.
Red tape Britain is a member of the EU. A valid passport is required for all overseas visitors for the duration of their visit. Citizens of Australia, NZ, Canada, SA and USA do not need a visa (check out www.fco.gov.uk for further information).
Speed limits Motorway (blue roads on maps) and dual carriageway (also blue) 70mph. Primary routes (green) and other roads 60mph in the country. In built up areas and where a lower limit is not shown assume 30mph, up to 40mph in urban areas. Speed limit on roads are also strictly enforced with many limits on primary routes. Other roads are usually very slow and where dual lane limits are enforced resulting in fines, and many roads are peppered with speed cameras.

Get out and explore Britain's coastline. There are some great waves and great communities out there.

Gabe Davies, former British Champion

they say – offering a bedroom in a private house and full English breakfast from £35-80 for a double. Prices vary through the season and deals can sometimes be struck if you're staying for more than one night. **Self catering** can often be the cheapest and easiest option for groups – tourist information offices have full lists of available properties.

Hostels There is a good network across Britain including independents, YHA www.yha.org.uk and SYHA hostels www.syha.org.uk with beds from around £15 or less per night. **Camping** From basic sites to activity filled holiday parks we have it all, prices vary accordingly. Some have on-site static caravans/chalets to rent – often a reasonable option. Groups may find camping options limited with many sites only accepting families or couples (often highlighted in the text). If you plan to do a lot of camping join **Caravan Club**, www.caravanclub.co.uk, or **Camping and Caravanning Club**, www.campingandcaravanning.co.uk, who, alongside plush sites, offer very basic options from £3 a night. Free-camping is not really an option in Britain.

Eating

British food has a bad reputation, but this is not strictly fair. The country has always been a melting pot of cultures, and now Britain's culinary tastes reflect this. It is as much the home of bangers 'n' mash, a full English breakfast and pub grub as it is the home of excellent Chinese, Indian, Thai, Italian and Middle Eastern cooking.

Getting there

Road Although an island, Britain is connected to continental Europe via the **Eurotunnel Shuttle Service**, T08705 353535, www.eurotunnel.com. A freight train transports you and your vehicle between Calais and Folkestone in about 35 minutes, 365 days a year. Book in advance for better deals.

Rail Eurostar, T08705 186186, www.eurostar.com. Travel as a foot passenger from Paris, Brussels or Lille to London Waterloo in less than 3 hours. If you're planning your connecting journey from anywhere else in Europe check out Rail Europe, www.raileurope.com, for details on linking with the Eurostar.

Air The main international airports for the UK are London-based Heathrow and Gatwick although there are also limited International services direct to Glasgow in Scotland, Birmingham in the Midlands and Manchester in the North. For cheap flights try **STA Travel**, www.sta-travel.com, or **Air Brokers International**, www.airbrokers.com. Flights from **Australia** and **New Zealand** are serious business, lasting 20-plus hours. The cheapest routes are usually via Asia. Try Trailfinders, www.trailfinders.com.au, for cheap flights from Australia or Usit Beyond, www.usitbeyond.co.nz, for good youth fares from New Zealand.

From **Europe**, travel to a wide range of regional British destinations is well serviced by the growing number of budget airlines. Try www.virginexpress.com, www.ryanair.com, www.flybe.com, www.easyjet.com, www.flybmi.com. Remember most budget airlines do charge for board carriage and they usually need to be booked on when you book your flight.

Sea From Ireland, ferries run to Scotland – Belfast to Stranraer is one of the cheapest routes. For **Wales** Rosslare-Pembrokeshire with **Irish Ferries** is one of the cheapest options. For crossings to **England**, Dublin-Liverpool takes about 7½ hours with P&O. For **France** and **Spain**, the South Coast is the gateway to Britain – Calais to Dover is the shortest and cheapest route. From **Northern Europe** entry is via Hull and Tynemouth in northeast (around 12-plus hours with a price tag to match). For full listings of routes check out the main carriers **Brittany Ferries**, www.brittany-ferries.com, P&O Stena Line, www.posl.com, Stena Line, www.stenaline.co.uk, and Irish Ferries, www.irishferries.com.

Getting around

Driving (left hand side) A good network of motorways and primary roads covers the country – all but a couple of which are toll free. In summer and on long weekends the M4 and M5 motorways to the Southwest become clogged making travel at non-peak times advisable. Distances and speed limits in Britain are indicated in miles not kilometres.

Maps An invaluable tool is a detailed Ordnance Survey Map which can reveal more than just where the roads lead.

Surfers' tales

Frenchie's Fantastical Pharmaceutical Voyage *by the Gill*

Frenchie and I didn't make the decision until after we'd watched the midnight weather chart on BBC2. Frenchie's car was out of action in the garage but luckily he had a courtesy car – a brand new Renault Clio with 750 miles on the clock. The opportunity was too good to miss. We wedged our boards inside, threw in some gear and were heading north long after most people were heading to bed. By the time we reached Birmingham we were ready to drop. Not even a quarter of the way there! I told Frenchie there was no way I could take over the driving, so he reached into his bag of goodies and pulled out some serious-looking pills and asked me to administer two of them. He swallowed them, smirking. "We'll be there in no time," he said. I read the warning on the side of the box. "Not to be given to a cow in calf." They were some sort of cattle steroid. "Great for keeping you awake," said Frenchie. Who was I to argue? It was 2.30 in the morning on the M6 with 600 miles to go.

Dawn was breaking around Glasgow, the halfway mark. I was dozing nicely when he rudely asked if I'd like to drive. I said that if he were to take two more tablets, he could probably make it all the way. He could tell the boys back home, impressing them no end. I regained consciousness on the farm track to Thurso East. He'd made it. We surfed all day and drank late into the night. By the time we arrived at Pat Keiran's, everyone was in bed and locked up. I slept soundly on my board bag in the garage. Frenchie however got no more than a couple of hours in.

After another day of sun and surf, we arrived at Pat's. There was only one spare bed, which we tossed for – with a coin. I won. Frenchie was on the floor again. Another sleepless night for him, on top of all the driving, surfing and sun. It was our last day. We made the most of it and surfed until three in the afternoon, when we ran out of steam and decided to head back to Swansea. We would arrive at 3.30 am if we drove non-stop. The final test for Frenchie's endurance. He took up the challenge and downed a few cattle steroids with his Big Mac in Inverness at about 6 pm. The next thing I knew the lights of Manchester were twinkling on the midnight skyline. Frenchie asked me to take over. I handed him another couple of pills and told him he would be a hero when we returned. Frenchie dropped me off at 4 am. He had to be up at 7.30 am the next morning to drop off the courtesy car. It was two days late. It would have been great to see the garage owner's face as Frenchie drove off leaving a brand new Clio with 1600 miles on the clock and a copy of the John O'Groats Advertiser on the back window ledge.

It's amazing what you can cram into a weekend break in Scotland with a good chart, someone else's car and a box of cattle steroids.

Frenchie speeding in Scotland

Car/van hire All the multinationals operate here but better deals can often be found with local companies if you're prepared to hunt around. You need to be over 21, have held a license for more than a year and usually have to pay by credit card. Try www.europcar.co.uk, www.e-sixt.co.uk, www.hertz.co.uk, www.wannavan.com. For VW camper van hire try Cornwall Campers, www.cornwallcampers.co.uk.

Public transport

Coach National Express, www.gobycoach.co.uk, and Citylink, www.city.link.co.uk, offer some of the cheapest travel in Britain but board carriage will be in the baggage hold and at the driver's discretion.

Rail The network covers the majority of Britain but services are often late and tickets pricey unless booked well in advance. Most companies will try and accommodate boards in the guard's van (some, like South West Trains, for a fee of £5 each way). For details try National Rail Enquiries, T0845 7484950, www.nationalrail.co.uk. The Underground, otherwise known as 'The Tube', www.thetube.com, offers good connections across London. Avoid travel with your kit across London during rush hour.

Air With a good network of airports across Britain, flying is a real option and with pre-planning can be the cheapest option. Try Air Southwest, www.airsouthwest.com (including flights Newquay-Gatwick), Fly Be, www.flybe.com (including flights Newcastle-Exeter) and Ryan Air, www.ryanair.com (flights include Newquay-Stanstead, London), as well as national airline British Airways, www.britishairways.com. Many budget airlines do charge for board carriage – usually around £10 per journey.

Tourist Information

Britain has good tourist information resources, try www.visitbritain.com for information about the country as a whole and www.visitengland.com, www.visitscotland.com, www.visitwales.com, for information on specific areas.

Tour operators

There are a number of surfing travel companies offering surf trips within Britain. Quite a few will also organize trips to Europe and destinations further afield.

Animal Surf Academy (operated by Wavehunters UK Ltd), 16 Tower Road, Newquay, TR7 1LR, T08702 422 856, Surf lessons: T07891 639 461, www.animalsurfacademy.com or

www.wavehunters.co.uk. The Surf Academy is at Polzeath, North Cornwall but they also run surf tours to Morocco.

Big Friday, Cornwall, T020 7793 1417, kate@bigfriday.com. Wave goodbye to the city! Big Friday organizes surfing weekends for landlocked Londoners. Great weekends to suit all budgets and surfing experience.

Freeride Surf Adventures, T07970 686 011, info@freeridesurf.com. Freeride is the new wave of surf travel with small groups heading to prime destinations. Check web site for information on current destinations.

Harlyn Surf School, 16 Boyd Avenue, Padstow, Cornwall PL28 8ER, T01841 533 076, www.harlynsurfschool.co.uk. Offer surf packages including full board residential throughout the summer season (pick up and drop off). Operates in Harlyn Bay and a variety of Cornish beaches to ensure optimum and safe conditions in which to learn to surf.

Oceanmotion, Bournemouth, T07941508531, oceanmotions2000@yahoo.com. Qualified BSA surf instructor and guide available for surf trips and lessons by arrangement. Own surf equipment and transport for groups up to 10 people.

Outdoor Adventure, Atlantic Court, Widemouth Bay, Bude, Cornwall EX23 0DF, T01288 361312, F01288 361153, info@outdooradventure.co.uk. Surf school and residential activity holiday centre with fantastic clifftop location at Widemouth Bay near Bude, on the north Cornish coast.

Pure Vacations Surfing Holidays, England, T01227 264264, F0870 922 3951, info@purevacations.com. Why not take advantage of a surfing holiday with Pure Vacations, the UK and Europe's leading surfing tour operator?

Surf South West, T01271 890400, F01271 890050, darren@surfsouthwest.com. Surfing holidays in Croyde Bay in Devon, Lanzarote, in the Canary Islands, and at Playa Jaco in Costa Rica, on the Pacific coast of Central America.

Surfersworld Ltd, T01271 890037, www.surfersworld.co.uk. Stylish surf accommodation in Croyde and Woolacombe with own bar and restaurant. Surf schools and surf hire. Surf guiding programmes and holidays in the UK and overseas.

TYF, St. Davids, Pembrokeshire, T01437 721611, F01437 721838, play@tyf.com. Adventure days surfing at BSA-qualified school. Also have coasteering, sea kayaking and climbing days out.

Wavehunters, London, contact Andy Cameron, T07815 059890, mail@wavehunters.co.uk or wavehuntersuk@wavehuntersuk.com. Low price weekend surf breaks for the frustrated city bound adventure seeker.

47 worldwide surfing destinations
6230
ATOL
PROTECTED
Break free ...
... take a surf trip
pure
vacations
www.purevacations.com
01227 264 264

England

DEMI TAYLOR

Cornish cream – Godrevy at its best
▶▶ *p62*

Motorway
A Road
B Road
Minor Road
✈ Airports
⛴ Ferries

SCOTLAND

Carlisle

Newcastle Gateshead   p133

p126   North Sea

Darlington

Middlesbrough

Scarborough   p117

Lancaster

York

Kingston upon Hull

Blackpool   Leeds   Bradford

Liverpool   Manchester

Sheffield   Doncaster

Newcastle-under-Lyme

Lincoln

Nottingham

p110

Telford   Derby

Norwich

Irish Sea

Birmingham   Leicester   Peterborough

Coventry   Cambridge

WALES   Northampton   Ipswich

Cheltenham   Milton Keynes

Gloucester   Oxford   Luton   Chelmsford

Swindon   Southend-on-Sea

Bristol   LONDON   p101

Bath   Reading

p41   Maidstone   Dover

Taunton   Southampton   Brighton & Hove   p99

Exeter   Bournemouth   Portsmouth

p51   Newquay   p93   p96

St Ives   Plymouth   English Channel

p55   p80

Penzance   p75

N

50 km
50 miles

Introduction

The dawn light is casting a pink hue across the eastern rim of the dark sky. Two figures are scrambling across a section of exposed reef towards the sea. There is no wind and the air is heavy with dew. Behind them towers a huge bleached wall, a quintessentially English geographical feature – the white cliffs. A welcome home sign visible from the window of a passenger aircraft or cross Channel ferry. Yet also a barrier, both physical and psychological. A sign to those who looked north across the Channel with envious eyes.

This morning it is a backdrop. Line yourself up with the dark scar in the cliff face and wait for the sets. This rock has witnessed many life-changing events. The Spanish Armada scattered by the English fleet, Spitfires harassing a retreating bomber. Today it sees two English surfers score the session of their lives on a coastline that doesn't officially have surf.

But come to think of it, there isn't any surf in the Northeast, Yorkshire or the Isle of Wight, is there?

England rating

Surf
★★★★

Cost of living
★★★★

Nightlife
★★★

Accommodation
★★★

Flat spells
★★★★

North Devon

Surfing North Devon

"Devon is still a vast swathe of countryside: it has a laid-back feeling and gentle pace of life. The backdrop of spectacular scenery where Exmoor meets the sea is awe-inspiring and is often taken for granted by the people who live there. There are fabulous beaches and great waves that work in a variety of conditions, [and] the place is small enough so that there is a real community feeling." Ester Spears, Woolacombe local and English Surfing Federation Secretary

Devon has always been one of the UK's biggest tourist destinations – exit the M5 and the epic green scenery envelops the traveller like a reassuring blanket. Postcard images of chocolate-box villages with thatched cottages and narrow country lanes attract holidaymakers from all over England and, as fishing and agriculture have become less lucrative, tourism now provides the county's main income.

Despite the image, Devon is not just a sleepy retirement community flooded every August with tourists. Vibrant, young communities of surfers are spread along the north coast in Croyde, Braunton, Barnstaple and Bideford. The influx of tourists does have positive effects – unspoilt areas of the coastline are now seen as a resource and are actively preserved, and water quality is improving as beaches have become seen as a valuable commodity.

For such a large county, the north shore of Devon has a surprisingly small coastline. When you think of the number of excellent surfers it produces, the number of visitors it attracts and its influence within the UK surf scene, it is amazing to see only ten breaks listed in this guide. Obviously there are others that we have not included, but this is a graphic illustration of how a limited resource like waves can come under ever increasing pressure.

Coastline

The coastline of North Devon can be as spectacular as any in Britain, a place where forest-shrouded sea cliffs drop off into the Atlantic and small villages like Lynmouth take shelter where stream-eroded valleys meet the sea. Between Ilfracombe and

Westward Ho! sit the county's main tourist and surfing beaches. These westerly-facing stretches of sand are a heaving mass in the summer months, but in the spring and autumn are home to quality waves. And in the biggest winter storms, sheltered points spring to life, allowing waves to be ridden on even the biggest Atlantic swells.

Localism

Most breaks will be crowded year round – it's just that they will be less crowded in the depths of winter. In the summer, Croyde will be packed every time there is a surfable wave (and even when there isn't). The standard of surfing here is very high. Putsborough or Woolacombe have more room and a more chilled-out vibe. Despite the crowding, it is still unusual to encounter out-and-out localism in Devon, though a surfer breaching the etiquette of the line-up may incur the wrath of the locals.

North Devon board guide

Longboard
Shaper: Gulf Stream Surfboards

- 10' x 23" x 3¼".
- Traditional noserider.
- 50/50 rails, rolled vee bottom, fixed pivot fin. Clark foam.
- Not just a summer board, we get some epic small days for hanging your pinkies over.
- Guaranteed to get you wet when your shortboard has come to a halt.

Thruster
Shaper: Gulf Stream Surfboards

- 6'3" x 18⅜" x 2¼".
- Classic squash tail shortboard.
- Clark foam, FCS fins.
- Single to double concaves.
- Ideal for the standard day of action on all the local beaches.
- Most of the local guys have a 6'6" or 6'8" pintail for the bigger low tide sessions.

Boards by **Gulf Stream Surfboards**
Factory: South Street, Woolacombe
T 01271 870831
www.gulfstreamsurfboards.co.uk

Top local surfers

Devon has produced some of the UK's best surfers. Riders like **Eugene Tollemache** and **Scott Rannochan** perform well in contest jerseys and freesurfing. Former British Champion **Sarah Whitely** is a Saunton local. As **Ester Spears** points out: "There are lots of good underground surfers in Devon, as proved by the fact that Croyde Surf Club and Woolacombe Boardriders are currently the top two clubs in Britain (British Interclub championships, November 2003). From Croyde there is **Ossian Pleasance**, Matt Jenkins, Dan Thornton, Nigel Cross, Matt Saunders, Ralph Freeman, Richard Carter plus a host of others. From Woolacombe **Neil Clifton** and **Nick Thorn**. From Westward Ho! and all places south **Sophie Hellyer** and her dark horses."

Getting around

The road network in Devon looks great on a map, but in reality it can be a bit of a nightmare. The so-called Atlantic Highway, the A39, is a single carriageway road that can be surprisingly narrow in places and frustratingly slow in summer traffic. Allow plenty of time to get to spots and take lots of patience with you. The roads north of Barnstaple, such as the A361, are also very busy during the summer.

> "The drawback of North Devon is the crowd factor... On a good day at Croyde you can hardly see the sea for wetsuits and boards. Despite the wide choice of waves, especially for learners, Croyde seems to be the focus, yet it's not ideal for beginners. On the bright side the vibe is mellow and in general the locals are very welcoming. Although how long that will last remains to be seen."

James Stentiford, Croyde local and top European pro snowboarder

Breaks...

1 Porlock Weir
2 Lynmouth ★
3 Woolacombe
4 Putsborough
5 Croyde
6 Saunton
7 Westward Ho!
8 Buck's Mill
9 Clovelly
10 Speke's Mill

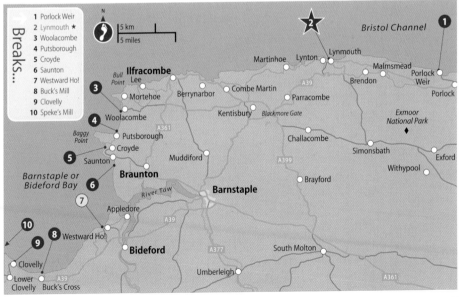

Breaks

1 Porlock Weir

- ◔ **Break type**: Left reef.
- ◕ **Conditions**: Big to huge swells, offshore in southerly/southwesterly wind.
- ❶ **Hazards/tips**: Crowds.
- ◒ **Sleeping**: Woolacombe ▸▸ p46.

Sitting in the heart of the Exmoor National Park, Porlock is actually just over the Devon border in Somerset and has a notoriously steep hill. It is a spot that is surfed on big swells, two hours before or after high tide. Parking above the break, but toll roads on the way in.

2 Lynmouth

- ◔ **Break type**: Long left point break.
- ◕ **Conditions**: Big swells, offshore in southerly winds.
- ◉ **Size**: 3-8 ft.
- ◍ **Length**: 300 m plus.
- ◐ **Swell**: Northwesterly.
- ◗ **Wind**: Light southerly/southeasterly.
- ◉ **Tide**: Through the tides, best at low.
- ◕ **Bottom**: Boulders.
- ◔ **Entry/exit**: Off the rocks.
- ❶ **Hazards/tips**: Crowds, rips, rocks.
- ◒ **Sleeping**: Woolacombe ▸▸ p46.

Lynmouth is one of the UK's finest point breaks. When a big swell hits Devon, long lefts are rideable for up to 300 m. Lynmouth works through all states of tide, with low being generally better, but needs light winds.

As the area's best point break, when it is on it will generally be crowded, especially on weekends or where big swells have been forecast well in advance.

Lynmouth, with long walls and hollow sections, is a break for experienced surfers as there can be bad rips, boulders and crowds to contend with. Car park on the headland to the west of the break.

ⓘ *If you like Lynmouth try Gills Bay in Scotland (see page 163) or La Fortaleza in Spain.*

3 Woolacombe

- ◔ **Break type**: Beach break.
- ◕ **Conditions**: All swells, offshore in easterly winds.
- ❶ **Hazards/tips**: Big beach, good place to escape crowds.
- ◒ **Sleeping**: Woolacombe ▸▸ p46.

A 2-mile stretch of beach with peaks and a high tide right at the northern end. Various peaks work at different states of tide. Can be a good place to escape the crowds at Croyde and ideal for beginners. Parking above the beach.

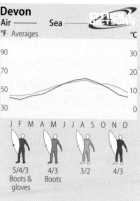

Devon
Air ——— Sea
°F Averages °C

90			30
70			20
50			10
30			0

J F M A M J J A S O N D

5/4/3 Boots & gloves | 4/3 Boots | 3/2 | 4/3

DEMI TAYLOR

4 Putsborough Peaks

4 Putsborough

- ⚙ **Break type**: Beach break.
- 🌊 **Conditions**: Medium swells, offshore in easterly winds.
- ⚠ **Hazards/tips**: Rips when big.
- 💤 **Sleeping**: Woolacombe/Croyde ›› *p46*.

The southern end of Woolacombe beach is protected from southerly winds by Baggy Point, so can be the place to check when Croyde and Saunton are blown out. Works at all states of tide. The waves here can be good, so it's worth checking if Croyde is packed as the beach can throw up good banks. Popular with beginners as is often 1-2 ft smaller than Croyde, but watch out for rips near the point in larger swells. Parking and toilets above the beach. The road down to the beach is narrow and windy if you are in a van.

5 Croyde

- ⚙ **Break type**: Beach and reef breaks.
- 🌊 **Conditions**: All swells, offshore in easterly winds.
- ⚠ **Hazards/tips**: One of the UK's most crowded beaches.
- 💤 **Sleeping**: Croyde ›› *p47*.

Croyde is the surf capital of Devon and as such attracts surfers from all around the UK. Add these surfers of mixed abilities to a hungry core of locals and the water can get pretty crowded. Keep your eyes open and don't drop in. The banks here can produce powerful, hollow waves, especially at low tide. If you're not an experienced surfer then it may be better to check out another spot. Croyde was crowded even before the recent surf boom.

The beach has some excellent banks and has often hosted the English or British surfing championships. It is offshore in an easterly wind and has the distinction of being privately owned. There are a number of car parks near the beach. Low tide can be a board-snapping experience.

"Croyde low tide on its day can look like Hossegor – people getting pitted everywhere," says James Stentiford, Croyde local and one of Europe's top pro snowboarders. "Above 4 ft it's heavy and fast but it needs the right swell direction and good banks to fire."

At the north end of the beach Baggy Point has a right-hand reef, **Baggy End Reef**, which works best on a spring high tide. It gets busy but doesn't really handle crowds well. The reef breaks in bigger swells up to three-quarter tide and is for experienced surfers only.

At the south end of the beach, **Downend Point** is probably the most surfed reef. It doesn't really work

2 Lynmouth

4 Putsborough Right

5 Croyde

England North Devon Breaks Putsborough to Croyde

below 4 ft and is best from low to mid tide on neap tides. It's also a good spot when it gets too big for the beach. It can be a bit of a cut-back wave but on its day it can produce a few barrels. It does get crowded but can handle a crowd pretty well. The reefs are shallow, rocky and popular with locals when they are on.

6 Saunton

- **Break type**: Long beach break .
- **Conditions**: Medium swell, offshore in easterly winds.
- **Hazards/tips**: Very mellow, popular longboard wave.
- **Sleeping**: Croyde/Braunton ›› p47/48.

This long stretch of sand runs from the headland south to the mouth of the

River Taw and works at all states of tides. It is a very gently sloping beach not renowned for the quality of its sandbanks. A great place for beginners and longboarders as the waves peel gently and lack punch. Miles of sand dunes and room to spread out. Car park off the main road. It's a pretty safe beach, with lifeguards in the summer.

7 Westward Ho!

- **Break type**: Beach and reefs .
- **Conditions**: Small to medium swells, offshore in easterly winds.
- **Hazards/tips**: Good spot to escape the crowds.
- **Sleeping**: Westward Ho! ›› p48.

Westward Ho! is the only town in Britain named after a book. It would make for a great review if we could say that the

break was a fairy tale, but it's a pretty average spot that can have its good days. The beach works through the tidal range and is much less busy than the breaks north of the Taw. It's a good spot for beginners, inexperienced surfers and those looking to escape the crowds. Easy parking at beach. Laidback line-ups.

8 Buck's Mill

- **Break type**: Left boulder reef.
- **Conditions**: Big swell, offshore in southerly winds.
- **Hazards/tips**: Not a wave for the inexperienced.
- **Sleeping**: Westward Ho! ›› p48.

When massive swells hit the West Country, local surfers head for sheltered breaks where quality waves come alive in locations that are usually as flat as a pond. In southwesterly gales and huge swells, Buck's Mill has a long left that breaks along a man-made boulder groyne. It is a low-tide break and can be crowded due to the quality of wave produced here. Park respectfully in the village.

9 Clovelly

- **Break type**: left point.
- **Conditions**: Huge swells, offshore in southeasterly winds.
- **Hazards/tips**: Very fickle.
- **Sleeping**: Westward Ho! ›› p48.

Clovelly is a fickle left point that is very hard to catch when it's on. Works at low tide on a massive swell, when long, walling lefts peel along a boulder-fringed sandy point. It's a really long walk down to the break from the expensive car park. Very sheltered spot that's offshore in southerly or southeasterly wind. The wave breaks

5 Croyde (Downend)

Robyn Davies *by Antonia Atha*

Robyn Davies sits opposite me; she is a difficult person to pin down – her concentration wavers and faults, half with me, half with a nursery rhyme book she found on my shelf. She is telling me about her first barrel, aged 15, at the beach on the Lizard, Cornwall, where she grew up. It was late September, the water a Caribbean turquoise, her brother Sam the only other person in the line-up. She describes taking off and making it to her knees as the water closed in around her. On her knees inside the barrel with a clear view of the exit, time stopped, and then she fell off. She says it was her first taste of how amazing the form of waves can be.

She tells me pockets of memories – of family trips to local beaches with her mother as driver and support technician, of her first surf at Porthleven aged 16 on a 2 ft, clean, nervous day. She stops briefly to comment how strongly she recommends no one ever surfs Porthleven (her home break) and that Newquay is a far better option. She tells me how surfing has shaped her life in more ways than just her career (Robyn is the best female surfer that Britain has produced and recently made history as the first female surfer ever to grace the cover of *Surf Europe* magazine). She has learnt to respect people, their countries and the ocean. Above all she has learnt that the importance of friends is everything.

As we both approach our 30th year, me with a sense of rising panic, I am amazed again by my friend's humility towards her talents and achievements and the positivity she brings to every day, saying that even with her worst surf, if she thinks hard enough, she can find something good in it. As for her future aspirations? She is a difficult person to pin down – she reads me a poem…

Antonia Atha and Robyn Davies have been friends for nearly a decade and have shared surf trips to Europe, Asia and Central America.

Robyn and Antonia

Surfers' tales

England North Devon Breaks Saunton to Clovelly

down the point towards the harbour. Access off the boulder beach or harbour if it gets big (once a decade).

10 Speke's Mill

- ⚑ **Break type**: Left and right reef.
- ❦ **Conditions**: Small to medium swells, offshore in easterly winds.
- ❶ **Hazards/tips**: Respect locals, difficult to find.
- ● **Sleeping**: Westward Ho! ▸▸ *p48*.

Once a secret spot, Spekes has always been a popular spot with Devon surfers as it hoovers up swell on small days. It is a shallow, rocky reef which can get crowded, so not for the inexperienced. Difficult to find the reef so you'll need to do some exploring. Respect the locals if it's on and if it's already busy head south to Cornwall's Sandy Mouth ▸▸ *p 52*.

ESTPIX

6 Saunton ▸▸ *p44*

Clovelly

Listings

Woolacombe

Just south of Morte Point sits Woolacombe and the 3-mile stretch of sand leading down to Putsborough.

● Sleeping

L-B Headlands Hotel, Beach Rd, T01271 870320, is a small family-run hotel offering B&B. Rooms have great views over the bay. Worth checking out off-season as they often do weekend deals. **Self catering Surfersworld**, Beach Rd, T01271 890037, www.surfersworld.co.uk, is the chic boutique end of the surf accommodation market offering stylish, modern apartments – sleeping 2-6 people – with outside 'wet' areas complete with board and wetsuit storage facilities. Based at the cool West Beach bar and restaurant, they are open year-round. A studio for 4 ranges from around £200-500 per week. **Camping** There are plenty of sites in the area. **Damage Barton**, T01271 870502, to the north between Lee Bay and Bull Point, is a working farm with campsite open Mar-Nov. **North Morte Farm**, T01271 870381, a mile to the north at Mortehoe, is open Easter-Sep with statics available to hire. **Woolacombe Bay Holiday Parcs**, T01271 870343, have 4 family-oriented sites dotted around with Golden Coast open year-round, call for details. **Woolacombe Sands Holiday Park**, Beach Rd, T01271 870569, with a 15-min walk to the beach with statics and chalets to rent. Open Easter-Oct, they don't take groups.

DEMI TAYLOR

● Eating/drinking

"The Red Barn, T01271 870982, is just a short walk from the beach and the perfect spot to watch the sun set and have a post-surf beer. It's popular with locals and the ceiling is covered in some interesting retro boards," recommends Devon local James Stentiford. They also do good, affordable food with a view. Gulf Stream's Andrew Cotton recommends **West Beach** on Beach Rd for good seafood – mains from £10 – and beach views.

⊕ Directory
Surf shops & facilities There are plenty of surf shops here including **Bay Surf Shop**, T01271 870961, just back from the beach on Barton Rd, stocking all the essentials and offering equipment hire and BSA-approved lessons. **Gulf Stream**, South St, T01271 870831, www.gulfstreamsurfboards .co.uk, have based their shop and surfboard factory here on South St. Jools and team have been shaping since 1993 and make boards for, among others, ex-British champion Sam Lamiroy, local charger Scott Rannochan and up-and-coming grom Stuart Campbell. **Hunter**, West Rd, T01271 872502, just back from the beach, sell hardware, hire equipment and run a BSA surf academy. **Shore 2 Surf**, West Rd, T01271 870870, stock hardware as well as hire out equipment. **Nick Thorn**, South St, T01271 871337, former European Ironman Champion, also runs a year-round BSA surf school. **Pure Vacations**, www.purevacations.com, offer complete year-round surf breaks in Woolacombe including B&B beachside accommodation, surf tuition and equipment hire from around £135 for 3 nights.
Tourist information Year-round on the Esplanade.

Croyde
Sitting on the B3231, Croyde, with its thatched roofs and little streets, has retained its chocolate-box feel despite being a summer tourist Mecca. The village, named after the Norse raider Crydda who landed here, also has a large population of surfers who surf to a high standard.

⊜ Sleeping
L-A **Home House Hotel**, St Mary's Rd, T01271 890541, www.homehousehotel .co.uk, offers deluxe B&B in a gorgeous 500-year-old thatched cottage – perfect for couples. A-B **The Thatch**, Hobbs Hill, T01271 890349. This central pub is the focus of village life with rooms over the pub or a (slightly) quieter option, over the road. Home House Hotel also offer a cheaper rate B&B in the same grounds at B **Wisteria Cottage** which sleeps up to 6 from £26 per person. Just along the road, they also run the chi-chi **Atlantico Bar & Grill** tapas bar.
B-C **Crowborough Farm B&B** in Georgeham, T01271 891005, between Croyde and Putsborough, is a quieter option with board storage facilities as well as an outside tap for rinsing suits. Other choices geared toward surfers and offering board storage include B-C **Moorsands House**, Moor Lane, T01271 890781, between the village and the beach; B-C **Oamaru**, Down End, T01271 890765; and B-C **Sandy Hollow**, Sandy Way, T01271 890556, which is also available to rent in its entirety as a self-catering cottage Jul-Aug. **Self catering Croyde Bay Holiday Village**, Down End, T01271 890890, have chalets to rent Apr-mid Nov. **Surfing Croyde Bay**, T01271 8901492, have several cottages to rent

⊗ Flat spells
Cinema Pendle Stairway Cinema, High St, Ilfracombe, T01271 863484, is the nearest place to catch the latest releases.
Clovelly A ridiculously pretty chocolate box of a village with a ridiculously expensive car park attached.
Golf There are a couple of 9-hole courses in the area: **Ilfracombe & Woolacombe Golf Range**, Woolacombe Rd, T01271 866222, and **Mortehoe & Woolacombe GC**, T01271 870255, in Mortehoe. **Saunton GC**, T01271 812436, has not one but two 18-hole courses for those with handicap certificates. **Royal North Devon GC**, Golf Links Rd, Westward Ho!, T01237 473817. **Horse riding** Go for a ride or get a lesson with **Folly Foot**, Burrows Park Rd, Westward Ho!, T01237 424856. **Skating SRP Skate Rock Park**, Pilland Way, Pottington Industrial Estate, Barnstaple, T01271 344465, is an indoor park with a street course and mini ramp. It's closed on Mon and you need to be a member (£5) to skate it, helmets are compulsory. A day pass is about a fiver. **Bideford Skate Park**, Bank End by the River Torridge, Bideford, has rails, banks, fun boxes and a spined mini ramp.

within walking distance of the beach, at around £150 for 3 nights.
Camping There are plenty of campsites in the area but as it is a popular holiday destination, camping is not a particularly cheap option and many places will not take groups. **Bay View Farm**, T01271 890501, has easy access to the beach and village as well

as statics available to hire. **Surfers Paradise Campsite**, Sandy Lane, T01271 890477, is open Jul-Aug and happy to accommodate groups. **Ruda Campsite** is the older brother of Surfers Paradise and open to families and couples only.

🍴 Eating/drinking

The Thatch on Hobbs Hill is the focus for village life and visiting surfers alike, serving good food at reasonable prices. It's always packed out, especially in the summer, so be prepared to wait for your post-surf pint. **Billy Budds** just up the road is another popular spot. Ester Spears also recommends **Blue Groove**, St Mary's Rd, a mellow restaurant run by a couple of surfers. The food is good with mains including wonderful tacos (beef/chick/veg) from around £7.

➊ Directory

Surf shops The Little Pink Shop, T01271 890453, is pink, in the middle of the village, sells all the surfing essentials and does equipment hire including boards, winter suits and women's wetsuits. Redwood Surf Shop, Hobbs Hill, T01271 890999, www.redwoodsurfshop.co.uk, is run by former British champ Richard Carter and stocks all the essentials as well as offering equipment hire. Surfing Croyde Bay, Hobbs Hill, T01271 891200, is open year-round selling a mix of hardware and pasties as well as hiring out equipment and running BSA-approved surf lessons. They count top Devon ripper Scott Rannochan among their instructors. **Surf South West**, T01271 890400, www.surfsouthwest.com,

based at the beach, run BSA-approved lessons as well as complete surf holidays to Croyde Mar-Oct.

Braunton

Off the A361, Braunton is a fair-sized market town with most amenities and is home to several UK brands including Tiki, Saltrock – who sponsor top Devon surfer Eugene Tollemache among others – plus made-to-measure wetsuit specialists **Second Skin**.

🛌 Sleeping

B-C **The Firs B&B**, Higher Park Rd, T01271 814358, is a mile from the village and 2 miles from the beach with board and bike storage. **Camping** **Lobb Fields Caravan and Camping Park**, Saunton Rd, T01271 812090, is about 2 miles to the beach and open mid Mar-end Oct.

🍴 Eating

The Sands Café Bar on nearby Saunton Sands beachfront is a lovely spot to grab a sundowner beer and a bite to eat with sea views.

➊ Directory

Surf shops Caen St is home to several surf shops including: Tiki, T01271 816070; Second Skin, T01271 812195, who've been making custom suits since 1972; and Gulf Stream, T01271 815490. Salt Rock HQ is at Velator Industrial Estate, T01271 815306, www.saltrock.com, and is open to the public. The Surf Shack, Saunton Rd, T01271 815619, www.surfshack.co.uk, deal with the board repair side for their sister shop Surf Station. Surfed Out,

Caen Fields Shopping Centre, T01271 812512, also offer surf hire. **Walking On Waves**, T01598 710961, www.walkingonwaves.co.uk, BSA school run by Saunton local and former English and British champion Sarah Whitely. **Tourist information** Caen St car park, T01271 816400, limited year-round opening.

Westward Ho!

The only town in England to be named after a book and be punctuated by an exclamation mark!

🛌 Sleeping

There are plenty of **B&B** options on Atlantic Way. Heading southwest along the A39 to Hartland, **Elmscott Youth Hostel**, T01237 441367, is about half a mile inland, open Mar-Sep, offering views over to Lundy Island. **Self catering** The Old Granary, T01237 421128, in Pusehill, Westward Ho!, sleeps up to 6 people for between £175-425. **Camping** Braddicks, Merley Rd, T01237 473263, www.braddicksholidaycentre.co.uk, overlooks the bay and is open year-round with statics to rent. Chalets sleeping 4 from around £165-515 per week. Camping (limited facilities) May-Oct. Heading west along the A39 to Clovelly, **Dyke Green Farm Campsite**, T01237 431279, in Higher Clovelly is open Apr-Oct. **Pusehill Farm Campsite**, T01237 474295, in Pusehill are open Apr-Oct. **Surf Bay Holiday Park**, Golf Links Rd, T01237 471833,is open Apr-Oct and rents statics accommodating up to 6 people for less than £500 a week.

Surfing North Cornwall

Kernow is a rugged land of rolling hills and wooded valleys, a place where the silhouettes of ruined tin mines overlook jagged, rocky coves. Cornwall is a Celtic land in both outlook and landscape. In places you could almost be on the west coast of Ireland, the north coast of Scotland or the northern seaboard of Spain. One thing that Cornwall shares with its Celtic cousins is its excellent surfing potential. And at the heart of the surf scene sits Newquay, a town with a very 'un-Cornish' feel to it.

Newquay would have been very happy to live on as a kind of Torquay of the northern Cornish coast, but what happened in the 1960s changed all that. The seeds were sown long before, due to the town's coastal geography, but the advent of Bilbo surfboards and advances in wetsuits made by Gul meant that surfing had gained a foothold in the town and it has stubbornly refused to let go. Today, with little encouragement from the council, surfing has become big business with the number of surf shops and shapers well into double figures. The annual Newquay Boardmasters attracts over 100,000 spectators and Newquay surfers have reached the highest levels in competitive surfing, with Russell Winter spending three years on the WCT, Spencer Hargreaves wining the European title and British Champion Alan Stokes performing well on the WQS circuit.

But there is more to Cornwall than just Newquay. Some would argue that the spiritual home of Cornish surfing sits to the south, in St Agnes, the heart of the 'Badlands'. This small village grew up around the tin mines, taking to surfing with a fierce passion and a strong will to protect its surf spots, from both outsiders and pollution. The first spawned the 'Badlands' legend, the second the national environmental pressure group Surfers Against Sewage. The tight-knit Badlands line-ups are home to surfing dynasties that span generations – Kents, Wards, Hendys, Bunts, Greens, Lascelles – something to bear in mind when you paddle out.

Overall, although Cornish breaks are crowded, the county has a vast coastline and miles of beaches to explore. The region also has a standard of surfing that would rival anywhere in Europe, although in a British, low-key way.

"Us Brits are hardcore and surf whatever the weather," says Joe Moran, editor of *Pit Pilot* magazine. *"In the past British surfers have been ignored when we deserve a lot more, but we don't go mad about the hype, we just get it done."*

Coastline

The coastline of Cornwall is rugged and crumbling due to the relentless onslaught of the North Atlantic. It was along this rocky shore that wreckers lured unsuspecting ships onto the rocks and the myriad tiny coves have, for centuries,

North Cornwall board guide

The PF Flyer
Shaper: Chops Lascelles, Beachbeat

▸▸ 6'2" x 20" x 2³⁄₁₆" the original hotdog shortboard.
▸▸ Models range from 5'4" x 19" x 2½ to 6'10" x 20½" x 2¾".
▸▸ Double winger spin machine for all sorts of waves.
▸▸ Aerial attacks a speciality.
▸▸ Single concave under the chest to help paddling in and a sprial V in the tail to help lay it on the rail when required.
▸▸ A great all-round board for Cornish summer waves.

Thruster
Shaper: Chops Lascelles, Beachbeat

▸▸ 6'0" x 18" x 2" for Shaun Skilton.
▸▸ For average Jo 6'6" x 19¼" x 2⁵⁄₁₆".
▸▸ Based on a fuller plan shape for sloppy summer surf.
▸▸ It has a single to double concave with a squash tail and tweaks to suit the ability of the surfer.

Boards by **Beachbeat Surfboards**
Factory: Laminations, St Agnes
T01872-553918
Lam2574@aol.com

been a smuggler's haven. Today it is the tourists who are lured to the Cornish coastline and although the beaches do reach bursting point during the months of July and August, there are still a few places off the beaten track for those who are willing to explore.

Localism

There is no doubt that a lot of Cornish breaks are already very crowded and every summer seems to bring a new influx of people into the water. This can lead to tension. With this in mind, if you are visiting the area, try to be honest about your ability and the types of waves you want to be surfing. Rather than small, tight-knit spots, it's probably best to head for the bigger open beaches where there is more room to spread out and less tension in the water. Breaks around St Agnes are crowded, ultra-competitive and home to powerful waves. Spots like Perran Sands and Godrevy/Gwithian have good waves, a more mellow vibe and more space. If you're heading to the Newquay area, Watergate holds more of a crowd.

Top local surfers

The level of surfing in Cornwall is as high as anywhere in Europe. It has spawned many world-class surfers and also some excellent local riders. **Russell Winter, Lee Bartlett, Spencer Hargreaves, Alan Stokes, Ben Baird, Shaun Skilton, Minzie, Robin** and **Jake Kent, Ben Skinner, James Hendy, Mark Harris** and **John Buchorski** are just the tip of the iceberg. Women surfers include British longboard champion **Dominique Kent-Monroe, Sarah Bentley** and **Nicola Bunt.**

Getting around

The road network in Cornwall is pretty good. The A39 and A30 act as the main arteries, and access to breaks by car is pretty straightforward. During the peak summer season, especially around the last two weeks in August, the roads can become very congested, often with massive queues leading into and out of Newquay. Allow more time for journeys crossing the border and try to avoid travelling at peak periods.

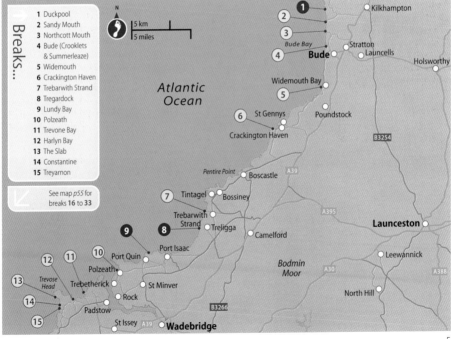

Breaks...

1 Duckpool
2 Sandy Mouth
3 Northcott Mouth
4 Bude (Crooklets & Summerleaze)
5 Widemouth
6 Crackington Haven
7 Trebarwith Strand
8 Tregardock
9 Lundy Bay
10 Polzeath
11 Trevone Bay
12 Harlyn Bay
13 The Slab
14 Constantine
15 Treyarnon

See map p55 for breaks 16 to 33

5 km
5 miles

Atlantic Ocean

Kilkhampton
Bude Bay
Stratton
Launcells
Holsworthy
Bude
Widemouth Bay
St Gennys
Poundstock
Crackington Haven
B3254
Pentire Point
Boscastle
A39
Tintagel
Bossiney
Trebarwith Strand
Treligga
Camelford
A395
Launceston
Port Isaac
Leewannick
Port Quin
Bodmin Moor
A30
Polzeath
Trebetherick
St Minver
Trevose Head
Rock
A388
North Hill
Padstow
B3266
St Issey
A39
Wadebridge

51

Breaks

1 Duckpool

- ○ **Break type**: Beach break.
- ● **Conditions**: Small to medium swells, offshore in easterly winds.
- ❶ **Hazards/tips**: Not really suitable for beginners due to rocks and rips.
- ● **Sleeping**: Bude ›› *p 67*.

A sandy cove flanked by rocky outcrops that works best from low to mid, on an incoming tide. Less busy than the breaks to the south, this spot can have some good waves at low tide, but needs easterly winds to work properly. Picks up plenty of swell. Easy access off the A39 with parking above the break.

2 Sandy Mouth

- ○ **Break type**: Beach break.
- ● **Conditions**: Small to medium swells, offshore in easterly winds.
- ❶ **Hazards/tips**: Watch out for rips and submerged rocks.
- ● **Sleeping**: Bude ›› *p 67*.

With the right banks this cliff-backed beach can produce high quality lefts and rights. Although an extension of the sandy bay leading to Bude, this is a better bet for escaping the crowds. Best from low to mid on a pushing tide – access limited at high tide. National Trust car park plus toilets near the break.

3 Northcott Mouth

- ○ **Break type**: Beach break.
- ● **Conditions**: Small to medium swells, offshore in easterly winds.
- ❶ **Hazards/tips**: Watch out for rips when big.
- ● **Sleeping**: Bude ›› *p 67*.

Good quality beach break that can produce powerful and hollow waves, best from low to mid tide. At high tide the beach can disappear so beginners should bear this in mind. Beach parking.

4 Bude (Crooklets and Summerleaze)

- ○ **Break type**: Beach break.
- ● **Conditions**: Small to medium swells, offshore in easterly winds.
- ❶ **Hazards/tips**: Crowds, rips, rocks.
- ● **Sleeping**: Bude ›› *p 67*.

Summerleaze has a number of waves that work in bigger swells. There is a quality left at low tide and a right at high tide near the swimming pool.

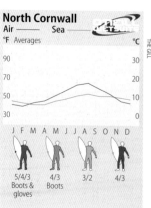

North Cornwall
Air —— Sea ——
°F Averages °C

90 — 30
70 — 20
50 — 10
30 — 0

J F M A M J J A S O N D

5/4/3 Boots & gloves | 4/3 Boots | 3/2 | 4/3

THE GILL

4 Paul Canning at Bude

There are also shifting sandbanks on the beach. **Crooklets** has a number of waves including sandbank peaks and a good right to the northern end and a left to the south. Watch out for rocky outcrops at high tide. Bude is a popular surfing location with a large local surfing community. Gets busy during the summer and during good swells. Suitable for beginners but watch out for rips near the river.

5 Widemouth

- **Break type**: Beach break.
- **Conditions**: Small to medium swells, offshore in easterly/southeasterly winds.
- **Hazards/tips**: Crowds, rocks.
- **Sleeping**: Bude ▸▸ p 67.

A long stretch of beach – almost a mile – with some quality banks. It produces lefts, rights and peaks depending on the banks and can get crowded as a result. Easy access off the A39 with a large car park overlooking the break. Beginners should watch out for rocky outcrops. There are a couple of good reefs worth checking to the south.

6 Crackington Haven

- **Break type**: Beach break.
- **Conditions**: Big swells, offshore in easterly winds.
- **Hazards/tips**: Rips, rocks.
- **Sleeping**: Bude ▸▸ p 67.

A sheltered, popular bay at the mouth of a valley, overlooked by 400-ft cliffs of limestone, sandstone and shale. The left-hand point break is surfable in even the biggest surf, with the right winds, hence the name 'Unmaxables'. Parking on the seafront.

7 Trebarwith Strand

- **Break type**: Beach break.
- **Conditions**: Small to medium swells, offshore in an easterly/southeasterly wind.
- **Hazards/tips**: Beach disappears at high tide. Parking at beach.
- **Sleeping**: Tintagel/Polzeath ▸▸ p 69.

A fairly good beach with lefts and rights, depending on the sandbars. Best surfed at low to mid tide as the beach is covered at high. Suitable for surfers of all abilities.

8 Tregardock

- **Break type**: Beach break.
- **Conditions**: Small to medium swells, offshore in easterly/southeasterly winds.
- **Hazards/tips**: Good place to escape the crowds.
- **Sleeping**: Tintagel/Polzeath ▸▸ p 69.

Remote stretch of beach with good peaks from low to mid tide. Access is on foot from Treligga which may explain why not too many people make the effort. Not suitable for beginners.

THE GILL

5 Alan Stokes at Widemouth

9 Lundy Bay

- **Break type**: Beach break.
- **Conditions**: Medium to big swells, offshore in south/southwesterly winds.
- **Hazards/tips**: Worth checking when other spots are blown out.
- **Sleeping**: Polzeath ›› p 69.

Sheltered northerly-facing bay that works best at low to mid tide. Needs a big swell to work. No car park near the beach. Follow footpath.

10 Polzeath

- **Break type**: Beach break.
- **Conditions**: Medium to big swells, offshore in southeasterly/easterly winds.
- **Hazards/tips**: Pentire Point provides some shelter in light northwesterlies.
- **Sleeping**: Polzeath ›› p 69.

Polzeath has a series of lefts and rights that work on all tides. There are peaks in the middle of the bay, with lefts to the south and rights at the northern end by the point. This is a popular and flexible break with parking by the beach. Suitable for surfers of all abilities.

11 Trevone Bay

- **Break type**: Beach break.
- **Conditions**: Big swell, southeasterly winds are offshore.
- **Hazards/tips**: Small bay with good peaks.
- **Sleeping**: Polzeath ›› p 69.

Small and sheltered bay that faces northwest and needs a decent swell to get going. Has peaks that are best from low to mid tide. Signposted from the B3276.

12 Harlyn Bay

- **Break type**: Beach break.
- **Conditions**: Big swells, offshore in southerly winds.
- **Hazards/tips**: Busy when it breaks, popular spot in winter storm surf.
- **Sleeping**: Polzeath/Newquay ›› p 69.

A popular beach due to its northerly-facing aspect. This means that it works in southwesterly winds with a big swell. Works best from low to three-quarter tide on the push. Parking by the beach. One of the few breaks that works in these conditions so can get crowded.

13 The Slab

- **Break type**: Right hand reef break.
- **Conditions**: Medium swells, offshore in southeasterly winds.
- **Hazards/tips**: Rips, rocks, crowds.
- **Sleeping**: Polzeath/Newquay ›› p 69.

Low tide reef that needs a decent swell to fire and has rips when big. Access to the break in Booby's Bay is on foot from Constantine Bay.

14 Constantine

- **Break type**: Reef break and beach.
- **Conditions**: All swells, offshore in easterly winds.
- **Hazards/tips**: Crowds, rips when big.
- **Sleeping**: Polzeath/Newquay ›› p 69.

To the south of the bay peels a left-hand reef break that can produce long, walling rides. The beach itself picks up any swell going and has some excellent banks. Popular due to the quality of the waves and its consistency. Easterly winds are offshore. Good spot for surfers of all abilities, but beginners should take care when the swell picks up. Parking by the beach.

15 Treyarnon

- **Break type**: Beach break.
- **Conditions**: Small to medium swells, offshore in southeasterly/easterly winds.
- **Hazards/tips**: Park near the beach.
- **Sleeping**: Polzeath/Newquay ›› p 69.

There are a series of peaks along this stretch of sand that break from low to high tide. There are also a couple of low tide sand-covered reefs worth checking. A popular spot with quality waves.

12 Harlyn Bay

> All my family surfs. My Dad surfs down here, my Mum surfs, my Uncle Drustan and my Uncle Dave. I remember when I was in primary school, my Dad would come and pick me up with the surfboard that they'd made me, and we'd go off surfing.

Cover star and Badlands local Josh Ward

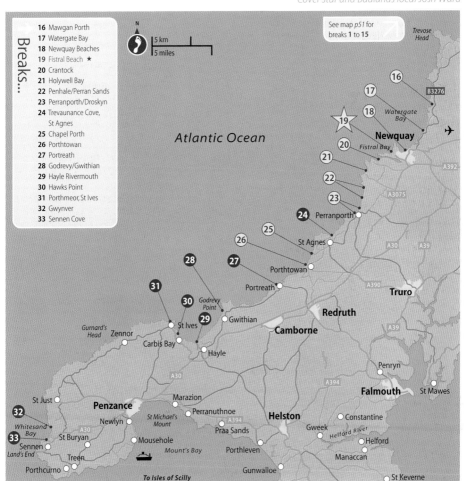

Breaks...

16 Mawgan Porth
17 Watergate Bay
18 Newquay Beaches
19 Fistral Beach ★
20 Crantock
21 Holywell Bay
22 Penhale/Perran Sands
23 Perranporth/Droskyn
24 Trevaunance Cove, St Agnes
25 Chapel Porth
26 Porthtowan
27 Portreath
28 Godrevy/Gwithian
29 Hayle Rivermouth
30 Hawks Point
31 Porthmeor, St Ives
32 Gwynver
33 Sennen Cove

See map p51 for breaks 1 to 15

England North Cornwall Breaks Lundy Bay to Trevarnon

19 Fistral Peak ▸▸ *p58*

16 Mawgan Porth

- **Break type**: Beach break.
- **Conditions**: Small to medium swells, offshore in southeasterly/easterly winds.
- **Hazards/tips**: Popular spot, rips when big.
- **Sleeping**: Newquay ▸▸ p 69.

This bay can produce fast, walling lefts and rights and works through all tides. There can also be an excellent left into the rivermouth. Parking off the B3276. It's also worth checking **Beacon Cove** to the south.

17 Watergate Bay

- **Break type**: Beach break.
- **Conditions**: Small to medium swells, offshore in southeasterly/easterly winds.
- **Hazards/tips**: Crowds, popular spot, good spot for beginners.
- **Sleeping**: Newquay ▸▸ p 69.

Watergate is a huge stretch of sand and a great place to head for when Newquay is heaving. Works on all tides.

17 Watergate bay

There are lefts and rights stretching north and south from the car park. Although it gets busy in the middle, there are usually some peaks further up the beach. In a good swell there can be excellent, punchy waves here. Watergate is a popular contest site for British and English surfing championships. It also helps take the pressure off Fistral and the Town beaches. Suitable for surfers of all abilities, many surf schools operate from here.

18 Newquay Beaches

- **Break type**: Beach breaks.
- **Conditions**: All swells, offshore in southerly/southeasterly/easterly winds.
- **Hazards/tips**: Crowded beaches, surf schools, flexible beaches.
- **Sleeping**: Newquay ▸▸ p 69.

Newquay is probably Europe's Surf City. It doesn't have the cafés and beach culture of Hossegor or the surf chic of Biarritz, but it does have a higher density of surf shops and shapers, and what it lacks in pastry shops, it makes up for in pasty shops.

Lusty Glaze is a privately owned, cliff-lined cove with some good waves in smaller swells at low to mid tides. Gets narrow near high. Site of an annual night surfing competition. Showers, café, toilets etc.

The **Town Beaches** (Tolcarne, Great Western, Towan) face north and are more sheltered. They work through all tides and need a much bigger swell to get going. There is a left near the harbour wall on Towan and assorted peaks heading east.

The **Cribbar** is a rocky point out past the Headland Hotel and an infamous big-wave spot that comes alive in huge clean swells. It is surfed, but only rarely, and has become the stuff of legends.

19 Fistral Beach

- **Break type:** Beach breaks.
- **Conditions:** All swells.
- **Size:** 2-8 ft.
- **Length:** 10-100 m.
- **Swell:** Northwesterly/westerly/southwesterly.
- **Wind:** Easterly/southeasterly.
- **Tide:** All tides.
- **Bottom:** Sand.
- **Entry/exit:** From the beach.
- **Hazards/tips:** Crowds, rocks at Little Fistral.
- **Sleeping:** Newquay ➤➤ p 69.

Fistral is Britain's most famous surfing beach. As the epicentre of the UK scene, it is an often maligned and underestimated break, but it is actually a very high quality spot that can produce hollow and powerful waves. The National Surfing Centre is based here and every year the Rip Curl Boardmasters surf contest attracts the best surfers in the world as well as hordes of holidaymakers. "That's the week when it really gets crazy. It's our peak time. All the car parks are full; even down at south Fistral people are squeezed in," explains

senior BSA coach Will Giles.

The main beach works through the tides and the waves vary with the quality of sandbanks. Although very busy in summer, the autumn and winter see the crowds drop off, but it is rarely quiet here. The beach has produced some excellent surfers including Russell Winter, Lee Bartlett, Alan Stokes, Spencer Hargreaves, Ben Baird. Even ex-world champion Martin Potter had a spell here. **Little Fistral** is a low tide spot to the north that can produce excellent waves with long walls and barrels. It breaks in front of the rocks so is not a good place for beginners.

ⓘ *If you like Fistral try Santa Cruz in Portugal or Praia Reinante in Spain.*

20 Crantock

- **Break type:** Beach break and rivermouth.
- **Conditions:** Medium swells, offshore in a southeasterly wind.
- **Hazards/tips:** Worth checking as a less crowded alternative to Fistral.
- **Sleeping:** Newquay ➤➤ p 69.

Just south of Fistral, this pretty northwesterly-facing beach has a rivermouth sandbank that can produce some excellent rights. It needs a decent

swell to get going. Works best from low to mid tide. The south end of the beach can produce good lefts.

21 Holywell Bay

- **Break type:** Beach break.
- **Conditions:** Small to medium swells, offshore in southeasterly winds.
- **Hazards/tips:** Less crowded than Newquay area.
- **Sleeping:** Newquay/Perranporth ➤➤ p 69.

Northwesterly-facing beach break that works on all states of tide, producing some good quality lefts and rights. Always worth checking as it can produce excellent waves but is dependent on the banks. Take turning off the A3075 Newquay road.

22 Penhale/Perran Sands

- **Break type:** Beach break.
- **Conditions:** Small to medium swells, offshore in easterly winds.
- **Hazards/tips:** Rips when big, OK for beginners when small.
- **Sleeping:** Perranporth ➤➤ p 71.

A huge, golden beach, stretching from Penhale corner south to Droskyn Head. An endless line-up of lefts, rights and peaks, varying in quality from mellow

23 Perranporth

22 Perran Sands

England North Cornwall Breaks Fistral to Perran Sands

58

peelers to reeling, hollow barrels. Works through all tides. A good spot for beginners and travelling surfers wanting to escape the crowded and competitive line-ups. Plenty of peaks to go around and a much more chilled-out atmosphere. Drive through the holiday camp to the pay and display car park overlooking the beach.

23 Perranporth/Droskyn

- ⚐ **Break type**: Beach break.
- 🌊 **Conditions**: Small to medium swells, offshore in easterly winds.
- ❶ **Hazards/tips**: Crowds in summer, good for beginners.
- 😴 **Sleeping**: Perranporth ▸▸ *p 71*.

Droskyn works best at low through to mid tide. At high the backwash from the cliffs makes the waves bumpy and unpredictable. It can have a good left in front of the cliffs. From here a huge expanse of westerly-facing sand stretches out north joining up with Perran Sands and Penhale. The **Perranporth** beach works on all tides but doesn't handle big swells. Parking on the cliff top at Droskyn or in

Perranporth. Chilled line-ups so a good spot for holidaying and travelling surfers to check.

24 Trevaunance Cove, St Agnes

- ⚐ **Break type**: Beach break.
- 🌊 **Conditions**: Medium to big swells, offshore in southeasterly winds.
- ❶ **Hazards/tips**: Very busy, localism, rips, rocks.
- 😴 **Sleeping**: St Agnes ▸▸ *p 71*.

This is a sheltered, sandy and rocky bay that faces northwest. It is also one of the few spots that works in big swells with southwesterly winds. Surfed through to three-quarter tide but best at mid. A small line-up which easily gets crowded with good surfers. Can hold a good size swell and has powerful, hollow, board-breaking waves. A strong rip to the left of the bay and crowds makes this a spot for experienced surfers only. The heart of the large Badlands surfing community, so rarely uncrowded. Parking near the Driftwood Spa pub. The birth place of SAS and still polluted, especially after heavy rain.

25 Chapel Porth

- ⚐ **Break type**: Beach break.
- 🌊 **Conditions**: Small to medium swells, offshore in southeasterly.
- ❶ **Hazards/tips**: Crowds, localism.
- 😴 **Sleeping**: St Agnes/ Porthtowan ▸▸ *p 71*.

Fast, powerful and hollow rights and lefts break in northwesterly or southwesterly swells. Chapel is a small beach that works from low to mid and has a big local crew. The standard of surfing is extremely high here and it is not a place for beginners. Visiting surfers may struggle to get a wave and there have been incidents of localism. Parking by the beach in small National Trust car park.

25 Chapel Porth

24 St Agnes

24 Joe tucking in atTrevaunance Cove, St Agnes ▶▶ *p59*

26 Porthtowan

- **Break type**: Beach break.
- **Conditions**: Small to medium swells, offshore in southeasterly winds.
- **Hazards/tips**: Crowds, dangerous rips, powerful waves.
- **Sleeping**: Porthtowan ›› *p 72.*

Heavy, punchy break that works through all tides, opening out at low tide to reveal Lushingtons to the south. Offshore in a southeasterly or easterly wind, but at high tide the cliffs provide some shelter from light southerlies. Porthtowan has powerful waves and broken boards are not unusual. Strong rips are a real danger so anything but small surf is best left to competent surfers. The excellent banks and beachfront parking has seen Porthtowan become a very crowded break with a strong local crew. Not recommended for the inexperienced.

27 Portreath

- **Break type**: Beach break and reef.
- **Conditions**: Medium to big swells, offshore in southeasterly winds.
- **Hazards/tips**: Sheltered bay. Gets crowded in summer.
- **Sleeping**: Porthtowan ›› *p 72.*

Portreath is usually about half the size of Porthtowan, but can be more sheltered from the wind. The right-hand reef that breaks off the rocks in front of the harbour wall is popular with bodyboarders and experienced surfers. The beach break is usually a short, fast, right that can easily become a close-out. Works best from low to near high. Car park and surf hire shop overlooking break. It can get crowded in the summer. Portreath was also at the epicentre of an amusing 'locals only' hoax in 2004 check out www.locals-only.co.uk for details.

DEMI TAYLOR

26 British kneeboard champion, Huey at Porthtowan

28 Godrevy/Gwithian

- **Break type**: Beach break.
- **Conditions**: All swells, offshore in southeasterly winds.
- **Hazards/tips**: Relaxed line-up, popular spot.
- **Sleeping**: Hayle ▸▸ p 73.

Huge stretch of sand that extends for 4½ miles from Godrevy south to Hayle, only broken by the occasional cluster of high tide rocks. This exposed beach can be fickle but is a good place for beginners and intermediate surfers on surf trips to head for due to the space and relaxed vibe. Godrevy, the headland at the northern end of the bay, picks up the most swell and can produce some quality waves with easy access from the National Trust car park. Although it does get busy in the summer, there are plenty of peaks to escape the crowds and the atmosphere here is pretty chilled. Good café in the car park. Rips by the river which can be polluted after heavy rains.

28 Godrevy

Secret spot

29 Hayle Rivermouth

- **Break type**: Rivermouth.
- **Conditions**: Medium to big swells, offshore in southerly/southeasterly winds.
- **Hazards/tips**: Crowds, rips.
- **Sleeping**: Hayle ▸▸ p 73.

Needs a decent swell to get going but can provide good quality waves around the rivermouth – usually half the size of Godrevy. Can get crowded when good. Watch out for rips and pollution after heavy rains. Access from Hayle town.

30 Hawks Point

- **Break type**: Beach break.
- **Conditions**: Big swells, offshore in southwesterly winds.
- **Hazards/tips**: Crowded, difficult access.
- **Sleeping**: Hayle/St Ives ▸▸ p 73.

A good left breaking off the western end of Carbis Bay. Needs a really big swell to get going so is a great place to check during a big southwesterly swell with southwesterly through to southerly winds. Works on all tides but if it's on, it will be packed. Access is also difficult.

31 Porthmeor, St Ives

- **Break type**: Beach break.
- **Conditions**: Medium to big swell, offshore in southerly winds.
- **Hazards/tips**: Crowds, parking.
- **Sleeping**: Hayle/St Ives ▸▸ p 73.

Overlooked by the St Ives Tate Gallery, Porthmeor is a sheltered beach that faces north and needs a decent swell to get going. This beach does get busy in the summer and parking can be a problem.

32 Gwynver

- **Break type**: Beach break with point.
- **Conditions**: Small to medium swells, offshore in easterly winds.
- **Hazards/tips**: Punchy waves, access on foot.
- **Sleeping**: Sennen ▸▸ p 73.

Gwynver is a quality beach break that joins up with Sennen at low tide. It picks up more swell than Sennen and in a good northwesterly swell, right-handers peel off the point at the north end of the beach over a rocky/sandy bottom. Also has a punchy shore break. Works best from low to near high. Watch out for rips. Access is from parking off the A30 and a 20-minute walk down the cliffs or via Sennen Cove.

33 Sennen Cove

- **Break type**: Beach break.
- **Conditions**: Small to medium swells, offshore in easterly winds.
- **Hazards/tips**: Rips in front of car park in bigger swells.
- **Sleeping**: Sennen ▸▸ p 73.

West-facing, good quality beach that works well from low through to near high. Due to its location on the toe of Cornwall, it picks up more swell than the other north coast beaches. Suitable for all surfers, but watch out for rips and rocks towards the southern end of the beach in front of the car park. A popular, year-round spot with a great view of Cape Cornwall about 4 miles to the north. Surf shop and toilets in car park.

Legends of the Badlands
Words by Chris Nelson with pictures by Demi Taylor

Another death in The Badlands, another victim no one will miss. The grim 8 miles of Germantown Avenue in north Philadelphia is controlled by the gangs and the drug dealers. To the residents, life in this urban hell is more Third World than world's only superpower.

South Dakota, a young geologist is out in the midday sun in the Badlands National Park. It is the hottest day and he's in one of the planet's most inhospitable places. There is no water, no animals or birds, no plants to lament the lack of wind. This truly is a bad land.

The world has many Badlands. To me, as a young grommet surfing in Yorkshire in the late 1980s, there was only one true Badlands – the 'locals only' breaks around St Agnes, Cornwall. The name alone was

enough to keep us away when we made the occasional foray to the Southwest. A magazine article here, an urban myth there. Tales of spontaneous acts of violence, regular drop-ins and a very warm welcome – but not of the pleasant variety. We didn't think our scruffy blue Datsun would really benefit from flat tyres and a 'locals only' wax job on the windscreen. Hey, there were other beaches, other waves. We never even ventured down to check the place out. But in my mind's eye, the waves of Chapel Porth seemed somehow mythical. Perhaps it was a perfect reef, named after a ruined church that overlooked waves so perfect that the local surfers swore to guard them by whatever means necessary. My young mind mixed images with another Cornish legend, perhaps these few surfers had found their Holy Grail?

The coastal land around St Agnes is harsh, fragile and unforgiving. Here,

St Agnes Girls Surf Academy

geography has dictated settlement patterns. Villages cling to the leeward sides of the water-hewn valleys and meander inland from the sandy borders of the beach. Just a few miles away from the shore the soil is rich and fertile; the living just that bit easier, the wind losing just enough of that bite. But there are people who have always been drawn to these coastal fringes – who have always been drawn to the sea. People who thrive on the edge. But the living here is no worse than other areas along the coast. This Badlands legend has a far more modern origin.

"I think it was between 1981 and 1985," says Steve Bunt, one of the original St Agnes surfers and owner of Best Ever surfboards. "We didn't like the outsiders coming in and taking over our break really. We decided to make it 'The Badlands' – put people off. It was bad karma to come down and surf here. It really did work and it still does. There are a lot of people who won't come down and surf around Aggie because it's The Badlands." "I think the original idea came from a sticker," reflects Martin 'Turnip' Ward, Badlands surfer and Lifeguard Supervisor at Chapel Porth. "But it does keep people away. They do let people come and have a surf, but if there's something they don't like about somebody, they'll close up." He smiles, "They can get a bit angsty sometimes, yeah. But then again I think some of the Badlands reputation came because they tend to go over the top on social outings. It's the same as surfing – if you can go harder, you do it."

Chops Lascelles of Beach Beat Surfboards first arrived in Cornwall in 1974. A talented young Aussie surfer, he'd been through Hawaii, the USA and South America, stopping off in Britain to visit his brother and earn some travelling money. "It was like pea soup, raining, cold and I hated it – I even rang my mum to see if she'd lend me the money to get home. I stayed the summer and returned again the next year. I fell in love with St Agnes because it was a community – it wasn't a tourist town. It had a good standard of surfing, good consistent waves, and I made

Josh Ward – from the roots of a strong surfing family

Chops, chilling out

good friends. The bottom line is I live here because this is where my soul is the happiest."

Chapel Porth is an idyllic sight on this late summer afternoon. The sun is low in the sky and head-high left-handers are peeling off the low tide sandbank. Turning the corner at the top of the hill reveals a familiar scene. The sandbanks may have changed over the years, but the names in the line-up remain constant. The Wards, Hendys, Bunts, Lascelles and Kents are just some of the surfing dynasties to be found in the line-up on any given day. "I've been surfing since before I can really remember," says Josh Ward, the latest in a long tradition of Badlands surfers to impact on the British surfing scene. His Volcom baseball cap is fighting to keep a lid on his shock of white hair. "All my family surf. My dad surfs, my mum surfs, my Uncle Drustan and Uncle Dave – they all surf."

Josh's dad Turnip has just finished a long day's work on the beach at Chapel, and is considering another surf. "My elder brother used to go off surfing for the day, cruising around. If I didn't go with him I'd get left behind. I think the younger generation get dragged along, like I dragged Drustan along and Josh drags his little brother Jamie along. They spend the day at the beach and if they don't surf they just kind of sit around doing nothing."

As surfing continues to grow, the younger generation here seem to empathize more and more with their community's unique identity. "There has always been a pride in coming from The Badlands," says Shaun Lascelles, Chops's

middle son. "Especially our rivalry with Newquay! Maybe it's because Newquay is so commercial and large and we have such a tight-knit community here." Josh agrees: "You hear stories as you're growing up and you watch things happening in the sea when you're young, and now you're out there in this super-competitive line-up. That's the thing – it's so hard for non-locals to get waves here."

Could it be however that the 'Badlands' phenomenon was born of an accident of nature – a result of the combined forces of geography, geology and geneology? "St Agnes is the only real classic village left on the north coast between Newquay and St Ives as it doesn't have a big, flat sandy bay," explains Chops. "Also, it's National Trust – so you can't build right down to the beach like at Newquay or Perranporth." The long track down to the bays of Chapel and Aggie both terminate in claustrophobic parking areas. New faces have always stood out, even on the busiest days. "The basic truth about The Badlands is that Chapel is a small beach

Robin Kent keeps watch over Chapel

with a very tight-knit line-up," explains British Longboard Champion Dominique Kent-Munroe. "The reason people find it intimidating is that you are surfing in amongst one big family. It's so close because you have so many generations out together, people who grew up together."

"At most beaches you get a few surfers who can rip," explains Dom. "At Chapel, the majority of surfers rip. Everybody watches out for everybody else. You know, someone might come here and drop in on a little grommet, but what they don't know is that his brothers, sisters, uncles and dad are all in the line-up with them. That's when the shit happens."

It's Wednesday evening and there are 30 girls ruling the line-up at Trevaunance Cove – not the image you'd expect from such a hardcore spot. It's 'Girls Surf Academy' night and the grommets are jostling for position in the 2-ft waves. Watched over by Dominique, Sarah Bentley and Antonia Atha, the next generation of Badlands rippers are taking

their first steps, riding their first waves. "We wanted to help girls learn in a friendly, safe, atmosphere, and encourage those who don't come from a surfing family to feel they are part of this family."

The decades have passed, and I now live just outside St Agnes. I know that there is no mythical reef, no ruined church giving the break its name. Chapel Porth is a small low tide break where the waves are as fickle as any beach break in Cornwall. But there is something special about this place, something mythical. A surf spot where locals can leave their cars unlocked and you know all your belongings will be there when you return to towel off. A line-up where the level of surfing is unbelievably high, but still has that tight-knit family feel. A spot where a new face still stands out, where a place in the line-up has to be earned. In a world of global surfing brands, crowded line-ups and lost identities, maybe this really is something worth fighting for. Maybe this is a surfing Holy Grail. Long live the Badlands.

Dominique Kent-Munroe, British Longboard Champion

Badlands surgeon, Minzie

Listings

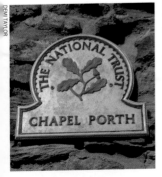

DEMI TAYLOR

Bude

The northernmost town in Cornwall, Bude is accessed off the A39 or the optimistically named 'Atlantic Highway' (more byway than highway). Built around a 19th-century canal and a stretch of golden beaches to the north and south, Bude is a pretty town with a relaxed attitude and has been a popular holiday destination since Regency times.

● Sleeping

Bude hosts an annual jazz festival in Aug during which accommodation gets booked up. **A-B Trevigue**, T01840 230418, is a beautiful B&B option serving up excellent farmhouse breakfasts and set in the courtyard of a working farm. A short walk from the sea, this is ideal for a weekend of loving and surfing. **B-C The Widemouth Manor**, T01288 361263, www.widemouthmanor.co.uk, overlooking Widemouth Bay is a popular choice with surfers (but also home to Manorism nightclub). **C The Bay View Inn**, T01288 361273, also overlooking Widemouth, is a quieter B&B option with board storage and a drying room. **C-D Pencarrol**, Downs View, T01288 352478, is a good B&B option near Crooklets beach. **E The Bunkroom**, T01288 355797, www.thebunkroom.com, is exactly as it sounds – a room with bunks sleeping 2-6 from £12 a night – with a small outdoor patio and BBQ. **E Northshore Backpackers**, T01288 354256, www.northshorebude.com, offer a fair deal with dorm beds from £12 a night. Double rooms are also available. **Camping** In terms of camping, there are plenty of choices; however many do not take single sex

groups so call before you rock up with a vanload of 20 mates. **Cornwall Campers**, T01208 832927, www.cornwallcampers.co.uk, provide sleeping and transport options in 1 package – a VW camper van! Van hire from £395 a week. **Cornish Coasts**, Poundstock, T01288 361380, is about 2 miles south of Widemouth on the A39. Open Easter-Oct with statics they are a friendly site, about the cheapest and one of the best options. **Redpost Inn & Holiday Park**, T01288 381305, is about 4 miles inland from Bude in Launcells. It is a small site, open year-round with the option of statics. **The Redpost Inn** on site serves up real ale and real food in 16th-century surroundings. **Upper Lynstone Caravan & Camping Park**, Widemouth Rd just south of Bude, T01288 352017, www.upperlynstone.co.uk, has bungalows, and is open Easter-Oct to couples and families only. **Budemeadows Touring Park**, T01288 361646, open year-round; **Bude Holiday Park**, T01288 355980, open summer only; and **Sandymouth Holiday Park**, T01288 352563, open Apr-Oct, are very family orientated and don't take same sex groups.

● Eating/drinking

For a basic approach, **Anne's Corner House**, Queen St, is the place to go for a cheap, filling 'with chips' menu. **The Coffee Pot**, Morwena Terr, is a good place to grab a coffee and access the latest charts on the internet. Jay Squire of the **Surf Spot** surf shop recommends **El Barco**, Bencoolen Rd, for the "best steaks in Bude, cooked by a Spanish chef with 30 years' experience". Overlooking Summerleaze, bistro/bar

✪ Flat spells

Cinema The Rebel Cinema, T01288 361442, 5 miles south of Bude in Poundstock, may not have the latest films but if it's flat… **The Plaza**, Lemon St, Truro, T01872 272894, gets all the current chart toppers.

Eden Project T01726 811911, www.edenproject.com. Just north of St Austell and signed off the A30, this former quarry has been transformed into a giant domed jungle with a couple of large biomes containing thousands of varieties of plants. When it's quiet (which is rare) you can escape to the top of the humid biome, lie on a bench and imagine you are far, far away. Do not go in the height of summer. Admission £12. Also keep an eye out for early summer music events hosted by Eden.

Extreme Academy Watergate Bay, T01637 860840, www.extremeacademy.co.uk, offers wave ski, kite surfing, mountain boarding and kite boarding tuition among other activities.

Golf Get a round in at **Bude and North Cornwall GC**, Burn View, T01288 352006. Green fees around £30. **Newquay GC**, Tower Rd, T01637 874354, is a links course but there are also a couple of pitch and putt greens overlooking Porth and Tolcarne beaches. **Holwell Bay GC** at the fun park, T01637 830095, is a cheap, short links course from £11.50. **Perranporth GC**, Budnic Hill, T01872 573701, is another links course and snuggled into the dunes is its own caravan park. There are a couple of courses around St Ives, the cheapest of which is **Treyanna Castle**

GC, T01736 797381, with parkland course fees from £15.

Skating Check out the mini skatepark on the seafront at Crooklets Beach, Bude. Newquay is home to **Wooden Waves**, T01637 853828. This indoor park has ramps and 1/4 pipes, costs around £4 for about 2 hrs and is based at Waterworld. Helmets are required. **Mount Hawke Skate Park**, T01209 890705, is an excellent indoor facility – sessions cost around £2. **Camborne Skate Park** on Cliff Rd is free with a nice concrete bowl, a mini bowl plus a couple of ramps.

St Ives The tightly packed streets of St Ives don't make the ideal base for a surf trip, but it is an excellent place to visit with a number of surf shops as well as great restaurants and bars. Try the **Saltwater Café**, Fish St, T01736 794928, for good seafood at a moderate price. If you're after a bit of culture with a sea view check out **Tate St Ives**, Porthmeor Beach, T01736 796226, www.tate.org.uk/stives.

DEMI TAYLOR

Camborne Skate Park

Life's A Beach is a popular and chilled place to grab a bite and watch the sun go down.

If it's real ale you're after, head south to the **Bay View Inn** at Widemouth Bay (see sleeping above). Or after dinner at El Barco, head to the **Bencoolen** bar on Bencoolen Rd for a drink. **The Carriers Inn** overlooking the River Neet is also popular.

At Crackington Haven, **The Cabin** on the beach serves a full range of snacks from pizza to cream teas and operates a BYO booze system for eating in. At Widemouth, check out the **Widemouth Manor** in all its guises as a pub, B&B, restaurant and 'Manorism' club.

❶ Directory

Surf shops and facilities Bude Surfing Experience, T08707 775111, www.budesurfingexperience.co.uk, runs BSA lessons as well as girls-only weekend sessions. **Celtic Connection Surfboards**, T01288 355545 www.ccsurfboards.com, Efford Business Park. Welshman Carl Welton has been shaping boards for some of North Cornwall's hottest talent including Joss Ash. Former British champion and local hero, Mike Raven runs BSA-approved **Raven Surf School**, T01288 353693, www.ravensurf.co.uk, for beginners through to competition level surfers. There are a good number of surf shops in Bude, including **Surf Spot**, Belle Vue, T01288 352875, www.surfspot.co.uk, who have been operating since 1968, and **Zuma Jay**, Belle Vue, T01288 354956, www.zumajay.co.uk.

Tourist information Open year-round in the crescent car park, www.visitbude.info.

Tintagel

Heading south along the A39, Tintagel is signposted from the main road. The castle may or may not be the birthplace of the legendary King Arthur, or the caves below home to the magician Merlin, but the castle ruins clinging to the 'island' are certainly worth exploring. Admission year round £3.20, T01840 770328. There are plenty of tat shops in the one-street town touting myths and magic to the willing.

Sleeping
E **YHA Hostel**, T01840 770334, at Dunderhole Point open 29 Mar-30 Oct with fantastic views along the coast (also available for hire off season). **Camping Bossiney Farm**, T01840 770481, just north at Bossiney, or **The Headland**, T01840 770239, on the Atlantic Rd, open Easter-Oct.

Polzeath

In the lea of Pentire Point nestles the pleasant seaside resort of Polzeath – popular with Middle England's guitar-toting, school-leaving population.

Sleeping
D-C **Pentire View**, T01208 862484, is just up from the beach. **Camping Trenant Steading**, T01208 869091. If you're not in a couple or with a family, camping in Polzeath is going to prove difficult – neither **Tristram Camping Park**, T01208 862215, which overlooks the bay, nor **The Valley Caravan Park**, T01208 862391, accommodate groups.

Eating/drinking
On the beach there are a number of eating opportunities serving up snacks. Just up from the beach sits **The Oyster Catcher**, a lively spot for an evening drink.

Directory
Surf shops Anns Cottage, T01208 863317, stocks a full range of gear. **Fluid Juice**, Old Airfield, St Merryn in Padstow, T01841 520928, www.fluidjuice.co.uk. Adrian Phillips has been creating custom boards for some of North Cornwall's chargers for more than 20 years. **Local Hero**, based just inland on Brook Rd, Wadebridge, T01208 814282, www.localhero.co.uk. Local Hero's Graeme Bunt brings more than 20 years of shaping experience to his north coast business. TJ's Surf Shop, T01208 863625, right on Polzeath beachfront, stocks a full range of hardware as well as offering equipment hire.

Newquay

Newquay is Europe's self-styled surf capital and deserves the title. There are surf shops on every corner and shapers galore. It even has good surfing beaches – if you can take the crowds. Although not an unpleasant resort, the summer nights can be a throng of stag nights, hen parties and a whole rainbow spectrum of football shirts.

Sleeping
Newquay is awash with hotels, B&Bs

DEMI TAYLOR

The Eden Project

and surf lodges. For cheap **B&B** accommodation within walking distance of Fistral, check out Headland Rd. There are also many **lodges** in town but check the rooms as standards vary from clean and compact to cramped and grubby.

L+ Headland Hotel, T01637 872211, www.headlandhotel.co.uk, sits in a commanding position, overlooking Fistral. This redbrick hotel formed the location for Roald Dahl's *The Witches* and sponsors the Fistral surf cam on Pentire Head. B&B budget doubles without views start at around £80; their best rooms in high season can command around £290. However, residents have access to the hotel's tennis courts, 9 hole golf course, swimming pools, sauna, jacuzzi etc. **A-C The Aqua Shack**, Island Cres, T01637 879611, www.aquashacksurflodge.co.uk, overlooks Towan Beach and has clean, bright B&B dorm accommodation from £20 p/p and doubles from £30 p/p with board storage. **A-C The Boarding House**, Headland Rd, T01637 873258, www.theboardinghouse.co.uk, has both dorms and quieter rooms for couples, a bar, restaurant and terrace with beach views and is home to a Quiksilver/Roxy surf school run by former European champion Grishka Roberts. **B-D Cribber Green Rooms**, Headland Rd, T01637 875082, overlooks Fistral and has bunk and room accommodation. **B-D Newquay Surf Lodge**, Springfield Rd, T01637 859700, is a self-catering lodge near the centre of town. **C-D Home Surf Lodge**, Tower Rd, T01637 851736, is a lively place that openly welcomes stag nights so might not be the best place if you need an early night. It has a late

bar and also does B&B. **C-E Fistral Backpackers**, Headland Rd, T01637 873146, is a short walk to the beach. It does dorms and doubles and has a board and drying room and kitchen facilities. **Self catering Headland Village**, T01637 872211, www.headlandvillage.co.uk, is a series of 22 modern cottages and apartments owned by, operated by and set in the grounds of **The Headland Hotel** (see above). 1-3 bed cottages furnished to a high standard come with sun deck, cleaning lady and all the leisure facilities of the hotel. 2 bed cottages from £625-1900 in peak Jul-Aug. **Camping** For camping the options are pretty limited for groups due to drunken antics in the past. Try **Rosecliston**, T01637 830326, **Smugglers Haven** at Trevelgue Holiday Park, T01637 852000, and **Sunnyside**, T01637 873338.

❼ Eating/drinking

For lunchtime 'caf' grub try **Breadline Café** on Beachfield Rd. **The Fistral Chef Café** over the road from the Red Lion on Beacon Rd is also a good place to grab a meal. For a more expensive slap-up meal, **The Fistral Blu** on Fistral Beach is worth trying, as is the **Lewenick Lodge** on Pentire Headline with a wide menu from seafood to steaks. Joe Moran, editor of *Pit Pilot*, recommends **The Phoenix** on Watergate Beach as a good place to eat day and night with a good value daily 'Surfers Special'. For traditional pub grub try **The Red Lion** on Beacon Rd, a popular spot with good value food.

Newquay is heaving with bars and clubs. **Berties** nightclub caters to the younger end of the spectrum, while **The Koola Bar**, T01637 873415, on

Beach Rd offers great sounds in a clean modern environment. **Jelly Jazz**, for the funksters out there, is not to be missed. **Sailors**, on Fore St, tends to be where everyone gravitates after a few pints to dance the night away to chart music. It's a bit like Woodstock – if you remember it, you obviously weren't there! **The Walkabout**, Cliff Rd, is another popular hangout.

❶ Directory

Internet Access at Tad and Nick's Talk 'N' Surf, Fore St, and at **Cybersurf @ Newquay**, Broad St. **Surf schools** Newquay is home to the smart-looking **National Surfing Centre**, www.nationalsurfingcentre.com, at Fistral beach. The complex houses the **BSA/NSC Surf School**, T01637 850737, plus showers, toilets, surf shops, hire shops, cafés and the smart Blu restaurant as well as the **BSA headquarters**, T01637 876474, www.britsurf.co.uk. **Hibuscus Surf School**, Fairfield Pl, T01637 879374, www.hibiscussurf school.co.uk, was the first women's- only surf school set up in the UK – run by women for women. It is BSA-registered and their instructors include BLU champion, Emma Fitzhenry. There are plenty of surf schools operating in Newquay, for a full listing see page 242.

Surf shops There is a massive selection of surf shops in Newquay. Here are just a few to get started. **Fistral Surf Company**, T01637 850808, is a long-standing surf retailer with a number of shops in town; the biggest is on Cliff Rd. **MMY**, Beach Rd by Towan Beach, T01637 852101, www.mmyworld.com, stocks MMY boards – whose team includes Steve Winter and Lee Bartlett – as well as other clothing and accessories.

North Shore, Fore St, T01637 850620, offers a good selection of hardware and clothing. **Ocean Magic**, Cliff Rd, T01637 850071, is run by shaper and former European champion Nigel Semmens who has been shaping boards under this mark and 'NS' for more than 30 years. **Revolver**, Fore St, T01637 873962, is a relatively new shop with a retro twist, run by surf photographer John Isaac and selling single fins, fish and old skool longboards including models by Fin, Skip Frye, Joel Tudor, Harbour as well as clothing and accessories. **Seabase**, Seabase Industrial Estate, T01637 875811, www.seabase.ltd.com, provide quality blanks and shape and finish boards for top brands. **Tourist information** Marcus Hill opposite the bus station, T01637 854020.

Perranporth

Perranporth is a pretty unremarkable resort town but it does offer plenty of cheap accommodation and access to a huge beach, complete with beach bar.

⊜ Sleeping

D **Perranporth Youth Hostel**, T01872 573812. There are also hordes of cheap B&Bs in town within a short walk of the beach. Perranporth also has a number of caravan parks including **Perranporth Caravan Holidays**, Crow Hill, T01872 572385, offering static caravans with sea views across Perran Sands. It's just a short scramble down to the waves.

❶ Directory

Surf shops There are plenty of surf hire stores and surf shops here

including **The Aloha Surf Station**, St Pirans Parade, T01872 571997, stocking a full range of hardware and accessories, and **Piran Surf**, T01872 573242, www.piransurf.com.

St Agnes

This picturesque ex-mining village off the B3277 is the heart of Cornwall's most tight-knit surfing community.

⊜ Sleeping

A **The Driftwood Spas Hotel**, T01872 552428, can be found down by the picturesque Trevaunance Cove and is home to a popular pub and Sun carvery. C-D **The Malthouse**, T01872 553318, is an excellent, eclectic, surfer-friendly B&B in a central location in Peterville, the lower part of St Agnes,

DEMI TAYLOR

25 Post-surf beer at Chapel ▸▸ *p59*

and comes highly recommended. C-D **Penkerris**, T01872 552262, is an ivy-clad house as you enter the village at the top end. **Camping Beacon Cottage Farm**, T01872 552347, offers camping and electric hook-ups for vans May to Oct. **Presingoll Farm**, T01872 552333, also offers camping and pitches for vans Easter-Oct and can be found on the main road into St Agnes near the film studio.

🍴 Eating/drinking
Chapel Porth Café on the beach at Chapel Porth is the ultimate take-away experience, somewhat an institution and not to be missed, especially the Croque Rosemary – hunks of granary bread with melted cheese and cream-cooked mushrooms. The hedgehog ice creams are also legendary – ice cream, clotted cream and roasted hazelnuts… **The Driftwood Spas** is a pub with a pool table and live bands as well as a Sun carvery. **The Peterville** is a traditional pub with live soccer and **The Tap House**, also in Peterville, is popular and crammed at weekends, even in the winter. The food is excellent and on Wed off-season does half-price pizzas. **The St Agnes Hotel** also does a good Sun roast and bar meals.

➊ Directory
Surf shops and facilities Aggie Surf Shop, Peterville, T01872 553818, has a full selection of hardware and clothing. St Agnes is the home of Chops Lascelles' **Beach Beat Surfboards**, T01872 553818, www.beachbeatsurfboards.co.uk. Chops and co shape boards for some of Cornwall's top surfers including barrel king Robin Kent, longboard champion Dominique Kent-Monroe, aerialist Josh Ward and ripper Shaun Skilton. Steve Bunt's **Best Ever Surfboards**, T07866 858343, www.besteversurfing.com, are also based in the heart of the Badlands and make boards for local chargers including Drustan Ward, Jamie Kent and rising women's star Nicola Bunt.

Porthtowan

Accommodation is pretty limited in Porthtowan but there is a campsite as you turn into the village at **Rosehill Touring Park** on Rose Hill, T01209 890802. It is in a nice shady valley but does have a slightly authoritarian list of rules. **The Blue** overlooking Porthtowan beach is a great place to enjoy a post-surf beer. The food is fairly pricey and can be hit or miss. Live music on a Sat night. **The Unicorn** set back from the beach may have a less glamorous location but is popular with locals for its well-priced menu, football screenings and regular bands and events.

Old tin workings hug the cliffs below St Just in West Cornwall

🛈 Directory

Surf shops Sick Lame & Lazy, at the top end of the village, T01209 891881, is open year-round and popular with bodyboarders. Stocks limited hardware and hires out equipment. **Sunset Surf School**, T01209 891699, www.sunsetsurfschool.co.uk. Run by top British surfer Eloise Taylor, this BSA-approved mobile surf school covers Porthtowan, St Agnes and Perranporth (depending on conditions) and caters for both mixed and girls-only groups. **Tris Surf Shop** just from the beach is open seasonally with a good range of hire equipment.

Gwithian

This little, pretty village on the coastal B3301 backs onto a 3-mile stretch of golden sands.

🛏 Sleeping

B-C Gwithian Holiday Suites, T01736 755493, www.gwithianholidays.com, offer reasonably priced holiday suites (room and lounge with tea-making facilities and toaster). Run by local ripper Tyson Greenaway, the accommodation is surfer-friendly; Tyson also offers equipment hire and lessons. **Camping Atlantic Coast Caravan Park**, T01736 752071, www.atlanticcoast-caravanpark.co.uk, is open to campers, with statics also available sleeping up to 6 from £205-470 per week. **Gwithian Farm**, Church Town Rd, T01736 753127, www.gwithianfarm.co.uk, is a relaxed site with simple facilities open Mar-Oct. It's a 15-min walk through the dunes to the beach and a stroll across the road to the local pub.

🍴 Eating/drinking

Godrevey Café, based in the National Trust beach car park, has views over the beach from the upper terrace. This is the perfect spot to enjoy a sundowner beer or post-surf snack from homemade cakes to sandwiches. It is even more perfect in the evening when the menu turns to fresh fish platters (around £10 for a main) – don't miss the Portuguese style monkfish stew! **Pendarves Arms**, opposite Gwithian Farm, is a relaxed spot for a pint or a bite to eat, with a popular summer beer garden.

🛈 Directory

Surf schools Gwithian Surf Academy, Prosper Hill, T01736 755493, www.surfacademy.co.uk, is BSA-approved and carries out lessons on Gwithian beach – perfect for learners and improvers.

Hayle

Hayle is an underestimated town that offers loads of potential as a base for a surf trip. It has easy access to St Ives Bay and has plenty of accommodation.

🛏 Sleeping

Camping Beachside Holiday Park, T01736 753080, sits in the dunes overlooking the sea and offers chalets, bungalows as well as pitches for vans and tents. **St Ives Bay Holiday Park**, T0800 317713, also overlooks the sea and has static caravans as well as pitches for tents and vans.

🛈 Directory

Surf shops Market Sq is the base for Down The Line Surf Co, T01736 757025, where they stock a good selection of hardware and clothing.

Sennen

This long, picturesque, crescent-shaped bay is a popular tourist destination and accommodation is pretty limited here. It is, however, one of Cornwall's most consistent beaches, and has plenty of room to spread out, has a pretty chilled atmosphere as well as new beach facilities including changing rooms, wet area, surf school, surf hire May-Sep and a café, www.sennenbeach.com.

🛏 Sleeping

A-E Whitesands Lodge, T01736 871776, www.whitesandslodge.co.uk, has been a popular option with dorm accommodation (from around £12.50), single and double rooms (en suite with breakfast around £60). It also has a café/restaurant. You could also try **C Myrtle Cottage**, T01736 871698, in the village. **Camping** Head to **Trevedra Farm Caravan and Camping Site**, T01736 871835, with pitches for tents and vans.

🍴 Eating/drinking

The Beach Restaurant in the seafront car park, T01736 877191, is fresh, modern and has some wonderful views across the bay.

🛈 Directory

Surf schools Sennen Surfing Centre, T01736 871227, http://sennensurfing centre.com, offer BSA surf lessons. **Surf shops** Chapel Idne Surf Shop in the beach car park at Sennen Cove, T01736 871192, stocks a good selection of hardware and clothing and has board hire facility as well.

Surfing South Cornwall and South Devon

Antonia Atha on the north coast is on the phone to Sam Boex on the south coast. She asks him what the surf is like. He goes quiet, then asks how many people she's bringing with her and where she's planning on going. "Two friends, Praa Sands," she replies. After a long pause, remembering years of friendship, but most importantly realizing she's not coming to his break, he decides to come up with the goods, "Yeah it's pretty glassy, about 3-4 ft." This is the real north/south divide.

The water laps on Porthcurno beach in tiny 6 inch glassy barrels. It is high summer and the golden sand runs up to the bottom of peach- and honey-coloured granite cliffs that are warm to the touch. The water is so clear that the huge mass of an offshore basking shark is clearly visible beneath the lumbering fin that extends skyward out of the water. The view is so serene that you wonder if there could ever be surf on Cornwall's southern shore. This shelter and calm has been a draw to generations of holidaymakers. When they think of Cornwall, it is scenes like this that they envisage. Thatched cottages, sheltered streams running down to sleeping coves. What they don't envisage when they decide to take a stroll along the harbour wall at Porthleven is 8-ft barrels unloading onto a shallow reef within plain view.

For although the south coast of Cornwall and Devon is home to many sleepy coves, sheltered beaches and hidden gems like the Minack, it is also home to some excellent surfing. All that is required to transform this sleeping coastline is any southwesterly or a big westerly swell. "The south coast is great… although it doesn't break as often as the north coast," says Porthleven local Sam Boex. "The waves are good when there is swell with more variety, from little coves to good reefs. Leven is a really good wave, but it can be busy with inexperienced surfers, which can be VERY dangerous. My advice is respect the locals: we are a

decent bunch of guys and girls, see how the line-up works… there is an unwritten etiquette within the water which is important to observe."

The south coast is also a cultural centre. "Falmouth mixes a buzzing and progressive arts scene with the rawer edge of the docks and the tangible feel of a real working town. The large student population keeps the place lively, and new cafés and bars are opening up all the time," explains *Stranger* magazine editor, Helen Gilchrist. Plymouth University offers a Surf Science degree, each new intake drawing in surfers from all over the UK. This diversity has produced a young and vibrant scene with locals including the Boex brothers and Robyn Davies – the best female surfer Britain has produced.

South Cornwall & Devon board guide

Fat Boy Flyer
Shaper: Chops Lascelles of Beachbeat Surfboards

- 7'2" x 20½" x 2⅝" the original hotdog shortboard.
- Versatile from 6'8" x 19¼" x 2⅛" up to 7'8" x 22" x 3".
- An aggressive mid-range retro style thrusters that will charge 10 ft and perform in 2 ft surf.
- Ideal for charging Praa from 2-6 ft.
- Built for big guys, beginner shortboarders, a perfect second board or a first board.
- The most popular model I've ever made.

Performance Shortboard
Shaper: Chops Lascelles of Beachbeat Surfboards

- 6'3" x 18½" x 2¼".
- Good high performance shortboard.
- Ideal for when the south coast reefs are pumping.

Boards by
Beachbeat Surfboards
Factory: Laminations, St Agnes, Cornwall, T 01872-553918
Lam2574@aol.com

The popularity of the south coast does lead to some pockets of overcrowding. Praa Sands, Leven and Whitsand Bay can be a hectic cocktail of locals, visitors and students all vying for the set waves. But it is also a coastline where, despite the large surfing population, it is still possible to strike out and find a quiet spot to share a few waves in a chilled-out line-up. It just takes a good map and a bit of exploring.

Coastline

The granite cliffs around Land's End have excellent climbing and stunning views, especially on a stormy winter's day. A steady stream of shipping slips out of the Channel and into the fury of the Atlantic bound for all corners of the world. Just to the east sit a myriad of smugglers' coves and open sandy beaches, each one holding a possibility of low tide waves. The weather-hardened Lizard is also a delight to explore. There really are some picture-book villages here, and coves where quiet waves can be found when the hugest of swells hit. South Devon lives a life torn between hosting hordes of holidaymakers in the summer and wild empty beaches in winter, the seafront parking of Portwrinkle, Whitsand and Bantham filled with board-laden cars and vans.

Localism

Many southern Cornish and Devon breaks are already very crowded. Sam Boex advises: "Don't bring more than two people with you – the beaches don't hold many surfers. Be friendly and you'll have a good time, and get some good waves." Breaks like Praa Sands are popular in the winter when northerly winds cut up the north shore. Try to check out new breaks. There is little localism on the south coast. As Sam puts it: "South coast surfers have no attitude, which is great. . . when we go to the pub, the last thing we talk about is surfing!" Certain breaks, like Leven, however do have very competitive line-ups. Try to be honest about your ability.

Top local surfers

South Cornwall is a hotbed of talent, including the likes of British women's champion, Robyn Davies; the brothers Boex (Jake, Sam and Will), Dan 'Mole' Joel and Falmouth local Kate Reeds. South Devon is home to respected surf photographer Alex Williams. When Leven is firing however you'll be sure to spot some of north Cornwall's finest including Minzie (who will be on it at first light), Robin Kent and James Hendy.

Getting around

A good series of A roads run the length of south Cornwall and Devon through Helston, Falmouth, St Austell, and Plymouth. Access down to many of the breaks however is via small country (often single track) lanes and narrow village roads.

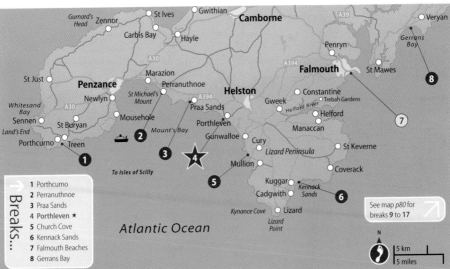

Breaks...
1 Porthcurno
2 Perranuthnoe
3 Praa Sands
4 Porthleven ★
5 Church Cove
6 Kennack Sands
7 Falmouth Beaches
8 Gerrans Bay

Breaks

South Cornwall

1 Porthcurno

- ⊙ **Break type**: Beach break.
- ⊛ **Conditions**: Medium to big swells, offshore in northerly winds.
- ❶ **Hazards/tips**: Beautiful spot, not too crowded.
- ⊜ **Sleeping**: Praa Sands ›› p84.

Cocooned by granite cliffs, at high tide this narrow bay almost disappears. At low the bay opens up with lefts and rights in the emerging bay to the east. Needs a southwesterly swell or a big northwesterly wrapping in to work. With crystal-clear water, this sheltered spot is a great place to see basking sharks on calm, flat summer days. The open-air Minack Theatre overlooks the bay.

2 Perranuthnoe

- ⊙ **Break type**: Beach break.
- ⊛ **Conditions**: Medium to big swells, offshore in northeasterly.
- ❶ **Hazards/tips**: Busy spot.
- ⊜ **Sleeping**: Praa Sands ›› p84.

Underestimated bay with a good right breaking off the rocks at the west. There is an A-frame reef, **Cabbage Patch**, which breaks over boulders to the eastern end of the bay. In between are peaks of variable quality. Works best from low to three-quarter tide as high tide sees the bay virtually disappear. It's usually a couple of feet smaller than Praa Sands. Parking near the beach. Used to be very quiet but as Praa has got busier, this spot has taken the overspill. With a more relaxed vibe, it is popular with beginners, intermediate surfers and longboarders.

3 Praa Sands

- ⊙ **Break type**: Beach break.
- ⊛ **Conditions**: Medium to big swells, offshore in northeasterly winds.
- ❶ **Hazards/tips**: Very crowded, can be heavy, rips.
- ⊜ **Sleeping**: Praa Sands ›› p84.

A popular, winter break that works in southwesterly or big northwesterly swells, to produce powerful, punchy waves. Offshore in northerly or northeasterly winds, it usually draws a big crowd because when Praa is on, the north coast is usually blown out. Gets packed at weekends on good swells. Works on all tides but at high can become a shore dump. There is parking overlooking the break.

4 Porthleven

- ⊙ **Break type**: Right-hand reef.
- ⊕ **Size**: 3-10 ft.
- ⊜ **Length**: 50-100 m.
- ⊚ **Swell**: Southwesterly.
- ⊘ **Wind**: Northeasterly.
- ⊜ **Tide**: Three-quarters to just off low.
- ⊛ **Bottom**: Rock reef.
- ⊛ **Entry/exit**: Off the rocks.
- ❶ **Hazards/tips**: Shallow near low, crowds, crowds, and more crowds!
- ⊜ **Sleeping**: Praa Sands ›› p84.

Porthleven is the most respected reef break in the south of England and, as such, when it is breaking it attracts a large crowd. Although 'Leven' breaks year round, it really comes to life during the big winter swells. The wave breaks onto a reef situated just to the west of the entrance to Porthleven harbour and provides some great vantage points for those watching. It is really a mid tide

South Cornwall

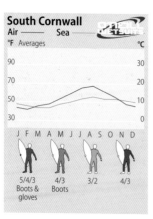

Air ——— **Sea**

°F Averages   °C

90   30

70   20

50   10

30   0

J F M A M J J A S O N D

| 5/4/3 | 4/3 | 3/2 | 4/3 |
| Boots & gloves | Boots | | |

break with low tide getting pretty shallow and high suffering from backwash. The reef is famed for its fast, hollow rights, which can be board-snappingly ferocious, but it also throws up some lefts.

The biggest factor in surfing Leven is the crowds. Most of Cornwall's best surfers will be in the line-up when it's firing and if you watch you will see that no waves go through unridden. The UK's most competitive line-up is no place for the faint hearted. Porthleven regular James Hendy says, "The thing about Leven is that when it's good, it's so competitive that there's only a handful of guys actually getting waves.

Some people just paddle out to say they were in." The rocks provide a great vantage point to watch all the action.

"Leven can be a real board eater," recalls Minzie. "I remember one session where I'd just snapped my board and I was scooting in on what was left of it and I saw Chops paddling out. He saw me and started laughing. I had a spare board with me so I grabbed it, put my leash on and jumped back off the rocks. I'm paddling out and guess who I meet coming in on the remains of his board?"

ⓘ If you like Porthleven try Thurso East in Scotland (see page 166) or La Sauzaire in France.

5 Church Cove

- ◉ **Break type**: Beach break.
- ◉ **Conditions**: Small to medium swells, offshore in northeasterly/easterly winds.
- ◉ **Hazards/tips**: Crowds.
- ◉ **Sleeping**: The Lizard ▸▸ *p84*.

Southwesterly-facing bay on the Lizard Peninsula that can produce some quality waves in southwesterly or big northwesterly swells. Works best from low to three-quarter tide. Winds from the northeast or easterly direction are preferable. Popular break in the winter.

3 Praa Sands

4 Porthleven

4 Cornwall's Russell Winter takes a break from the World Tour to drop in at Porthleven ▶▶ *p76*

6 Kennack Sands

- **Break type**: Beach break.
- **Conditions**: Big swells, offshore in northwesterly/northerly winds.
- **Hazards/tips**: Crowds.
- **Sleeping**: The Lizard ▸▸ *p84*.

Southeasterly-facing beach on the eastern side of the Lizard. There are two beaches separated by a large rocky reef known as the Caerverracks. Only works in massive northwesterly or big southwesterly swells. At low tide the beach opens out with a long stretch to the east and a small section to the west. Can have lefts and rights. Gets busy when working. Parking by the beach.

7 Falmouth Beaches

- **Break type**: Beach and reefs.
- **Conditions**: Big swells, offshore in north/northwesterly winds.
- **Hazards/tips**: Crowds.
- **Sleeping**: Falmouth ▸▸ *p86*.

The three beaches closest to Falmouth – Maenporth, Swanpool and Gyllyngvase – can break in big southwesterly swells and the occasional easterly in the channel. Between Swanpool and Gyllyngvase lies Falmouth Reef.

❝❞

On its day, Porthleven is as good as any wave in the world, but with such a small take-off zone, the crowd factor can be horrendous. Like any high performance wave, Pipeline for example, there are only a handful of people getting the waves, the really ruthless, focused ones. The rest are floating around just to say they've been in.

James Hendy, top Cornish surfer

8 Gerrans Bay

- **Break type**: Beach break.
- **Conditions**: Big swells, offshore in northerly winds.
- **Hazards/tips**: Check in winter on huge swells. Parking at beach.
- **Sleeping**: Falmouth/Pentewan ▸▸ *p86/p87*.

Beautiful setting for this long, sheltered bay. Access from the west to car park overlooking beach with rocks. Can have some lovely peaks from low through to three-quarter tides. There is another access point through Veryan to the east of the bay where sandy peaks work all through the tide.

DEMI TAYLOR

3 Praa Sands looking east ▸▸ *p76*

9 Caerhays

- ⊕ **Break type**: Beach break.
- ☁ **Conditions**: Big swells, offshore in northerly winds.
- ❶ **Hazards/tips**: Picturesque bay.
- ⊜ **Sleeping**: Falmouth/Pentewan ›› p86/p87.

Beautiful beach facing south into Veryan Bay. A winter break that needs a huge westerly storm or a decent southwesterly swell. Works through the tides but needs northerly winds.

10 Pentewan

- ⊕ **Break type**: Beach break
- ☁ **Conditions**: Big swells, offshore in westerly winds
- ❶ **Hazards/tips**: Check in huge winter storms
- ⊜ **Sleeping**: Pentewan ›› p87

This spot sits directly to the south of St Austell and is only worth checking in the biggest of storms. However, westerly winds will be offshore here and the beach can deliver nice, clean waves – better on the push.

11 Seaton

- ⊕ **Break type**: Beach break
- ☁ **Conditions**: Big swells, offshore in northeasterly winds
- ❶ **Hazards/tips**: Watch out for rips when big
- ⊜ **Sleeping**: Fowey/Whitsand Bay ›› p88

Beach break that works from low to mid tide on the push. Doesn't pick up as much swell as the breaks to the east. Worth checking the reefs at Downderry on a good clean swell.

12 Portwrinkle

- ⊕ **Break type**: Beach break.
- ☁ **Conditions**: Big swells, offshore in northeasterly winds.
- ❶ **Hazards/tips**: Popular break.
- ⊜ **Sleeping**: Whitsand Bay ›› p88.

Long stretch of beach close to Plymouth and as such attracts a crowd when it's working. This beach break, which sits sheltered below cliffs, has decent rights and lefts when a good southwesterly swell hits. Works from low tide on the push, but high can be rocky.

13 Whitsand Bay

- ⊕ **Break type**: Beach break.
- ☁ **Conditions**: Big swells, offshore in northeasterly winds.
- ❶ **Hazards/tips**: Popular break.
- ⊜ **Sleeping**: Whitsand Bay ›› p88.

When a southwesterly or westerly swell hits, Plymouth surfers will head here. for

Although a crowd magnate, it's a big beach so there are always plenty of peaks to go around. Works on all tides. Access around Tregantle is regulated by the military, so look out for the red flags. Offshore in northeasterly winds.

South Devon

14 Bovisand Bay

- ⊕ **Break type**: Reef break.
- ☁ **Conditions**: Big swells, offshore in northeasterly winds.
- ❶ **Hazards/tips**: Rips, shallow.
- ⊜ **Sleeping**: Whitsand Bay/South Devon ›› p88.

A jacking, right-hand reef that works best from mid to low tide. There is a tight local crew on it when a big southwesterly swell arrives. Just in the mouth of Plymouth sound. Head west from Down Thomas village. Experienced surfers only.

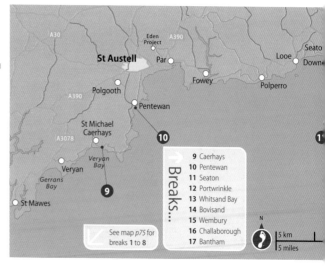

See map p75 for breaks 1 to 8

5 km
5 miles

15 Wembury

- **Break type**: Left point.
- **Conditions**: Big swells, offshore in northeasterly winds.
- **Hazards/tips**: Crowds, rips.
- **Sleeping**: South Devon ›› p89.

In good swells a left will break off Blackstone Rocks producing long walling waves. When it's on there will be a crowd of Plymouth surfers on it. Not a wave for novices.

16 Challaborough

- **Break type**: Beach break.
- **Conditions**: Big swells, offshore in northeasterly winds.
- **Hazards/tips**: For advanced surfers.
- **Sleeping**: South Devon ›› p89.

There is a decent low tide right-hand point at the north end of the bay, breaking off the rocks into deeper water, and also a decent left breaking

16 Challaborough

off the cliffs. There are waves through the tide in the bay which can have rips in big swells. Parking at the beach.

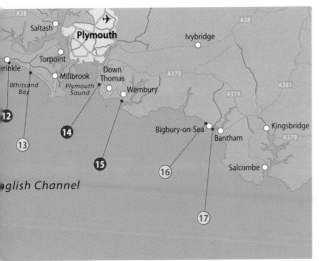

17 Bantham

- **Break type**: Rivermouth and beach break.
- **Conditions**: Big swells, offshore in northeasterly winds.
- **Hazards/tips**: South Devon's top break, quality beach, rips.
- **Sleeping**: South Devon ›› p89.

Not only does Bantham pick up more swell than other South Devon beaches, it also has excellent banks to handle it. There are long waves reeling along the sandbars near the rivermouth and in the middle of the bay there is a right and left peak. Inexperienced surfers should watch out for rips near the river, especially on a dropping tide. Popular beach that can even get waves in the summer. Car park in the dunes, so can get crowded.

DAVID RASTOVICH

TRIPLE COVER

CREATURES OF LEISURE
TRIPLE WHEELY

CREATURES OF LEISURE
BIG FIVE

CREATURES OF LEISURE
LONGBOARD DOUBLE

SEABASE

South Cornwall

Praa Sands

A popular winter haunt, Praa is inundated every time a good swell is running and northerly winds tear up North Cornwall's shores. The vibe however remains good. With the opening of the Sand Bar, Praa has cemented itself as South Cornwall's surf centre.

● Sleeping

C Brambles B&B, Pengersick Farm, T01736 762123, www.bramblesbed andbreakfast.co.uk. Adjacent to Pengersick Castle, set in beautiful gardens and just a short walk to the beach, this rustic B&B has a welcoming feel with wonderful organic breakfasts.
C Quikkyns B&B, T01736 719141, set just to the west overlooking Perranuthnoe, this relaxed B&B is a short walk from the beach and used to surfers – additionally, they have secure storage for boards and bikes. **Camping** There are several small campsites in the area around Praa. The larger sites include **Kenneggy Cove Holiday Park**, T01736 763453, www.kenneggycove.co.uk. Overlooking the cove to the west of Praa, this is a pretty and relaxed spot to camp, open Apr-Oct. They also have statics sleeping 4 which cost from around £150-450 per week. Try out the rope shortcut to the bay. **Praa Holiday Village**, T01736 762201, www.praa-sands.co.uk. Set just back from the seafront and open Mar-Nov to couples and families only, they offer camping

plus statics – a 4-berth caravan costs between £105-255 to hire for a week.

● Eating/drinking

Chris Old's Restaurant. Right on the seafront, he serves up chish and fips, Yorkshire-stylee. **Sandbar**, T01736 763516, with massive windows overlooking the beach *and* a pool table in the background, this is *the* place on the south coast to head to for a post-surf chow down, sundown beer or even just a hot choc. At weekends there's music and great food on offer – a surf 'n' turf grill for around £15 for a couple. You know it makes sense!

● Directory

Surf shops Stones Reef Surf Shop, T01736 762991. Right on the seafront, they are open year-round (even New Year's day!) and sell a range of hardware and essentials. They also carry a good range of hire equipment, including winter suits.

The Lizard Peninsula

Forming the most southerly point on mainland Britain, the Lizard Peninsula has a wild western coast – home to the Devil's Bellows blowhole – and sheltered eastern coastline popular with the blue rinse brigade.

● Sleeping

West There are plenty of good sleeping options around Mullion including **C Colvennor Farmhouse B&B**, T01326 241208. Just to the north in Cury, this is a beautiful stone, former farmhouse. **C Meaver Farm**

B&B, Mullion Cove, T01326 240128, with lovely log fires. **C-D Criggan Mill**, T01326 240496, www.crigganmill.co.uk, offers a B&B service in their pretty timber lodges just above Mullion Cove with breakfast in their on-site coffee shop.

Self catering Criggan Mill also has year-round self-catering timber lodges sleeping 4 from £195-515 per week. Pretty location, pretty lodges. Bring a bag of coins for the electric.

Camping Mullion Holiday Park, T0870 444 5344, www.weststar holidays.co.uk. This is a real family resort with swimming pools and cabaret, open Apr-Sep with camping facilities and statics.

Kennack Sands B-C **Kennack Bay Guest House**, T01326 290780. This former telegraph station in Ruan Minor is a good base. They also have a self catering 1-bed apartment. E **Coverack YHA**, School Hill, Coverack, T01326 280687. Just north of Kennack and 2 mins to the sea with camping also available, open Mar-Oct. Drying room and meals available. **Self catering Mount Herman**, Ruan Minor, T01326 240496, www.crigganmill.co.uk. Owned by the people from Criggan Mill, this beautiful granite and serpentine cottage sleeps 6 from around £325-750 per week.

Camping Welcome to the land of the family holiday park – take your pick!

Gwendreath Farm Caravan Park, T01326 290666, May-Sep to tents, caravans but not to vans! Statics from around £125-325 per week for 4. **Kennack Sands Park**, Kuggar, T01326 290533, open Easter-Oct with statics from £125-285 per week for 4. **Sea Acres**, T0870 220 4649. 20 acres to be precise! Open Mar-Sep, statics from £120-415 sleeping 4. **Seaview**, T01326 290635, www.seaviewcaravanpark.com. A 10-min walk to the beach with statics and chalets. **Silver Sands**, T01326 290631, www.silversandsholiday park.co.uk, is probably the best bet: 600 m from the beach, open Mar-Sep for camping, and statics sleeping 4 available from £130-350 per week.

DEMI TAYLOR

Evening sun in south Cornwall

Flat spells

Diving Whitsand Bay Divers, Seaton Beach, T0845 2002313, www.whitsandbaydivers.com. Book in for a try-dive or a snorkel safari or something more adventurous…go poking around the wreck of a WWII Liberty Ship sunk off Whitsand Bay – the UK's first artificial reef.

Golf There are plenty of courses dotted along this stretch of coastline. Praa Sands GC, Germoe Crossroads, T01736 763445, www.praasandsgolclub.com, is a reasonably priced 9-hole course – around £20 for the day.

Sights Minack Theatre, T01736 810181, www.minack.com. Created in the 1930s, and cut into the cliffside, this outdoor theatre overlooks Porthcurno and is the ultimate summer evening experience – just remember to wrap up warm and take a picnic.

Scilly Isles Thirty miles off the coast of Land's End lies this granite archipelago, home to white sands, hidden coves and an almost sub-tropical collection of flora and fauna. Fly, sail or go James Bond-style and jump on a helicopter (T01736 36871, www.scillyhelicopter.co.uk, from around £75 day return). Tourist information,T01720 422536, www.islesofscilly.co.uk. **Trebah Gardens**, near Falmouth, T01326 250448, www.trebahgarden.co.uk, is recommended by *Stranger* magazine editor, Helen Gilchrist: "A beautiful subtropical garden in a ravine that tumbles down to a lovely beach on the Helford river – probably one of the best skimming locations in the world!"

Skating Penzance Bowl, Princess Way recreational ground, Trenere Estate, is home to a massive, beautiful, brand-new concrete bowl – go and practise your lines. **Pig Pen**, Praceana Av, Falmouth has a good selection of ramps and 1/4 pipes.

Playing Place, just off the A39 to Truro, is this mellow, old skool concrete bowl.

DEMI TAYLOR

Beware of dragons…

Eating/drinking

Halzephron Inn, Church Cove Rd, Gunwalloe, T01326 240406 and close to Culdrose airstation. This excellent inn serves up top-quality lunch and dinner – from traditional pub fare (scampi 'n' chips) to local cheeseboards, to something a little more exotic – all at moderate prices. They also have a lovely beer garden and B&B facilities (around £80 for a double).

Falmouth

With its art college, plethora of students and town beaches backed by a myriad of cool bars and cafés, Falmouth almost has the feel of Brighton to it. It is also home to *Stranger* magazine, www.stranger-mag.com, a true reference point for what's really going on in Cornwall: music, art and surf.

Sleeping

There are plenty of B&Bs in the town – many on Melvill Rd. E **Falmouth Lodge Backpackers**, Gyllyngvase Terr, T01326 319996, www.falmouthbackpackers.co.uk. Next to the Princess Pavilion, this is a very homely hostel and some of the rooms have a sea view. Also has internet access, kitchen, TV lounge.

Camping **Mill Farm Chalets & Camping**, Pennance Mill Farm, Maenporth Rd, T01326 317431, www.pennancemill.co.uk. Set on a working dairy farm and open Easter-Nov, they are about ½ mile to the beach with good camping facilities including free showers. Wooden chalets also available from £150-500 per week.

Eating/drinking

Blue South, Arwenack St, is recommended by *Stranger* magazine editor, Helen Gilchrist, for the "huge plates of Nachos, great burgers and interesting salads in a chilled-out atmosphere with sofas and good tunes." **The Boat House** on Trevethan Hill above the old High St has a decking area overlooking the harbour with BBQs in the summer. "In the winter they serve up roaring fires and innovative pub grub washed down with local Skinners ales," says Helen. She also recommends **Bodene's** on Arwenack St, for "a great menu and killer cocktails". **Gyllngvase Beach Café**, Cliff Rd, T01326 312884. Good food, good tunes, good views. **The Quayside Inn**, Arwenack St. Local surfer Emily Caulfield recommends the Chilli Hands and giant Jenga. **Remedies**. Dance the night away downstairs to funk and hip hop, or head upstairs for classic tunes. **The Three Mackerel**, Swanpool Beach, has it all: drinks, food and a great view.

ⓘ Directory
Surf shops and schools Big Wednesday, Church St, T01326

211159, www.bigwednesday surfshop.co.uk, has been stocking a full range of hardware and accessories since 1989. **Falmouth Surf School**, T01326 212144, www.falmouthsurf school.co.uk. This BSA-registered mobile school also offers deals with the backpackers in town. **Freeriders**, based at The Moor, T01326 313456, www.freeridersonline.co.uk, carries a full range of surf, skate and snow products. **Quiksilver Boardriders Store**, Discovery Quay, T01326 311123, stocks hardware plus accessories. **Tourist information** Killigrew St, T01326 312300.

Pentewan

This private beach is managed by **Pentewan Sands Holiday Park**, with several campsites in the area.

🛏 Sleeping
B-C **Piskey Cove B&B** on the village square, T01726 842817, is a 5-min walk to the beach. **Self catering St Margaret's Park**, Polgooth, T01726 74283, is just south of St Austell and has great wooden chalets from £170 per week for 4. **Camping   Penhaven Touring Park**, T01726 843687, set about a mile back from the beach, is a serious ark with pools and family facilities. **Pentewan Sands Holiday**

DEMI TAYLOR

Fishing is an important industry around the Cornish coast with a big fleet based at Newlyn.

6 Kennack Sands ▸▸ *p79*

Park, T01726 843485. Open Apr-Oct to families and couples only, this park with camping pitches and statics sprawls over 32 acres. **Polrudden Farm**, T01726 843213, is a basic site open year-round. **Sun Valley Holiday Park** is just off the B3273 Pentewan Rd, T01726 843266, about a mile form the beach. Open Apr-Oct with statics and apartments available.

🛈 Directory
Surf shops Ocean Sports, Westend, T01726 842817, stocks surf essentials as well as hiring out surf equipment and bikes.

Fowey

Centred around the estuary and overrun by yachts during the Aug regatta, this pretty little harbour town has links to novelist Daphne du Maurier, of *Poldark* and *Jamaica Inn* fame. There is the annual Daphne du Maurier Festival of Arts & Literature which last for around 10 days in May

🌙 Sleeping
Par Sands Holiday Park, behind the dunes at Par Beach, T01726 812868, this park is open Mar-Oct with free shower facilities for campers. Statics sleeping 4-8 available from £175-450 per week for 4.

🛈 Directory
Surf shops Object Boardrider, T01726 832175, South St. Stocks a few basics including wax.

Whitsand Bay

This massive stretch of golden sands (around 4-miles long) is a great ending to Cornwall…

🌙 Sleeping
Camping Carbeil Caravan & **Camping Park**, T01503 2500636, Treliddon Lane, Downderry. At the westernmost edge of Whitsand, 5 mins from the beach and open Apr-Oct. **Whitsand Bay Holiday Park**, Millbrook, T01752 822597, www.whitsandbayholidays.co.uk. Open year-round, overlooks the bay from a cliff-top position. Full family facilities. Statics available from £105-405 per week sleeping 4. Wooden chalets sleeping 6-8 available from £385-1015. Touring pitches not currently available.

🛈 Directory
Surf shops South Coast Surf, T01579 347557, www.south-coast-surf.com, is on the A38 just south of Liskeard and stocks a good range of hardware and accessories.

South Devon

Bantham/Bigbury/Salcombe

You've crossed the River Tamar. Welcome to Devon!

🌐 Sleeping

L-A The Sloop Inn, Bantham, T01548 560489, www.sloopatbantham.com, offers B&B accommodation in 14th-century surroundings, just a short walk from the beach. They also do excellent food from reasonably-priced sausages and chips and sandwiches (around £3-4) to Dover sole (around £16). **B Folly Foot B&B**, T01548 810036, overlooking Challaborough, this is an excellent, surfer-friendly stopover with a drying room for wetsuits and even a little outdoor pool. **E Plymouth Backpackers**, Citadel Rd, Plymouth, T01752 225158, www.backpackers.co.uk, are used to surfers and have good showers. **E YHA Salcombe**, Sharpitor, T01548 842856 has gardens. **Camping Mount Folly Farm**, Folly Hill, Bigbury-on-Sea, T01548 810267, is a simple site in a family-run farm. Open year-round overlooking the bay. They also have a self catering wing of the farmhouse sleeping 2-6.

🌐 Directory

Surf schools Discovery Surf, Plymouth, T07813 639622 www.discoversurf.com. Martin Connolly runs his BSA school from his Plymouth base with year-round lessons at Bigbury Bay.

ALEX WILLIAMS

South Coast

Surfing the South Coast

There is an enduring image of South Coast surfing – the cluster of surfers found around Brighton Pier on cold, onshore winter's days. Longboards glide along mushy, windswept waves, ridden all the way to the shore under the watchful eye of pensioners promenading along the wooden walkway far above. It is a day that would normally see most surfers nestled safely next to the fire, waiting for the next *real* swell to arrive. But here on the South Coast every swell, big or small, is the cue for local waveriders to drop everything and head for the sea. For if there is one characteristic that the South Coast scene has, it is that the locals are the most enthusiastic surfers in the whole of the UK. There are also many hidden spots that this dedicated crew can head for to make the most of the waves while they last. General conditions here have also lead to a switched-on crew that tend to ride boards suited to local waves. Lots of longboards, hybrid shortboards or fish with the volume and drive to get round the flat spots and to rip those onshore, short period swells.

Yet this isn't the whole story. The South Coast does have some quality waves breaking onto some classic set-ups. Breaks around Kimmeridge and the Isle of Wight are on a par with breaks anywhere on the south coast of Devon and Cornwall and the local crew like to keep their secret spots secret. The IOW picks up the most swell on this coastline. It sticks out into the Channel hoovering up both southwesterly and easterly swell. "We have a diversity of the waves due to the unique shape of the island," explains local surfer Joe Truman. "Whatever the conditions it's nearly always possible to find somewhere that's offshore," expands IOW local Nick Whittle. As a result local surfers have progressed to become some of the best on this stretch of coastline. Johnny Fryer is a future star in the making having already finished as runner-up at the 2004 O'Neill British Nationals.

There is also some rich history southside. The Witterings is home to Shore Surf Club, founded back in 1969, just one of the many clubs and societies that help to keep the stoke alive through the flat spells and cold winters. An amazingly extensive network of surf shops, surf schools and shapers cater to this ever-expanding community. With such a stoked and committed group of surfers, it looks like this is the region destined to boast the UK's first artificial reef – Bournemouth Pipeline here we come?

South Coast board guide

Fish
Shaper: Chris 'Guts' Griffiths, Guts Surfboards

- 6'4" x 20½" x 2⅝" for Joe Davies.
- Available from 5'10" x 6'6" long.
- Flexible board for those who want to shortboard on the South Coast.
- Fun board for anything up to 6-ft surf.
- Swallow tail for snappy turns.
- Good all round board for when the surf is on.

Mullet
Shaper: Chris 'Guts' Griffiths, Guts Surfboards

- 6'8" x 21½" x 2⅝" for Guts.
- It's easy to recommend a longboard for the South Coast, but this board is a new idea for longboarders who want a shorter board with the same paddle power and drive.
- Slight rolled V, straight and wide tail template for maximum drive – less squirly.
- As used by Guts to win the 2004 Welsh Masters shortboard title.

Boards by **Guts Surfboards**
Factory: The Gower, Wales, T 01792-360555 or T 07779 583445, www.gutssurfboards.com or contact admin@gutssurfboards.com

Coastline

The South Coast of England includes some of the country's most remarkable and contrasting scenery and geography. The great symbol of Britishness, chalk white cliffs, provide a stunning backdrop to a few hidden surf spots, yet many breaks sit nestled under Victorian piers or in front of bustling promenades whose beaches are riddled with sand-marshalling groynes. Some parts of the South Coast are restricted areas and cordoned-off for the military. Swathes of land around Kimmeridge fall within a firing range and are only accessible at certain times – a frustration to local surfers when a perfect swell hits the Bench.

Localism

It's a familiar tale on the South Coast. Increased numbers in the water, more competition at popular breaks, and consequently a lot more drop-ins and hassles. This is also compounded by the fact that swells in the Channel tend not to last very long, so everyone is frantically trying to make the most of the waves while they are there. As JB and Tom of Ocean Sports Surf Shop explain: "Brighton's waves are fickle and never consistent but there are still a huge number of dedicated surfers – there can be up to 40 people out when it's only 2 ft and messy." Mostly it's a relaxed vibe on the South Coast, but there can be friction at the main breaks. With regards to the IOW, surfer Gail Sheath explains: "The absence of surf hire facilities at our main breaks helps to prevent the overcrowding experienced at Cornish beaches during the summer season."

Top local surfers

On the South Coast, **Johnny Fryer** is the real standout. **Nick Whittle**, **Joe Truman**, **Dominic Ward** and **Jamie Ransom** are

also Isle of White chargers. Other South Coast names include **John Copley**, **Mark Morgan**, **Eric Davies**, **Heather Colebrook** and **Joe Hart**. Jez at Smallplanet rates local shortboarders: Masters champion **Cliff Cox**, **Kevin Hemsley**, **Luke Palmer**, **Tim Elmanbrown** and longboarders **Tom Frost**, **James Frost**, **Paul Turner** and **Jock Patterson**. "What amazes me is the *overall* standard of the quiet shortboard old school who just appear from nowhere as soon as the surf gets above 3 ft," says Adam from www.nosurfinbrighton.tk. "These cat-like individuals absolutely rip. Considering many people would consider any Channel coast area to be longboards only, Brighton has some really amazing shortboarders."

Getting around

Most of the South Coast breaks are very easy to access. There is an excellent road network and usually a major route following the coastline, or just inland. A few breaks are more difficult. Kimmeridge is accessed by a series of minor B roads and a toll road down to the bay. For the Isle of Wight, a short ferry crossing can be an expensive and time-consuming hurdle but it also helps keep the crowds down.

Josh Jupe – South Coast snap

11 Compton line-up ▶▶ *p97*

Breaks

1 Lyme Regis

- ◕ **Break type**: Left and right.
- ◕ **Conditions**: Big swells, offshore in northerly winds.
- ❶ **Hazards/tips**: Parking by the harbour.
- ◔ **Sleeping**: Isle of Purbeck ›› p102.

There is a left- and a right-hand wave by the harbour wall in Lyme Regis that come to life in big southwesterly swells. Best at low to mid tide.

2 West Bay

- ◕ **Break type**: Right-hand boulder reef.
- ◕ **Conditions**: Big swell, offshore in northerly winds.
- ❶ **Hazards/tips**: Parking above the break.
- ◔ **Sleeping**: Isle of Purbeck ›› p102.

Found at the southern end of Chesil Beach, this wave needs a big clean swell to work. Chesil Beach is a shingle shore dump that drops off into deep water.

3 Weymouth

- ◕ **Break type**: Beach break.
- ◕ **Conditions**: Huge swell, offshore in westerly/northwesterly winds.
- ❶ **Hazards/tips**: Sheltered spot in westerly storms.
- ◔ **Sleeping**: Isle of Purbeck ›› p102.

Definitely worth a punt when the swell's up in the Channel. An unremarkable beach that can produce fun lefts and rights. Mainly a winter break.

4 Kimmeridge

- ◕ **Break type**: Reefs.
- ◕ **Conditions**: Medium/big swells, offshore in northerly winds.
- ❶ **Hazards/tips**: Toll road down to bay, parking.
- ◔ **Sleeping**: Isle of Purbeck ›› p102.

Kimmeridge is a break local surfers mention in hushed tones – as you do when discussing a secret. For a well-known break, there are surprisingly few photos and it has avoided the surf mag spotlight. Not only are the breaks here very good when they work, but they are elevated even more by the poor quality of the other South Coast breaks.

There are a number of waves here. **The Bench** is a right-hand flat reef with a short left breaking off the western side. It

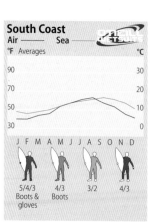

South Coast

Air —— Sea ——

°F Averages °C

5/4/3 Boots & gloves	4/3 Boots	3/2	4/3

J F M A M J J A S O N D

6 Bournemouth Pier

South Coast reef

can produce hollow and shallow waves which are surprisingly powerful. It works through all tides but can be sketchy at low. The reef is a long paddle out to the outer western edge of the bay and is off-limits a lot of the time as it sits in an army firing range. Can get big.

The Bay is a left and right breaking over rock. A lot more mellow than the Bench and a popular spot. Too rocky at low. **The Ledges** are a left- and right-hand reef that are popular with longboarders. They sit outside the bay to the east and can have pretty strong rips in big swells. They work best from mid to high tides and are exposed to the wind. Best on light northerlies. All these breaks are best left to experienced surfers. There is a large, committed crew who are on these waves whenever they break. Don't expect to be a welcomed addition to the line-up, but there is no localism. The lack of photos, the fact it is notoriously fickle and the fact it is fiercely protected, all add to the mystery and allure of this break.

5 Chapman's Pool

- ➔ **Break type**: Reef break.
- ☁ **Conditions**: Medium to big swells, offshore in northeasterly winds.
- ❶ **Hazards/tips**: Access on foot.
- ▬ **Sleeping**: Isle of Purbeck ›› p102.

This cove is found to the southeast of Kimmeridge and is home to a left and a right-hand reef, each breaking down the sides of the cove over a reef. Drive through Worth Matravers and park in the National Trust car park. It is a walk down to the breaks from here. Don't miss the view from St Aldhelm's Head.

6 Bournemouth Pier

- ➔ **Break type**: Beach break.
- ☁ **Conditions**: Big swells, offshore in northerly winds.
- ❶ **Hazards/tips**: Crowds.
- ▬ **Sleeping**: Bournemouth ›› p103.

This Victorian resort town is slightly sheltered by Durlston Head at Swanage and so needs a good sized, southwesterly swell to get into the sand- and pebble-lined bay. Bournemouth Pier acts as an aid to sandbank formation and has banks to the east and west of the structure, which break in any decent swell. Typical conditions would be waist high and crowded. Every now and then it can be very good, rewarding one of Britain's most committed surf communities with good walling lefts and rights. Watch for rips if it gets big.

7 Boscombe Pier

- ➔ **Break type**: Beach break.
- ☁ **Conditions**: Big swells, offshore in northerly winds.
- ❶ **Hazards/tips**: Crowds.
- ▬ **Sleeping**: Bournemouth ›› p103.

Another centre for South Coast surfing, the pier breaks are slightly better than the rest of the beach, with peaks forming to the east and west of the pier structure. If the pier gets good,

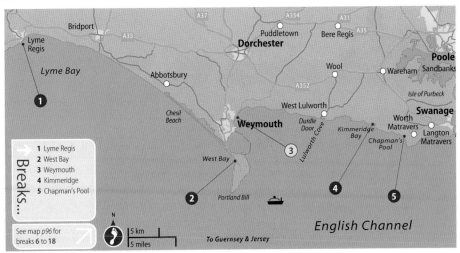

Breaks...

1 Lyme Regis
2 West Bay
3 Weymouth
4 Kimmeridge
5 Chapman's Pool

See map p96 for breaks 6 to 18

Johnny Fryer

We have a friendly, enthusiastic local surf population. There's a strong local identity and sense of history. The Isle of Wight Surf Club was formed in about 1967 and is still going strong. I see people in the line-up that I was first photographing back in the 1970s.

Roger Powley, surf photographer

DEMI TAYLOR

8 Southbourne groynes

word will be out and the line-up will quickly fill with people ditching work and students ditching lectures. Again, fairly average waves that rarely get over waist high and rarely break during the summer months. The new artificial reef proposal seems to be following the great tradition of British millennium projects.

8 Southbourne

- 🌐 **Break type**: Beach break.
- 🌀 **Conditions**: Big swells, offshore in northerly/northeasterly swells.
- ❶ **Hazards/tips**: Groynes.
- 🛏 **Sleeping**: Bournemouth ▸▸ *p103*.

Attractive beachside resort town that merges with Bournemouth to the west. The beach has a series of chalets and a sea wall that drops down onto a sandy beach held in place by a series of large groynes. Low tide sees waves breaking off the end of the barriers, giving short, punchy rights and lefts into the gaps.

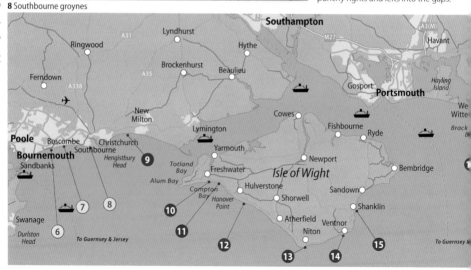

9 Highcliffe

- 🌀 **Break type**: Beach break.
- 🌊 **Conditions**: Big swells, offshore in northerly winds.
- ⓘ **Hazards/tips**: Rips.
- 💤 **Sleeping**: Bournemouth ›› p103.

Past Hengistbury Head there are a series of beaches with groynes that can hold good waves in solid southwesterly swells. Highcliffe has a number of low tide rights but watch out for rips on big tides and big swells.

ROGER POWLEY

15 Hope Bay line-up ›› p99

10 Freshwater Bay

- 🌀 **Break type**: Right-hand point.
- 🌊 **Conditions**: Medium to big swells, offshore in northerly winds.
- ⓘ **Hazards/tips**: Crowds, backwash, rips.
- 💤 **Sleeping**: IOW - West coast ›› p104.

Freshwater is one of the best known breaks on the IOW with right-hand point waves breaking over a reef on the west of the bay. In medium and big southwesterly swells the point will work from low tide until the backwash starts to affect wave quality. The point can hold swells up to 8 ft and can produce excellent waves. Around the corner **Alum Bay** can have reasonable beach break waves when the banks and swell combine. There is a heavy reef on the left of the bay, but for experienced surfers only. The winds need to be from a southerly or southeasterly direction to be offshore on this coast. **Totland** is only worth checking in the biggest of storms

with southerly winds. The groynes mean it only breaks around low tide. Watch out for the rips here as the water moves around a lot with the tides.

11 Compton Bay

- 🌀 **Break type**: Beach and reef.
- 🌊 **Conditions**: Medium swell, offshore in north/northeasterly wind.
- ⓘ **Hazards/tips**: Popular spots.
- 💤 **Sleeping**: IOW - West coast ›› p104.

Just south of Freshwater, this bay has three main set-ups. **Fields** is a fairly consistent beach with peaks that work in medium swells. **Middle Compton** is worth checking if Hanover Point is too crowded. It can have nice peaks in medium swells and smaller but more powerful waves here. **Hanover Point** is an A-frame reef with pretty mellow waves which always attracts a crowd when it's on. Best in a medium swell from mid to high tide. Compton is a popular Summer and Autumn spot due to the fact it can fire in small swells upwards.

12 Chilton Reef

- 🌀 **Break type**: Reef.
- 🌊 **Conditions**: All swells, offshore in northeasterly winds.
- ⓘ **Hazards/tips**: Heavy with rips when big.
- 💤 **Sleeping**: IOW - West coast ›› p104.

This is a heavy reef with hollow lefts and rights in the right swells. Works through the tides and can handle powerful southwesterly swells of a decent size. Best in light winds. Experienced surfers only due to rips and hollow, shallow waves.

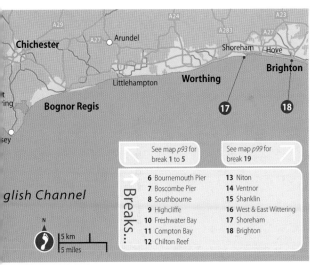

See map p93 for break **1** to **5**

See map p99 for break **19**

glish Channel

N
5 km
5 miles

England South Coast Breaks Highcliffe to Chilton Reef

10 Freshwater Bay line-up ►► *p97*

13 Niton

- 🌀 **Break type**: Right point.
- 🌊 **Conditions**: Medium to big swells, offshore in northerly winds.
- ⓘ **Hazards/tips**: Rips.
- 💤 **Sleeping**: IOW - West coast ▸▸ p104.

This right point is worth checking in clean, southwesterly groundswells when rights can be found by the point. Watch out for rips and rocks. There are other waves nearby.

14 Ventnor

- 🌀 **Break type**: Beach with rocks.
- 🌊 **Conditions**: Medium swells, offshore in northwesterly/ northeasterly winds.
- ⓘ **Hazards/tips**: Heavy shore break, rocks. Experienced surfers only.
- 💤 **Sleeping**: IOW - East coast ▸▸ p105.

There are a number of options here depending on the swell direction. Watch out for the shore dump and the rocks. The new harbour wall here has thrown up a nice peak when the sandbanks are good. With long walling

lefts that work best at low tide, and a short wedgy right at high, it offers some shelter from the wind.

15 Shanklin

- 🌀 **Break type**: Beach break.
- 🌊 **Conditions**: Big swells, offshore in westerly/ northwesterly winds.
- ⓘ **Hazards/tips**: Check in huge southwesterly Channel swells or storms.
- 💤 **Sleeping**: IOW - East coast ▸▸ p105.

This big beach – including **Hope Bay** – offers some shelter when a big swell is pushing up the channel

or a storm is hitting the island from the west. The swell wraps into the bay and cleans up providing some fun waves. Watch out for rips and the longshore drift.

16 West and East Wittering

- 🌀 **Break type**: Beach break.
- 🌊 **Conditions**: Medium to big swells, offshore in northeasterly winds.
- ⓘ **Hazards/tips**: Pebble beach with groynes.
- 💤 **Sleeping**: Witterings ▸▸ p106.

This is a rather inconsistent, windswept stretch of coastline that is

ROGER POWLEY

14 Ventnor

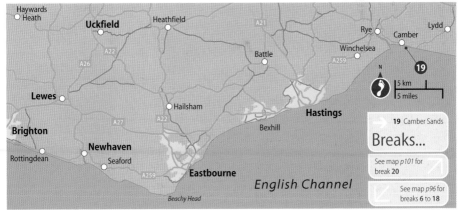

Haywards Heath
Uckfield
Heathfield
A21
Rye
Lydd
Camber
A22
Battle
Winchelsea
A26
A259
19
Lewes
Hailsham
N
5 km
5 miles
Brighton
A27
A22
Bexhill
Hastings
Newhaven
Rottingdean
Seaford
A259
Eastbourne
Beachy Head
English Channel

Breaks...

19 Camber Sands

See map *p101* for break **20**

See map *p96* for breaks **6** to **18**

Surfers' tales

Brighton rocks…
By JB/Tom, Ocean Sports, Brighton

When I first arrived in Brighton, I was still quite new to surfing. There was a huge southwesterly gale and I noticed some big sets rolling in, so stupidly I thought I would get in there. After waiting for what seemed like an hour for a break in the sets I ran in and paddled like a maniac to get past the shore break which was at least double head high and straight onto the stony beach. After about five minutes in the water I realised I had made a bad move. The tide was approaching high and the only waves to be had were breaking about two metres from the shore. I pondered what to do for a few minutes then thought the only thing to do was catch a wave in and hope for the best. I started paddling and a wave picked me up. As I dropped in all I saw was a bed of rocks looming below me, the next thing I remember is crawling up the beach attached by a stretched leash to half of my board. I decided from that day on maybe I needed a little more local knowledge…you live and learn…

www.nosurfinbrighton.tk

Cold winter's shore dump

as popular with windsurfers as it is with waveriders. It does pick up southwesterly Channel swells and when there are waves it will generally have an enthusiastic and committed group of mainly longboarders. Watch out for the rips when big, the groynes and the high tide shore break onto large pebbles. Home of Shore Surf Club since 1969.

17 Shoreham

- **Break type**: Beach break.
- **Conditions**: Medium to big swells, offshore in northerly winds.
- **Hazards/tips**:
- **Sleeping**: Brighton »» *p106*.

There are a number of spots worth checking here. The harbour wall can produce nice wedgy waves in a decent swell, but has a small take-off area. The **Hot Pipe** is a decent peak that will also attract a crowd when it's on. Check breaks from near the harbour.

18 Brighton

- **Break type**: Beach and sand-covered reef.
- **Conditions**: Medium to big swells, offshore in northerly winds.
- **Hazards/tips**: Crowds, rips, long flat spells.
- **Sleeping**: Brighton »» *p106*.

One of the centres of the South Coast surf scene, Brighton has an enthusiastic scene with stoked surfers regularly taking to the 2-ft onshore mush. But good waves can be had here, and competition can get serious. **The Piers** can have a build-up of sand around the pilings providing rolling rights and lefts, but beware of debris around the all but derelict West Pier. Popular with longboarders; drop-ins are common. There is a chunky right known as **The Wedge**, breaking off a large stone breakwater onto the beach. It is sheltered in westerly winds and popular with local bodyboarders. Further to the west sits a couple of breaks known as **The Marina**, found coincidentally next to the marina. This is one of the area's main breaks. The waves here need a big swell to work and can provide short, powerful rights and lefts onto a sandy/flint reef. Experienced surfers only.

faces in a south-southwesterly direction and so is more exposed to swell. Best from mid to high tide. Don't expect too much and you might be pleasantly surprised.

20 Joss Bay

- ⚐ **Break type**: Beach and reef breaks.
- 🌊 **Conditions**: Big swells, offshore in westerly/southwesterly winds.
- ⓘ **Hazards/tips**: Popular beach with Kent surfers.
- 🛏 **Sleeping**: Isle of Thanet ▸▸ p107.

This break sticks out into the southern part of the North Sea where it works in solid easterly or northeasterly swells.

The shallow, sloping geography of the seabed can rob swells of some of their power, but check here in the same swells that see the east coast pumping during the autumn and winter. There is a beach break as well as a couple of reefs on either side of the bay. Surfing in Kent is becoming increasingly popular and a dedicated crew can be found at breaks around Folkestone – including the bay and harbour wall, Dover, Ramsgate, Margate and Herne Bay. A good resource to check out before heading to this stretch of coast is www.thebigchill.co.uk. Surf on this coastline is notoriously fickle so this can also be a good way of making contact with local surfers.

19 Camber Sands

- ⚐ **Break type**: Beach break.
- 🌊 **Conditions**: Big swells, offshore in north/northeasterly winds.
- ⓘ **Hazards/tips**: Big tidal range.
- 🛏 **Sleeping**: Camber Sands ▸▸ p107.

This long, flat beach has a huge tidal range and this affects the quality of the waves. In its favour is the fact that it

18 Brighton

18 Brighton – SAS annual paddle round the pier

Isle of Purbeck

So it's not strictly an isle, but you can hop on a chain ferry from Sandbanks to get there (often the quickest choice if coming from Bournemouth). Swanage, the main village, is full of pubs and cafés. They also play host to an excellent New Years' Eve fancy dress party – all the roads close and the isle rocks out. The area from Durlston Head to Durdle Door, nicknamed the Jurassic Coast, is a geologist's dream and has been granted World Heritage status.

Sleeping
West Purbeck   A-B Black Manston Farm, Steeple, T01929 480743, is about a mile inland from Kimmeridge so is well placed for surfing the reefs here. The B&B is based in a beautiful 16th-century working farm. **A-C Castle Inn**, off the B3070 to West Lulworth, T01929 400311, is a good pub with meals and a beer garden offering B&B. **E YHA Lulworth Cove**, School Lane, West Lulworth, T01929 400564, is a basic timber hostel, open year-round (call first), with a bike store.

Camping   Durdle Door Holiday Park, Lulworth Cove, T01929 400200, open Mar-Oct with field and wooded camping areas and statics from £155-485 per week for 4. Pretty, simple with good bar and restaurant.

Swanage   There are loads of B&Bs here, with a good selection on Kings Rd. **B Eversden Hotel**, Victoria Rd, T01929 423276, is a good choice – a comfortable B&B with drying room and secure board lock-up. **D-E YHA Swanage**, Cluny Cres, T01929 422113, overlooks the town, is open all year with dorms, doubles, a drying room and cycle store. **Camping**   There are plenty of holiday parks and campsites here including **Acton Field Camping Site**, T01929 439424, a simple site. **Swanage Bay Holiday Park**, Panorama Rd, T01929 422130, www.swanagebayholidaypark.co.uk. Open Mar-Nov with statics sleeping 6-8 from £170-410 per week, it also houses a bowling alley, bar, sauna,

www.sharkbait.co.uk

Brighton pier fire ▸▸ *p100*

pool and gym in the new 'Vista Club'. **Tom's Field Campsite**, west of Swanage at Langton Matravers (a 20-min walk), T01929 427110, www.tomsfieldcamping.co.uk. This is the best choice for cheap, relaxed, non-'park'-style camping. Token showers. Not open to caravans. On-site shop selling fresh bread and free-range eggs. They also have the **E Walkers Barn** on the same site, open year-round – basic bunk rooms with simple kitchen. Bedding and cooking equipment not provided.

❶ Directory
Surf shops Freeride Surf, Haven Rd, Canford Cliffs, Poole, T01202 708555. **Just Add Water**, Kingland Cres, T01202 680268. Over the water in Poole, stocks hardware and accessories. **Underground Surf**, The Esplanade, Weymouth, T01305 789822, stock some surf equipment alongside kiteboarding and skate gear. **Tourist information** By the beach on Shore Rd, T0870 4420680, www.swanage.gov.uk.

Bournemouth

Arching golden beaches stretch out around Bournemouth, traditionally drawing in crowds of the blue rinse brigade. Just 2 hrs from London, with a strong student culture, Bournemouth has an eye on what Brighton has achieved, and is slowly trying to reclaim itself.

⊕ Sleeping
D-E Bournemouth Backpackers, Frances Rd, T01202 299491 www.bournemouthbackpackers.co.uk, is a cheap, handy and fairly friendly choice for impromptu surf trips to the South Coast with beds from £13-17. Also accommodates long-term residents. **Camping** There are several sites in the area although none of them offer sea views – you will need your car to get to the breaks. **Meadowbank Holidays**, Stour Way, Christchurch, T01202 483597, is open Mar-Oct to vans and caravans but not tents. They also have statics from £160-410 per week sleeping 4. No

single sex groups. **Mount Pleasant Holidays**, Matchams Lane, Christchurch, T01202 475464, www.mountpleasant-cc.co.uk, have 2 sites, both very French in look and style. Open Mar-Nov, with limited winter bookings, they are reasonably priced and about 5 miles from Bournemouth.

❶ Directory
Surf shops Animal Surf Shop, Post Office Rd, T01202 311334, stock hardware and essentials. **Just Add Water**, Commercial Rd, Bournemouth, T01202 319999, have a good range of hardware and skateboards to tempt you for when it's flat. **Quiksilver Boardriders**, Old Christchurch Rd, also stock hardware and essentials. **Sorted Boardriders**, Sea Rd at Boscombe Pier, T01202 399099, www.sortedboardriders.co.uk, stock hardware and essentials as well as offering BSA-approved lessons. The site has a webcam at Boscombe Pier updated at 0900 everyday. **Surfing Centre**, Bellevue Rd, Southbourne,

DEMI TAYLOR

Heather Colebrook

T01202 433544,
www.bournemouthsurfing.co.uk,
stock a good range of appropriate
boards and equipment. They also offer
BSA-approved lessons and equipment
hire. Their website is a useful resource
with a surf report and webcams for
Southbourne and Bournemouth. For a
surf report call T01202 434344. **Tourist
information** Westover Rd, T01202
451700, www.bournemouth.co.uk.

Isle of Wight

Covering 23 by 13 miles, the Isle of
Wight has more than 60 miles of
coastline and is best known for its
prestige yachting event, **Cowes week**,
and its maritime history. It is also home
to the Isle of Wight Music Festival,
taking place in Jun,
www.isleofwightfestival.com, and the
Oct White Air Festival,
www.whiteair.co.uk, which combines

surfing, wakeboarding, skateboarding,
luge and windsurfing.

⊖ Getting there
Ferries Red Funnel, T02380 334010,
run a vehicle service between Cowes
and Southampton every 50 mins.
Crossing takes just under 1 hr and costs
around £85 for car plus 2 passengers.
Wightlink, T0870 5827744, run a more
regular service for cars and passengers
between Portsmouth and Fishbourne
as well as a service between
Lymington and Yarmouth. Similar
prices to Red Funnel.

Freshwater and West coast
To avoid the hordes of holidaymakers
rushing for the east coast resorts, jump
off the ferry and head straight for Niton
and the less commercialized side of the
island. For magnificent views to the
offshore Needles, follow the B3322 from
Freshwater to the westernmost tip.

⊖ Sleeping
L-A **Sandpipers Hotel**, Coastguard
Lane, Freshwater Bay, T01983 758 500,
www.fatcattrading.co.uk. Just back
from the seafront, they also offer
dinner, B&B from £45 per person. Look
out for ferry/B&B deals with Wightlink.
Self catering Grange Farm (see
below) have 4 excellent barn
conversions on their land sleeping up
to 10 people. Prices for a barn sleeping
6 from £295-655. **Camping** There are
plenty of large, commercial sites on
the island. **Chine Farm Camping Site**,
www.chine-farm.co.uk, is on the
coastal Military Rd in Atherfield. Handy
for Compton or Niton. Roger Powley
recommends **Grange Farm**, Military
Rd, Brighstone, T01983 740296,
www.brighstonebay.fsnet.co.uk. An
excellent, activity-free site on a
working farm for people who enjoy
natural surroundings. Perched on the
clifftop overlooking the reefs a few

South Coast surfers

miles down the coast from Compton, they offer camping and statics as well as free showers. Statics sleeping 6 from £220-655.

Eating/drinking
Fat Cat Bar, part of the Sandpipers Hotel. Either sink a beer or slip next door to Fat Cat on the Bay Restaurant and go all out with the surf and turf menu on offer – local bass from £15. **Sun Inn**, Hulverstone, and **Crown Inn**, Shorwell, are both traditional village pubs with good food.

Sandown and East coast
Sandown and Shanklin are classic twin resort towns with all the trimmings – amusements, holiday parks and wide seafront promenades. For many visiting the island, this is what it's all about.

Sleeping
A-B **Spyglass Inn**, Esplanade, Ventnor, T01983 855338. An olde worlde pub with B&B rooms. A-B **The Steamer Inn**, The Esplanade, Shanklin, T01983 862641, is a clean and airy seafront B&B with pub and restaurant attached. E **The Firs YHA**, Fitzroy St, Sandown, T01983 402651. Open Jul-Aug with limited opening for the rest of the year. Doubles, dorms and meals available. **Camping** Castlehaven Caravan Site, T01983 855556, www.castlehaven.co.uk, on the cliffs at Niton. Open Mar-Oct, statics sleeping 6 overlook the break from £175-350 per week . As surf photographer Roger Powley comments: "Straight out of your caravan into the line-up!"

Eating/drinking
Buddle Inn, Niton, just above the break with views over the English

Channel, is a decent village pub. **Spyglass Inn**, Esplanade, Ventnor, does good seafood, as recommended by Roger, and overlooks the beach and line-up, as does **The Steamer Inn**, on the Esplanade, Shanklin, also recommended. **The White Lion**, Niton is another decent village pub.

Directory
Surf shops Offshore Sports, Atherley Rd, Shanklin, T01983 866269, are *the*

surf shop on the island with a good range of boards, wetsuits and accessories. They have a 2nd shop in Cowes. **Wightwater Adventure Water Sports**, Orchardleigh Rd, Shanklin, T01983 866269/404987, www.wightwaters.com, offer a whole raft of watersports tuition including BSA-approved surf lessons. **Tourist information** High St Shanklin and Sandown, T01983 813818, open year-round.

> ❝❞
>
> The scene has a really concentrated energy and momentum. It isn't just maintained, it progresses. There are surf clubs, comps and all the bits and pieces you might expect to find in a place with a proper swell catchment, as opposed to our fickle and short-lived waves.
>
> *Adam Tarry, www.nosurfinbrighton.tk*

DEMI TAYLOR
Waiting for inspiration. . .

✦ Flat spells

Bikes Beat the crowds, get on yer bike on the Isle of Wight. Hire from **Offshore Sports**, Shanklin, T01983 866269.

Cinema Bournemouth IMAX, Pier Approach, T01202 200000, www.bournemouthimax.com, the latest in 3D experiences. **The Odeon Brighton**, West St, T0870 5050006, is a massive multiplex within walking distance from the pubs. **The Odeon Hastings**, Queen's Rd, T0871 2244007, has all the recent releases.

Golf Isle of Purbeck GC, T01929 450361, www.purbeckgolf.co.uk. They have 2 courses – 9 holes at Dene from £10, 18 holes at Purbeck from £35. **Solent Meads GC**, Rolls Dr, Hengistbury Head, Christchurch, T01202 420795. 18-hole course with driving range – £2 for 50 balls. **Brighton & Hove GC**, Devil's Dyke Rd, T01273 507861, is a 9-hole course with sea views from £15 for 18 holes.

Kitesurfing If the onshores get too much at Camber, try kitesurfing or windsurfing with **Rye Water Sports**, New Lydd Rd, Camber, T01797 225238.

Sights The Surfing Museum, www.thesurfingmuseum.co.uk, in Brighton, founded by surfer Pete Robinson and aided by board restorer, Steve Frost, they have pulled together resources from around the country and the globe to create Britain's first true surfing museum. Visited by 15,000 people in the first year of opening, it will be permanently housed on Brighton seafront from May 2006.

Skating A few of spots to get you going: **Poole Skate Park**, Baiter Park, Catalina Dr, www.funseaker.org.uk. This is a good-sized free park with a street course and spined mini ramps. **Slades Farm**, Slades Farm Rd, Bournemouth, fun concrete bowl. **Lipton Xtreme Skatepark**, Kings Rd, West Pier, Brighton, T01273 323200. £2.50 buys you 2 hrs on the ramps. Helmets compulsory. Popular with the younger crew.

Witterings

West and East Wittering are backed by Bracklesham Bay, a stretch of golden sand punctuated by groynes leading to Selsey. Popular with windsurfers and yachties, East Wittering is also home to the Shore Surf Club, established in 1969.

● Sleeping

A **The Beach House**, Rookwood Rd, West Wittering, T01243 514800, www.beachhse.co.uk, is a modern and clean hotel-cum-B&B with an onsite restaurant. **Camping** There are several sites in the area including **Gees Campsite**, Stock Lane, East Wittering, T01234 670223, open Mar-Oct. **Nummington Farm Campsite**, West Wittering, T01243 514013, is open to families and couples only, Easter-Oct. They also have a 'pet park' with cattle, goats, sheep, chickens.

🍴 Eating/drinking

Boulevard Café, Shore Rd, East Wittering is a great place to grab a cup of tea, a wonderful cooked breakfast or even a Sun roast. **The Shore Inn** has been the hosting ground for the **Shore Surf Club** for many years.

● Directory

Surf shops Shore Water Sports, Shore Rd, East Wittering, T01243 672315, www.shore.co.uk, stock a good range of boards, equipment and accessories.

Brighton

Just an hour and a half from London, packed with artists, bars, cafés and clubs, Brighton is a bustling, beachside bohemia. Which is perfect because if it's flat, there's plenty to do.

● Sleeping

There are hundreds of sleeping options here ranging in price, style and cleanliness. **A-B Oriental Hotel**, Oriental Pl, Hove, T01273 205050, a lovely little hotel, just out of the way. **D-E Baggies Backpackers**, Oriental Pl, Hove, T01273 733740, is an excellent, homely hostel with several long-termers. If you want a good night's sleep, try to avoid the main dorm. **D-E Brighton Backpackers**, Middle St, T01273 777717, www.brightonbackpacker.com. Another independent hostel, can be a bit grubby. **D-E St Christopher Inn**, Palace Hotel, Junction Rd, www.st-christophers.co.uk, has dorm facilities plus it houses its own bar and club, but no kitchen facilities.

🍴 Eating/drinking

"The best local surf-friendly cafe is **Carat's** at Shoreham Harbour, run by Chris – a wicked guy," recommends Small Planet's Jez. There have been reports of break-ins at Carat's car park so watch your things. **Food for Friends**, Prince Albert St, is a good and cheap spot for vegetarian food. "After a surf grab a few beers at **The Fortunes of War** on the seafront. Most summer nights the beaches are rammed," recommends James at www.sharkbait.co.uk. **Woodies Longboard Diner**, Kingsway, Hove Beach, is a 1960s-inspired American retro diner where you can get a stack of sweet pancakes for breakfast from £3. Lunch and dinner burgers, wraps, pizzas and the rest are on the menu. Reasonably priced.

Directory

Surf shops and resources Filf, West St just back from the beach in Rottingdean, T01273 307465, www.filf.co.uk, have been going strong since 1995. They stock an excellent range of hardware and boards including Filf boards shaped by Matt Adams, and offer ding repair. Riders include south coast charger Cliff Cox and Luke Palmer. www.nosurfinbrighton.tk is home to an awesome photo gallery. **Ocean Sports Boardriders**, Kingsway, Hove T01273 412241. www.sharkbait.co.uk is an excellent resource for South Coast surfers combining local news with a daily surf report and webcams, break info as well as a photo gallery to inspire. **Small Planet**, T01273 727237, www.smallplanetsurfshop.com, on Victoria Terr, Hove, was opened by Jez in 2000. They stock a good range of longboards and skateboards as well as other surf essentials.

Camber Sands

With a decent stretch of golden sands, Camber Sands, just northeast of Hastings, is famous for its smuggling past and has now turned into a resort village. Nearby Hastings, is famous for that battle of 1066 (which actually took place up the road at Battle).

Sleeping

L Place, New Lydd Rd, T01797 225057, www.theplacecambersands.co.uk. Although it is just down the beach from the nearby holiday village, this beautiful little boutique hotel is a million miles apart. Egyptian cotton sheets on the bed, spa therapy products in the bathroom, perhaps it is worth splashing out upwards of £75 on a double room. **Self catering Poundfield Farm**, Farm Lane, T01797 223967, offers modern rooms for 4 (2 on a sofa bed) in converted stables from £190-300 per week. Just a 10-min walk to the beach. **Camping** Camber **Sands Holiday Village**, T0870 429284. Just back from the beach, this is a purpose-built family park complete with pools, sauna, spa, crazy golf and anything else you can imagine. Statics and chalets available to rent Mar-Nov from £120-650 per week.

Eating/drinking

Mermaid, Hastings seafront, serves up better than average fish and chips. **The Mermaid Inn**, Mermaid St, inland at old skool, artistic Rye, is something quite different, good pub grub at reasonable prices in glorious surroundings. **The Bell Inn**, The Mint, Rye, is a good choice for hearty, reasonable pub food. **The Place**, New Lydd Rd, Camber Sands. Part of the hotel, this brasserie serves up delicious local fare – local fish and Romney Marsh lamb. Main meal around £12.

Isle of Thanet

The fact that the Isle of Thanet isn't an 'isle' isn't Thanet's only claim to fame. Son of Margate, Benjamin Beale invented the bathing cubicle allowing bathers to subtly slip into the sea for a swim. We happily strip off in freezing car parks, before encasing ourselves in rubber, 250 years on – now that's evolution! The isle is also home to the old skool seaside resorts of Margate and Ramsgate.

Sleeping

D-E Margate YHA, The Beachcomber, Royal Esplanade, T01843 221616, overlooks Westbrook Bay. Open Apr-Sep with flexi-opening Jan-Apr. **E Broadstairs YHA**, Osborne Rd, T01843 604121. A more basic hostel, open Mar-Sep with some flexi-opening off-season. **Camping** Nethercourt **Touring Park**, Nether Court Hill, Ramsgate, T01834 595485. Set in the grounds of Nethercourt Park, open Apr-Oct with free hot showers.

Eating/drinking

Churchill Tavern, The Paragon, Ramsgate Harbour, decent fish 'n' chips.

Directory

Surf schools Ocean Jack, T0208 3039223, www.oceanjack.com. Stuart Clark is an avid sailor, windsurfer and surfer, running BSA lessons at Joss Bay and Viking Bay.

ROGER POWLEY

11 Joe Truman, Compton ▸▸ *p97*

Surfing the Channel Islands

The Channel Islands always conjure up images of a little piece of Britain moored just of the French coast. Strictly speaking the Channel Islands are not part of Britain, but are part of the British Isles. This element of independence made it famous as a tax haven for rich Brits. It is also home to the UK's oldest surf club and has had surfers riding the waves here since the 1920s. Its exposure to Atlantic swells on westerly-facing coastlines along with its mild temperatures make it a natural place for surfing to thrive. There is a strong competitive history here dating back to the early 1960s, and Jersey was the venue of early European Championships. The Channel Islands Surfing Federation runs a number of events throughout the year and there is a healthy number of talented youngsters pushing through the ranks and snapping at the heels of the more established surfers.

The islands of Jersey and Guernsey are at the heart of Channel Island surfing. A hundred miles south of the British coastline, they benefit from summer water temperatures that can rise to 19°C. Every year, thousands of tourists flood the islands for the summer months – roads on the tiny islands become busy and a sea of towels fill the sandy beaches.

The main breaks on **Jersey** are focused around the west coast of the island. These tend to work best in winds from the east and with an Atlantic swell from the west. The main surf destination is the 5-mile-long St Ouen's Bay. Stretching from just south of the break at Stinky Bay, there are a number of spots to check including 'Goldies' by the slipway, 'Secrets' at Le Grosse Tour and the 'Watersplash' out in front of the café. It works through the tides but is best off low on the push. There are also a number of other spots worth checking heading south to Le Braye. When big swells kick in, the north and south coast are the places to check.

On **Guernsey** there are a series of bay and reefs following the west coast from north to south from L'Ancresse Bay through Portinfer, Vazon and Perelle. One thing to always bear in mind is that the Channel Islands have a massive tidal range – up to 40 ft. Watch out for rips and stay at breaks where you feel comfortable.

There are a number of **hot locals** on the islands making an impression at a national and international level. They include Ian Battrick, Sam George, Scott Eastwood, Andy Cummings, James Hick, Johnny Wallbridge and Andre Le Geyt. When it comes to localism and crowds, these small islands really do have a limited number of breaks and an increasing number of local surfers. Add to this the number of visiting surfers and some spots can get very crowded. Just remember to follow the rules, stay chilled and the line-up will remain a friendly place.

Getting there
Getting to the Channel Islands is relatively easy. There are flights with BMI from Cardiff, Durham, Manchester and East Midlands from as little as £20 return. VLM Vlaamse fly from the City of London Airport, BA from Gatwick and Flybe from a whole host of airports including most major cities as well as Exeter in the Southwest. Prices vary greatly so check online.

If you are travelling by car to Jersey there are also good ferry options. **Condor Ferries**, www.condorferries.co.uk, T01305 761551, offer a weekly 9 hr crossing from Portsmouth, a twice-daily 4 hr crossing from Poole and a daily 3¼ hr crossing from Weymouth. Crossing times to Guernsey from Poole and Weymouth are a little shorter at 2½ hrs. For a car and 2 passengers travelling midweek in Sep it will cost roughly £200 for a return ticket.

Sleeping
Guernsey does not accept camper vans or any van that can be slept in and Jersey will only do so with a special permit obtained from the council. The council likes visitors to frequent local hotels and B&Bs. Try D **Prince of Wales Guest House**, Greve de Lecq, St Ouen, Jersey, T01534 482085.

🍴 Eating/drinking

The **Watersplash**, www.watersplashjersey.com, beachfront bar, café and club has been the hub of the Jersey scene for decades and has been the venue for many surf comps. You can get an all-day breakfast here and sandwiches from £4, salads from £7.

➊ Directory

Surf shops There are plenty of surf shops on the islands. On **Jersey** try **SDS**, 13 La Colomberie, St Helier, T01534 736209; **Freedom**, 8a Quennevais Precinct, St Brelade, T01534 744601. **Jersey Surf School**, The Surf Shack, T01534 484005, at the Waterplash run BSA-approved lessons and hire out surf equipment.

On **Guernsey** try **Freedom Guernsey**, L'Islet Crossroads, St Sampsons, T01481 243282.

Websites In terms of websites check out www.jerseylongboarders.com and www.cisurf.com, who have a webcam at St Ouens. For information about what's happening on Guernsey, check out www.bbc.co.uk/guernsey/surfing/index.shtml.

AL McKINNON

Jersey's Ian Battrick tucks in

Surfing East Anglia

"The local scene is pretty laid-back and very friendly. The highs are: warm water in summer (can reach almost 20°C); uncrowded breaks the majority of the time; three points of the compass to surf – north, east and south – so it picks up swell from all directions (even southwest can give 3-4 ft waves); it's easy to get to all breaks. The lows are cold water in winter (as low as 5-6°C); not as consistent as the Atlantic Coast; just beachie, no reefs; isolated breaks (also an advantage!) so not safe for beginners; and it's very hard to get hold of surf gear – we only have one shaper (Paul Nicker) in East Anglia!" Mark, www.eastcoastsurf.co.uk.

By all rights Cromer and East Runton should be up there among Britain's top surf spots. They sit on a part of England that juts out in the North Sea, with better exposure to passing lows than Whitby and Scarborough. They are also further south than the surf zones of Yorkshire and the Northeast. Hefty arctic swells have a much greater fetch and so should be cleaner and more lined by the time

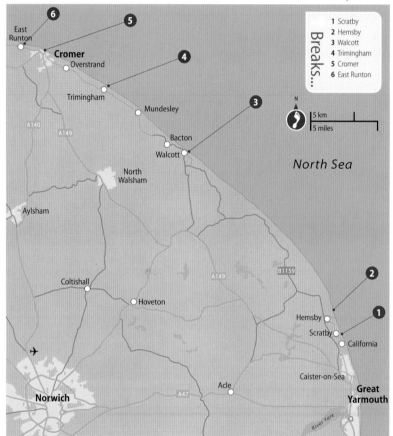

Breaks...
1 Scratby
2 Hemsby
3 Walcott
4 Trimingham
5 Cromer
6 East Runton

East Anglia board guide

Airborne
Shaper: Pete Lindsell, Lindsell Surfboards

▸▸ 5'4" x 19½" x 2½" for Matt Hiller.
▸▸ Versatile shape ranging from 5-ft to 6-ft.
▸▸ Bullet nose hybrid shortboard.
▸▸ Makes the most out of small to head-high waves.
▸▸ Deep nose concave and flat rocker to get you up and riding quickly.
▸▸ Moveable rear fin system allowing the board to be loosened up to suit wave conditions.

Retro Fish
Shaper: Mark Lindsell, Lindsell Surfboards

▸▸ 5'10" x 20½" x 2¾" for Matt Hiller.
▸▸ Versatile shape ranging from 5'6" to 7'.
▸▸ Retro twin fin, ideal for steady summer surf.
▸▸ Double foiled wooden twin fins, flattened rocker and subtle single concave running into flat double concave.
▸▸ Flattened rocker aids paddling speed and helps the board through flat sections.
▸▸ Ideal for East Coast around East Runton, bottom contour to give the board lift.

(i) Boards by **Lindsell Custom Boards**
T 07796 398805 (M)
www.lcboards.co.uk
lcboards@hotmail.com

be explored. And just because the swells lose some of their stored energy, it doesn't mean they can't be devastatingly powerful. This is, after all, the part of Britain where the sea is eroding huge swathes of land at an alarming rate. Groynes and sea defences take tons of sand and deposit them onto an array of shifting and changing sandbanks. It is a coastline in a state of flux. It is an exciting coastline. The next storm might just deposit a 'superbank' with reeling lefts rolling down the coast. It's just a case of getting out there and searching.

"I could never understand it really," says John Isaac, owner of Revolver Surfboards. "There are so many people trapped in London without surf, and two hours up the M11 there are some great waves – much better than the South Coast." While John was in London he realized that this stretch of coastline was a real undiscovered gem that can salvage the sanity of those marooned in and around the capital. "I love the place. There are some great little surf spots along that coastline."

Coastline
The breaks along this coastline are usually beach or sand and shingle breaks. The longshore drift along the coastline of East Anglia has caused serious coastal erosion to certain areas, where the crumbling, fragile land has gradually fallen into the sea. In some places houses and even villages have been lost. The sea defences set up to try to protect regions of the coastline can help sediments deposit into sandbanks. In some regions the process is reversed and land is advancing into the sea. As sediments are deposited into mud flats, it becomes rich with bird life and attracts birdwatchers in huge numbers.

Localism
While the breaks around Cromer and Runton can get busy on a weekend, the atmosphere in the line-up is fairly chilled. Bring a board with some volume or you'll be at the bottom of the chain. It's worth chatting to the locals – they will know which of the breaks are worth checking, which will save you driving around looking for that elusive sandbank. The line-ups of East Anglia are very friendly. "Most of the time you are happy to see someone else in the water! It does get crowded in the summer especially if the West Coast is flat. In summer you could easily be talking 40-50 people in at East Runton. This dwindles to maybe 12 or so in the winter," says Mark of www.eastcoastsurf.co.uk. "Because of limited

they hit. They should be – if it weren't for two tiny factors, oceanography and geology. Whereas the accumulated kinetic energy deposited onto the beaches and reefs of the north come out of deep water, by the time the swell lines pass Hull they are starting to run into shallower water. Energy is lost through friction with the ocean floor. The waves breaking on the beaches of East Anglia are now about half the size of their Yorkshire cousins.

But although the region lacks the awesome slate reefs of Yorkshire, or the crystal-clear point waves of Northumbria, there are some very rewarding surf spots along this coastline. Besides East Runton and Cromer, there is an endless stretch of beaches with easy access just waiting to parking, there are never that many at Cromer – about 20 max'" explains Mike at www.surfriders.co.uk. It is possible (and usual) to surf many of the breaks heading south alone.

Top local surfers

"The original East Anglian surfer was **Maurice Butler**," says Mark of www.eastcoastsurf.co.uk. "His son **Neil Butler**, a longboarder, and grandson still surf. **Neil Watson** is one of the old skool, and his son Dan is also a keen shortboarder." Others include **Adam 'Chippie' Chipperfield**, **Danny Cotgrove**, as well as longboarder and local shaper, **Paul Nicker**. "The scene has a growing number of surfers – more than 70 took part in a 2004 event won by local shortboarder **Luciano Huergo**," says Mike of Surfriders.

Getting around

The M11 to Cambridge followed by the A11 is a picturesque run up from London to Norwich. From here the breaks between Great Yarmouth and East Runton are within easy reach. The A140 heads directly north to the weathered seaside resort of Cromer. An intricate series of B roads will take you southeast along the coast through a chain of small hamlets, each with their own beach access. Heading west from Norwich along the main A47 takes you to Great Yarmouth. The optimistically named California plus Scratby and Hemsby are just a short hop from here along the A149 and B1159.

East Runton is the most reliable break in the region, well exposed to northerly swells coming down the North Sea from Scotland, with various peaks all the way down to Cromer.

Mark, Lindsell Surfboards

Chris Nelson, East Anglia

5 Cromer sunset ▸▸ *p114*

Bruce McIver

Breaks

1 Scratby

- ○ **Break type**: Beach break.
- ○ **Conditions**: Medium to big swells, offshore in westerly winds.
- ○ **Hazards/tips**: Longshore drift when big.
- ○ **Sleeping**: Cromer ▸▸ *p115*.

Stretch of sandy beach between Scratby to the north and the optimistically named California to the south. In good, clean northeasterly swells, this beach offers some quality lefts as the swell rolls down the shore. This action can create longshore drift so watch out for rips. There are also rights here in a decent southeasterly swell, though it tends to be a shorter swell period and less clean.

2 Hemsby

- ○ **Break type**: Beach break.
- ○ **Conditions**: Medium to big swells, offshore in westerly winds.
- ○ **Hazards/tips**: Rips.
- ○ **Sleeping**: Cromer ▸▸ *p115*.

This stretch of sandy beach near the little town of Hemsby is home to some good quality lefts and rights. Works mainly from low to mid tide, there is a bad longshore drift to watch out for in big swells.

3 Walcott

- ○ **Break type**: Beach break.
- ○ **Conditions**: Medium swells, offshore in southeasterly winds.
- ○ **Hazards/tips**: Groynes, rips.
- ○ **Sleeping**: Cromer ▸▸ *p115*.

Further north on the B1159 is the tiny hamlet of Walcott. There is a good left-hand bank that breaks far out at low tide in decent swells, and from the end of the groyne in smaller swells. Best low to mid tide when it can be a consistent, quality spot with a good reputation among locals. Lovely sandy beach.

4 Trimingham

- ○ **Break type**: Beach break.
- ○ **Conditions**: Medium swells, offshore in southwesterly winds.
- ○ **Hazards/tips**: Groynes, quiet spot.
- ○ **Sleeping**: Cromer ▸▸ *p115*.

This is a quiet beach break with groynes. It is not as good quality as Cromer but it can have some good banks with decent lefts. Works on all tides but can have rips in big swells. Less crowded spot, empty during the week. Also try **Mundesley** and **Bacton** to the east for short, punchy lefts. The road hugs the coast heading west towards Cromer – keep your eyes open, you never know what you will find.

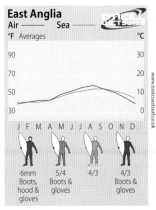

East Anglia
Air ——— Sea

°F Averages °C

90		30
70		20
50		10
30		0

J F M A M J J A S O N D

6mm Boots, hood & gloves	5/4 Boots & gloves	4/3	4/3 Boots & gloves

www.eastcoastsurf.co.uk

1 Scratby

www.eastcoastsurf.co.uk

4 Trimingham

113

5 Cromer

- **Break type**: Beach break with pier.
- **Conditions**: Medium swells, offshore in southwesterly winds.
- **Hazards/tips**: Groynes, pier pylons, rips.
- **Sleeping**: Cromer » p115.

Check the waves near the pier where there are short rights and longer lefts. Again, needs a clean north to easterly swell, and light southwesterly winds – but there will be crumbly waves for the committed in light onshores. Works on all tides, but watch out for the groynes. Rips when big. Can be busy on a good weekend. Cromer is the region's surf capital with easy access and consistent banks. Holds less of a crowd than Runton due to parking.

6 East Runton

- **Break type**: Chalk-flint reef.
- **Conditions**: Medium swells, offshore in southwesterly winds.
- **Hazards/tips**: Flinty reef, rips.
- **Sleeping**: Cromer » p115.

The best known of the east coast breaks, East Runton is a chalk-flint reef offering short rights and long lefts out from the sandy beach. Works best from mid to three-quarter tide in clean north, northeasterly or easterly swells. Like many breaks here it is exposed to wind and works best with light southwesterlies. The waves have a patented brown colour, due to fine sediments, common on this stretch of coast. When Scarborough and Whitby are 6 ft, the swell will be half the size here in East Anglia.

Bruce McIver cutting back

6 East Runton

5 Cromer barrel, Danny Cotgrove

East Anglia peak

Cromer

Although this corner of England actually comprises Norfolk, Suffolk, Essex and Cambridgeshire, the main focus for East Anglia's surfers is the Norfolk coastline – also a popular spot with the Queen, who has a small country pad in Sandringham. Cromer, with its pier, faded grandeur, cliff-top presence and popular break, is the area's surf capital.

Sleeping

B-C Cambridge Guest House, East Cliff, T01263 512085. With sea views and comfortable rooms, this is just one of a selection of good B&Bs in the area. **D-E Sheringham Youth Hostel**, Cremer's Drift, west of Cromer at Sheringham, T01263 823215. Open Apr-Nov with limited low period opening, it also has a drying room and lock-up. Doubles available.
Camping Seaview Caravan Park, T01263 514569, www.seaviewcaravanpark.net. Just to the west, on the cliffs overlooking the popular East Runton, the park is open Apr-Oct to over-25s, with statics to hire from £180-385 per week for 4. **Woodhill Camping Park**, Cromer Rd,

East Runton, T01263 512242, www.woodhill-park.com, has camping and statics available from £180-495, open Mar-Oct with free showers. No single sex groups. **Woodland Park**, Trimingham, T01263 579208, www.woodland-park.co.uk, also has on-site pool and sauna facilities.

Eating/drinking

Cliff Top Café, Cliff Rd to the east of Cromer in Overstrand. Open during the summer, this is an excellent spot to grab some decent food at reasonable prices. Sea view at no extra charge. **Dave's Fish & Chips**, Co-op St, do excellent fish suppers, eat in or take away. Try the 'special' cod, chips, peas, bread 'n' butter and a mug of tea for around £7. **Sea Breeze**, High St, Sheringham, does good value traditional fare: pies; ham, egg 'n' chips, as well as limited vegetarian options.

Directory

Surf shops and resources Orca Mountain Surf Centre, T01328 711722. Heading west out of Cromer on the coastal A149 to Wells-next-the-sea, they sell surf basics and equipment. **Just Add Water**, Bedford St, Norwich,

Flat spells

Cinema The Regal Cinema, Cromer, T01263 510151, www.regalfilmcentre.co.uk. Small but perfectly formed with multi-screens showing the latest and greatest releases.
Golf Royal Cromer GC, Overstrand Rd, T01263 512884, www.royalcromergolfclub.com, might be a bit rich for some – green fees from £30-50. **Mundesley GC**, Links Rd, Mundesley, T01263 720279, is a cheaper, nearby alternative – the 9-hole course is pretty exposed to the elements but fees are from £12.
Skate The Strip at the Splash Leisure Centre in Sheringham has a mini ramp plus a 1/4 pipe. **Stoke Holy Cross Skate Park**, Playing Fields. Heading south of Norwich on the B1332, Holy Stoke is near Povingland. This is a free wooden skatepark with ramps.

T01603 662428, all the surf essentials. **Board talk**, Battery Green Rd, Lowestoft, Suffolk, T01502 517992, www.boardtalk leisure.co.uk, sell a full range of surf equipment including boards and suits. There are also a couple of excellent websites. www.eastcoastsurf.co.uk includes local break information, a weekly forecast plus regularly- updated webcams at Cromer and Lowestoft, tide tables and a 'for sale' section – a great tool in an area with limited surf shops. www.surfriders.co.uk offers similar tools including break info and a raft of images plus webcams for Cromer and Lowestoft.

www.eastcoastsurf.co.uk

5 Cromer Pier

Surfing Yorkshire

Surfing might not be the first thing that springs to mind when Yorkshire is mentioned – it is probably more likely to be puddings, cricket, Dales, a nice cup of tea and dark Satanic mills. However, the coastline that fringes Britain's largest county just happens to be a veritable surfer's playground. The slate geography, with its flat, tapering reefs, is perfect for producing waves of stunning quality. Eroded and smoothed over the millennia, they form the perfect platform for the long travelled Arctic swells to break onto. The dominant wind direction is offshore. Some people say that with a bit more consistency, and a bit more sunshine, it would be Yorkshire and not Cornwall that attracts surfers in their droves, with the Victorian resorts of Whitby and Scarborough as surf Meccas lined with surf shops and a massive local crew. Today, this is not far from the truth. Yorkshire has a thriving surf scene. Local numbers are swelled by an influx of students and city surfers from towns such as York, Newcastle, Leeds, Sheffield and Manchester all taking advantage of the fact that they can hit the coast, surf twice and still be home in time for Emmerdale.

Yorkshire surfers are a pretty hardy lot. With winter water temperatures dipping to 4°C, it is a place that tests wetsuits to their maximum limits. They are also chart watchers – as a low drops into the slot, a gentle summer of 2-3 ft days can explode overnight with the timely arrival of 8 ft corduroy, converting the reefs for a day or two into a brown water Indo. The crew will be out in the line-up before the sun has crept over the horizon – meaning 4.30 am in the summer – knowing the next day it could be completely flat.
"There's a good variety of waves, but as conditions change so quickly, you need to build up a good local knowledge to be on it," says Secret Spot shop owner Tommo. As a result they have learned to be patient through the flat spells and charge hard

when the surf kicks in. As the sea turns to black and the stars illuminate the beach, faint figures will be just visible in the line-up, waiting for a last wave in. To be a Yorkshire surfer means to really appreciate every swell and every wave ridden.

Coastline

The geology of the Yorkshire coastline makes for excellent reefs. The flat, slate rock juts out from the base of towering cliffs, fringes open bays or forms long, tapering points. The sedimentary rock also holds hidden treasures such as rare dinosaur skeletons of species never before seen in Europe. Whitby is famous as a source of the precious gemstone jet. Areas of the coastline are inaccessible by road and classic set-ups are know to a few tight-lipped locals who have spent time scouring

Yorkshire board guide

Fish
Shaper: The Gill, ODD Surfboards

▸▸ 6'2" x 19½" x 2⅜" .
▸▸ For average surfer 6'4" x 19½" x 2⅜" .
▸▸ Flat bottomed with a fuller nose to help wave catching and aid stability in manoeuvres.
▸▸ Double concave through the swallow tail for drive, designed for small summer surf.
▸▸ When the surf picks up, use with bigger fins to create a loose board in good surf.

Semi-gun
Shaper: The Gill, ODD Surfboards

▸▸ 6'7" x 18½" x 2⅜"for Isaac Kibblewhite.
▸▸ Narrow screwdriver or rounded pintail.
▸▸ Double concave bottom for rail to rail down the line speed..
▸▸ Designed for 6-8 ft hollow waves, good for the Cove.

ⓘ Boards by **ODD Boards**
Factory: Freelap Surfboards, Porthcawl, Wales
T00 44 (0)1656-744691, www.oddsurfboards.co.uk
or contact gill@eurotelemail.net

the coastal footpaths and secluded bays. The waves here have a very distinctive brown hue, but it is not pollution or sewage that colours them. Fine, silty sediments left from the ice age are suspended in the coastal waters, yet not far from the shore the sea is as blue and clear as anywhere in the UK. Staring hauntingly out at the north sea, the jagged, Gothic ruins of Whitby Abbey are silhouetted above the harbour where Bram Stoker's Dracula first set foot in England.

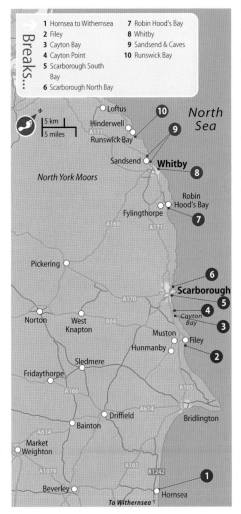

Breaks...

1 Hornsea to Withernsea	7 Robin Hood's Bay
2 Filey	8 Whitby
3 Cayton Bay	9 Sandsend & Caves
4 Cayton Point	10 Runswick Bay
5 Scarborough South Bay	
6 Scarborough North Bay	

> ❝ ❞
>
> **There was only a handful of us who knew about the reef and we did our best to keep it like that. I remember once some surfers came down to check a nearby break and we all ducked down in the line-up and hid under the kelp.**
>
> *Andrew Harrison, Zero Gravity Surfboards, Whitby*

England Yorkshire Surfing

Localism

As a whole, the line-ups of Yorkshire are very friendly. Even though numbers have been rising for many years, there is little in the way of localism or intimidation. However, as with northeast Scotland, a couple of spots have started to suffer due to over exposure in the surf media; while locals are currently tolerant of visitors who follow the etiquette, this could quickly change. These breaks are not listed in this book, but are surprisingly good, and surprisingly heavy. Drop-ins can result in substantial beatings by cold, dark waters. If you do stumble across them, the advice is only to take to the line-up if you're very proficient and always surf respectfully.

Top local surfers

The original Whitby crew of **Andrew Harrison** of Zero Gravity, **Sedge**, **Greenie** and **Joe Botham** can still be found patrolling the reefs to the north with **Si Stephenson** and **Bod**. In Scarborough, **Roger Povey** and **Tommo** of Secret Spot are at the heart of an exploding scene. Big wave charger **Del** is still the region's hellman.

Getting around

The coastal roads along the Yorkshire coastline allow access to all the major breaks. The A165 heads north to Scarborough where the A171 takes over. Along the coast are country lanes and hidden footpaths that are jealously guarded secrets. It really is an area with plenty of potential still to explore. Check parking as many coastal villages have strictly enforced no parking areas.

117

Breaks

1 Hornsea to Withernsea

- **Break type**: Beach break.
- **Conditions**: Medium to big swells, offshore in westerly winds.
- **Hazards/tips**: Dangerous longshore drift in big swells.
- **Sleeping**: Filey » p123.

Accessed via the coastal B1242, these are not really a surfer's first choice, but are worth checking in a clean northeasterly or easterly swell if you're in the area. As the groynes show, when the surf picks up, there is a longshore drift from the north, so keep a beach marker in view. Better on low to mid tide. Not many surfers here, so not really a good spot for the inexperienced.

2 Filey

- **Break type**: Beach break.
- **Conditions**: Big to huge swells, offshore in southwesterly winds.
- **Hazards/tips**: Rips in big swells, parking on the seafront .
- **Sleeping**: Filey » p123.

Filey has a long, flat crescent shaped beach, the northern end of which is sheltered by Filey Brigg, a rocky headland. The southern end of the bay picks up the most swell, the northern end is worth checking in big, storm surf. Not renowned for the quality of its waves, but worth checking if everywhere else is maxed out.

3 Cayton Bay

- **Break type**: Beach breaks.
- **Conditions**: Small to medium swells, offshore in southwesterly winds.
- **Hazards/tips**: Busy spot, suitable for all surfers.
- **Sleeping**: Scarborough » p123.

Bunkers is the most popular and consistent spot with lefts and rights breaking off the sandbanks formed in front of WW2 concrete bunkers. Best from mid to high tide and with a southwesterly wind. There is also the fickle **Pumphouse** that produces lefts and rights in front of the pumping station, but needs a southeasterly swell. Pay parking available above the bay. Popular break with Scarborough surfers, students and even visitors from as far as Manchester due to the good road links. There are also showers and pay toilets.

Yorkshire
Air ——— Sea ———
°F Averages °C

90												30
70												20
50												10
30												0

J F M A M J J A S O N D

6mm Boots, hood & gloves	5/4 Boots & gloves	4/3 Boots & gloves	4/3 Boots & gloves

SCOTT WICKING

4 Cayton Point

4 Cayton Point

- **Break type**: Left point.
- **Conditions**: Medium to big swells, offshore in southwesterly winds.
- **Hazards/tips**: Access, crowds, heavy wave, rocks, experienced surfers only.
- **Sleeping**: Scarborough ›› *p123*.

Excellent and powerful left-hand point that breaks over a bouldery reef. Definitely a wave for experienced surfers, this grinding left breaks up to 10 ft, wrapping around the point at the northern end into the sheltered bay. Too shallow at low, it's best surfed from quarter tide up. Needs a good northeasterly swell to get going. Locals enjoy pushing each other deeper until they are taking off virtually on the rocks.

Check from the A165 where the point is visible through the trees. There is access through the woods.

5 Scarborough South Bay

- **Break type**: Beach break.
- **Conditions**: Big swell, offshore in northerly to westerly winds.
- **Hazards/tips**: Crowds, average waves.
- **Sleeping**: Scarborough ›› *p123*.

Poor quality, flat beach fronted by amusements and fish and chip shops. Needs a really big northeasterly to work, so is a popular spot in huge winter gales. Best peaks are in front of the Spa, from low to three quarter tide, and there is limited pay parking here too. In the winter there can be Fistral-like

numbers. Waves are short and pretty weak. OK for beginners. On smaller swells there are waves to the south between the Spa and the headland.

6 Scarborough North Bay

- **Break type**: Beach break.
- **Conditions**: All swells, offshore in southwesterly winds.
- **Hazards/tips**: Beachfront parking on Marine Drive overlooking the surf.
- **Sleeping**: Scarborough ›› *p123*.

North Bay is a northeasterly-facing beach with scattered rocky outcrops. It can have some good quality banks, which produce both lefts and rights. It picks up plenty of swell and works in north, northeasterly and easterly swells.

DEMI TAYLOR

THE GILL

Peak and ye shall find

THE GILL

Bunkers

6 Scarborough North Bay

Yorkshire point

The beach is fronted by a sea wall, which means it's only surfable from low to mid tide. These defences have recently undergone reinforcement with boulders, but this doesn't appear to have affected the surf. As Billabong rep Shaun Thomas says: "North Bay hasn't been dramatically affected by the new defences. It still works at low to mid tide with a 2- to 5-ft swell – any bigger it closes out. I think the long term effects still remain to be seen over the next couple of years."

7 Robin Hood's Bay

- **Break type**: Reefs.
- **Conditions**: Medium to big swells, offshore in southwesterly winds.
- **Hazards/tips**: Rips, rocks, shallow, big tidal range.
- **Sleeping**: Robin Hood's Bay ▸▸ p124.

There are a number of flat, slate reefs in the bay that work on big northeasterly or any southeasterly swells. Best from low to three-quarter tide as beach disappears at high. Quiet spot. The point can be good in big swells. There is a car park in town. Not a good spot for inexperienced surfers. Long walk to breaks deter crowds.

8 Whitby

- **Break type**: Beach break.
- **Conditions**: Small to medium swells, offshore in southwesterly winds.
- **Hazards/tips**: Parking in town or on cliff top.
- **Sleeping**: Whitby ▸▸ p124.

Popular with grommets in small swells and one of the few spots sheltered in a southeasterly wind due to the harbour wall. Works best on low to mid tide near the harbour.

9 Sandsend and Caves

- **Break type**: Beach and reef.
- **Conditions**: Small to medium swells, offshore in southwesterly winds.
- **Hazards/tips**: Heavy beach break, rips, can be crowded.
- **Sleeping**: Whitby ▸▸ p124.

Sandsend is a high quality beach that works through the tides. Hollow, powerful lefts and rights spring up on shifting banks. Southwesterly winds are offshore. Works in northeasterly, easterly and southeasterly swells. Not really for beginners when over 3 ft. Hell

DEWI TAYLOR

9 Sandsend

THE GILL

If you're not local, you're barred

Jesse Davies – home comforts

paddle, bad rips and packs a punch when big. Parking available by the beach. Becoming a very popular spot.

Caves is a flat, mid tide reef that sits under the headland at the southern end of Sandsend Bay. It is one of the few spots sheltered in a northwesterly wind. Breaks well between 3 and 4 ft but maxes out easily. Usually looks better than it is. At high tide backwash ruins the waves and exiting the water is difficult. Beware.

10 Runswick Bay

- 🔀 **Break type**: Reefs.
- 🌊 **Conditions**: Medium to big swells, offshore in southwesterly/westerly swells.
- ⚡ **Hazards/tips**: Dangerous rips, Cobbledump is a shallow, rocky reef.
- 🛏 **Sleeping**: Whitby ▸▸ p124.

This northeasterly-facing bay has three quality, right-hand reefs found on the southern side. Slabs of flat slate form excellent reefs for fast, walling right-handers that break from low through to mid tide. The inner reef is the most sheltered and needs more swell to get going, the middle reef is the most popular. Watch out for rips next to the reef, which can be strong.
Cobbledump is a left-hand reef breaking over rocks, found on the north side of the bay near the village. Runswick offers some shelter so is traditionally surfed when big swells max out the exposed beaches.

SCOTT WICKING

Yorkshire. Bitter?

Filey

Often overlooked in favour of Scarborough, its more glamorous neighbour, Filey's massive stretch of beach is a real pull for families.

🛏 Sleeping
Camping There are plenty of campsites in the area including **Centenary Way Camping & Caravan Park**, Muston Grange, T01723 516415, just a short walk to the town and beach, open Mar-Oct. **Crows Nest Caravan Park**, T01723 582206, 2 miles north of the town on the coastal A165, is a large, family resort with camping and statics to rent Mar-Oct. **Filey Brigg Touring Caravan Park**, T01723 513852, this clifftop site is set in 9 acres of land, open Jan-Oct. **Muston Grange Caravan Park**, Muston Rd, T01723 512167, just south of the town.

Scarborough

A real Jekyll and Hyde resort. Garish and brash amusements line South Bay, yet explore just a short way from the neon and it becomes clear that Scarborough hides its real light under a bushel.

🛏 Sleeping
C **Rockside Hotel**, Blenheim Terr, T01723 374747, overlooking North Bay, is run by local big-wave charger, Del. C **The Selomar Hotel**, T01723 364964, Blenheim Terr. Just a few doors up, this is another surfer-friendly B&B with good breakfasts and a late bar. E-F **Scarborough YHA**, Burniston Rd, T01723 361176, heading north out of town. **Self catering** Brompton **Holiday Flats**, Castle Rd, T01723

364964, are a good option.
Camping   Scalby Close Park, T01723
365908, and **Scalby Manor Caravan
Park**, T01723 366212, both offer
camping and van pitches and are on
Burniston Rd.

🍴 Eating/drinking
Café Italia on St Nicholas Cliff near the
Grand is a great place to grab a coffee
and pastry. **Florio's**, Aberdeen Walk off
Westborough, T01723 351124, does
good Italian food in a central location.
Roger from Secret Spot recommends
Old Mother Hubbard's on
Westborough for "the best fish and
chips in the town", eat in or take away,
£4.95 lunchtime special. **The
Scarborough Tandoori**, Thomas St,
T01723 352393, serves great Indian
food at very reasonable prices.

When it comes to bars, on the
recommended list are **Cloisters** wine
bar on York Place, the nearby
Privilege Lap Dancing Club and **Red
Square**, Somerset Terr. Secret Spot's
Tommo recommends **Murray's**,
www.murraysmusicbar.com, on
Westborough, where they have

regular surf nights with films, as well as
live bands.

❶ Directory
Surf shops   Cayton Bay Surf Shop,
Killerby Cliff, T01723 585585, is
something of an institution. They stock
hardware and run the car park next
door – £2, no questions asked.
Although it costs 10p to pee they do
have free hot showers. **Secret Spot
Surf Shop**, Somerset Terr, T01723
500467, www.secretspot.co.uk, is
Scarborough's longest running surf
shop, stocking hardware and clothing.
Roger and Tommo will offer advice to
travelling surfers and are happy to give
an update on surf conditions. **Tourist
information**   Pavillion House, Valley
Bridge Rd, T01723 373333.

Robin Hood's Bay

This pretty, traditional, Yorkshire
fishing village discourages traffic –
there's a large pay and display car
park at the top of the hill overlooking
the bay, just a 5-min walk down to
the village.

💤 Sleeping
B **Boathouse**, T01947 880099, with
the Boathouse Bistro downstairs,
upstairs is run as a B&B. They also let
The Little House, a small, self-catering
stone cottage sleeping 2 from £300
per week. **B-C Bay Hotel**, T01947
880278. Set just back from the
seafront, they offer year-round B&B in
comfortable surroundings. E **Boggle
Hole YHA**, T0870 7705704, is a
popular but basic hostel open
Feb-Nov. **Camping   Middlewood
Farm Holiday Park**, T01947 880414
(0900-1900 only!), Middlewood Lane,
Fylingthorpe is a 10-min walk to the
beach with statics sleeping 4 from
£120-360 per week mid Feb-early Jan
and camping Easter-Jan.

Whitby

One of Yorkshire's seaside gems, this
town is now as famous for its Gothic
connection with Dracula (it hosts an
annual Goth Weekend over
Hallowe'en) as it is for its picturesque
harbour with cobbled streets and
excellent seafood.

Yorkshire streets

Local delicacies

DEMI TAYLOR

DEMI TAYLOR

Sleeping

B The Shepherd's Purse, Church St, T01947 820228, in a central location, with pretty rooms set around a courtyard to the rear of the shop, plus it does a good vegetarian breakfast.
B The White Horse and Griffin, Church St, T01947 604857, has a number of rooms above the popular restaurant. There are also a vast number of average B&Bs to choose from on West Cliff. **E-F Whitby Backpackers**, Hudson St, T01947 601794, has bunks and private rooms with no curfew. **Camping Sandfield House Caravan Site**, Sandsend Rd, T01947 602660, overlooks the sea north of Whitby, open Mar-mid/late Oct.

Eating/drinking

Bar 7, Pier Rd, is recommended as one of the best nights out by Ben Pepler at Zero Gravity. Ben also recommends the **Duke of York** at the end of Church St for cheap pub grub. **Elsinore** is a busy pub and popular with visiting Goths. **Finleys**, Flowergate, is worth a check for light meals and live music. **The Greedy Pig** takeaway café at the bottom end of Flowergate is *the* place

for mega roast pork, apple sauce and crackling served up in a white bap – you won't go hungry again!
Green's, Bridge St, T01947 600284, is mid-priced and one of the best spots for a sit-down dinner in Whitby.
Java café, Flowergate, serves up light, cheap snacks and has internet access.
The Magpie Café, Pier Rd, has a reputation for serving up the best fish and chips and seafood. Expect big queues during peak times of the year, but it is worth it! **The Shambles** on Market Pl is a popular and busy spot that also has a restaurant attached. The intimate **White Horse and Griffin**, T01947 604857, has a wide-ranging if fairly expensive menu, served by candlelight.

Directory

Surf shops Zero Gravity Surf Shop, Flowergate, T01947 820660, was opened by shaper Andrew Harrison in 1995 and sells the full range of hardware and clothing. 'Harry' is one of the east coast's best known surfers and first started shaping in 1987 for Freespirit Surfboards. **Tourist information** New Quay Rd near the train station, T01947 602674.

Flat spells

Cinema Hollywood Plaza, North Marine Rd, T01723 507567, Scarborough shows the latest releases from £5.
Golf Bridlington is home to a couple of courses: the parkland **Bridlington GC** on Belvedere Rd, T01262 672092, and the slightly cheaper **Bridlington Links**, T01262 401584, at £15-20 per round. **Filey GC**, West Av, T01723 513293. This links course is about a mile south of the town centre, £20-30 per round. **Scarborough North Cliff GC** is 2 miles north of the town on North Cliff Av, T01723 360786, while **Scarborough South Cliff GC** on Deepdale Av, T01723 360522, is a mile to the south, both around £20-30 green fees. **Whitby GC**, Sandsend Rd, T01947 600660, is a dramatic 18-hole cliff top course overlooking the sea.
Sights Scarborough Castle sits in a commanding position overlooking both north and south bays and is worth a visit for the views alone. **Whitby Abbey** was the inspiration for Bram Stoker's *Dracula*. Climb the hill for the great views over Whitby Bay.
Flamborough Head Check out this 'Lands End of the Eastcoast' minus the extortionate parking and tourist tat. You'll be surprised at what you might find.
Skating Scarborough North Bay Skatepark is free, overlooks the sea and is lit until about 2200 with metal banks, ¼ pipes and rails.

DEMI TAYLOR

Look through the square window...

Surfing Northeast England

The early autumn sun is dropping down below Dunstanburgh Castle, a dark shadowy silhouette on the headland. The only other surfer in the bay paddles up and strikes up a conversation. "It's nice to have a bit of company," he says. "Nice to see new faces in the line-up." In 20 years of surfing this is a first, but then Northumbria isn't like many other destinations in Britain. It is still a place where a car with boards on the roof stands out. Still a place where complete strangers strike up conversations when you're checking the surf. It's like it used to be everywhere else.

The Northeast was once England's secret realm. A small population of hardcore locals went about their surfing, without shouting about their breaks. Occasional travelling surfers returned with fantastical tales of reeling reefs and points, but these were put down to too much cold water on the head. Even when Newcastle surfer Nigel Veitch took the British title and headed onto the world tour, the east coast still avoided the limelight.

It was not until the surfing boom of the 1990s that the waves around Saltburn and Newcastle came into the surf media spotlight. Surfers like Gabe Davies and Sam Lamiroy were making an impression both at UK and European levels and locals like Robbie Hildreth and Jesse Davies were featured in surf mags charging big swells at home. Today spots that at one time saw a small local crew are suffering from overcrowding, and breaks that were once secret are common knowledge. Still, for those with a spirit of adventure, and a need to get back to how surfing used to be, the A1 always beckons. Ninety minutes north will take you 20 years back to a time when surfers were still an oddity to be stared at, and a new face in the line-up is excuse enough to strike up a conversation.

Coastline
The coastline from Saltburn to the Scottish border has some of England's most varied surfing terrain. From flat, slate reefs, to long, rocky points and heavy, hollow beach breaks, this area has it all. Northumbria has miles of white sand beaches interspersed with point breaks, whereas Cleveland has some amazing slate reefs as well as grinding man-made rivermouth breaks. The Gare and Black Middens, nestled in the mouths of the Tees and Tyne respectively, are probably the most bizarrely polluted in the UK. The Tees carries away effluent from steel works, an ICI plant the size of a small town, and a nuclear powerplant – a heady cocktail of warm, fragrant, discharge with a radioactive threat balanced like a cherry on top!

A tell-tale trademark of these northern waves is the brown colour of the coastal waters. Although certain breaks are polluted, most are coloured by

See map p133 for breaks 9 to 20

Breaks...
1 Saltburn
2 The Gare ★
3 Seaton Carew
4 The Pier, Hartlepool
5 South Shields
6 Black Middens
7 Tynemouth
8 Hartley Reef

the silty composition of the soil and coastal sediments. However, north of Newcastle the sea clears, the line-ups clear and crystal-blue waves peel in front of the silhouettes of once-great castles.

Localism

Compared to Cornwall and Devon, most of the Northeast is relatively uncrowded. But since the mid-1990s, some of this region has undergone a massive boom in the number of surfers in the line-up. Tynemouth and Hartley Reef are now popular breaks where numbers can be high. This has caused some tension but there have been no incidents of localism. The line-ups here are quite tight-knit however, and it helps to take a good attitude with you. Problems arise when surfers paddle out at crowded breaks that are well beyond their ability – both dangerous and frustrating.

Top local surfers

Sam Lamiroy and Gabe Davies are successful WQS surfers, the late Nigel Veitch was a national champion and ex-world champion Martin Potter was born in the Northeast. Local chargers include Jesse Davies, Steve Crawford, Robbie Hildreth, Chris Eire, Nick Noble, Owain Davies and 2004 British Master Champion Gary Rogers. Surf filmmaker Mark Lumsden (of Cold Rush fame) is a resident of Berwick-upon-Tweed.

Getting around

The road network in the Northeast is very good. Northumbria and Newcastle are serviced by the A1, while the A168/A19/A172 feeds up from the A1 heading northeast to Saltburn. Access to breaks is excellent from the coast road. Check parking as many coastal villages have strictly enforced no parking areas.

“ ”

I don't think people are surprised anymore by the quality of surfers coming out of the Northeast. Not now that they've seen in the magazines and on videos the quality of waves up here.

Sam Lamiroy, former English and British Champion

Northeast England board guide

Fish
Shaper: The Gill, ODD Surfboards

▸▸ 6'2" x 19½" x 2⅜".
▸▸ For average surfer 6'4" x 19½" x 2⅜.
▸▸ Flat bottomed with a fuller nose to help wave catching and aid stability in manoeuvres.
▸▸ Double concave through the swallow tail for drive, designed for small summer surf.
▸▸ When the surf picks up, use with bigger fins to create a loose board in good surf.

Performance Thruster
Shaper: The Gill, ODD Surfboards

▸▸ 6'1" x 18" x 2⅛" for Isaac Kibblewhite.
▸▸ For average surfer 6'4" x 19" x 2¼".
▸▸ Screwdriver square tail for extra bite in the face.
▸▸ Sunken double concave.
▸▸ Ride in clean medium sized powerful surf.
▸▸ Good for heavy waves like The Gare and Hartley Reef.

ⓘ Boards by **ODD Boards**
Factory: Freelap Surfboards, Porthcawl, Wales. T 01656-744691
www.oddsurfboards.co.uk
or contact gill@eurotelemail.net

Igor Harris surfing a Northeast point

KIRRA CHOCOLATE

KIRRA MILITARY

KIRRA KHAKI / CHOCOLATE

ROBB KALANI

FIND THIS STYLE AND A DEALER NEAR YOU AT:
WWW.GRAVISFOOTWEAR.COM
RIDER SERVICE EUROPE 00 800 744 72 847 (TOLL FREE).

Breaks

1 Saltburn

- **Break type**: Beach break.
- **Conditions**: All swells, offshore in southwesterly/southerly winds.
- **Hazards/tips**: Good beach for all surfers.
- **Sleeping**: Saltburn ›› p137.

Fairly good quality beach break with the best waves near the pier. Very popular spot due to parking access and surf hire on the beach. Great place for beginners.

To the south under the cliffs, **The Point** is a quality wave that comes to life at low tide in big, clean swells when hollow right-handers reel off the flat reef. In the corner **Penny Hole** is a low tide peak with short rights and long lefts, which can be excellent. This beach has been one of the central hubs of Northeast surfing due to the beachfront Saltburn Surf Shop, first opened in 1986, one of the first surf shops in the northeast. Many of the region's surfers caught their first waves on Nick and Gary's hire boards. Pollution was always a problem here but things seem to have improved with a new treatment works.

2 The Gare

- **Break type**: Right-hand point break.
- **Size**: 3-10 ft.
- **Length**: 50-150 m.
- **Swell**: Big easterly or southeasterly swells.
- **Wind**: From the south or southwest.
- **Tides**: Works on all tides.
- **Bottom**: Small, sharp, hard boulders.
- **Entry/exit**: Off the rocks at the end of the break.
- **Hazards**: Bad pollution, heavy wave, long hold-downs, cold water.
- **Sleeping**: Saltburn ›› p137.

On its day, the Gare is a world-class wave that is the Northeast's best right-hander. In big easterly and southeasterly swells, this man-made

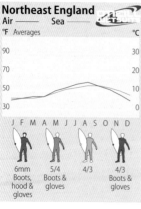

Northeast England

Air ——— Sea

°F	Averages											°C
90												30
70												20
50												10
30												0
	J	F M A M J J A S O N D										

6mm Boots, hood & gloves	5/4 Boots & gloves	4/3	4/3 Boots & gloves

DEMI TAYLOR

1 Saltburn

breakwater inside the mouth of the River Tees is transformed from bleak rocky pier into a brown Jeffrey's Bay with long, walling, hollow waves reeling along the sharp boulders. This is a heavy wave best left to experienced surfers only. Holds big swells up to 10 ft, and is very powerful – even at 6-8 ft, surfers have had two-wave hold-downs. Works through all tides. Water quality has been absolutely diabolical with sewage combining with petrochemical outflows, but this is supposed to be slowly improving. The white water fizzes and has a strong aftershave/ chemical smell. The Gare needs very specific conditions to work: strong southeasterly winds blowing over 24 hours. This normally means it breaks only a handful of times a year, in the depths of winter. However in 2000 the Gare broke for about 14 days in one month. There were 30 guys out the first day, 20 the second, 10 the third…

There is only so much exposure to the pollution that the human body can take. "Every year we vow not to surf it any more," says northeast surfer Nige Rodwell, "but then you see a chart and know it's gonna break and you find yourself ringing round the crew saying 'You on for the Gare tomorrow?'"

3 Seaton Carew

- **Break type**: Beach break.
- **Conditions**: Big swells, offshore in southwesterly winds.
- **Hazards/tips**: Pollution is supposed to be getting better.
- **Sleeping**: Saltburn ▸▸ *p137*.

Seaton Carew has a sheltered beach with harbour at the north end and a groyne with sandbar. Doesn't pick up as much swell as other beaches in the area. Rarely surfed. Traditionally very polluted, reputedly getting better.

4 The Pier, Hartlepool

- **Break type**: Beach break.
- **Conditions**: Small to medium swells, offshore in southwesterly winds.
- **Hazards/tips**: Good waves but polluted water, bad rips near houses on the seafront, not for beginners.
- **Sleeping**: Saltburn ▸▸ *p137*.

Stunning location. Huge, empty sandy beach overlooked by the shells of once-mighty northern engineering plants. This huge industrial pier allows sandbars to form either side and produces heavy waves in clean swells on all tides. Can produce epic waves with hollow powerful lefts and rights. Bleak and industrial backdrop with derelict factories casting their shadows over the dark North Sea. Park on Old Cemetery Road and check the waves through the graveyard or on the seafront at Hartlepool and walk.

DEMI TAYLOR

SCOTT WICKING

4 The Pier, Hartlepool

2 The Gare

5 South Shields

- **Break type**: Beach break.
- **Conditions**: Medium swells, offshore in southwesterly winds.
- **Hazards/tips**: Beachfront parking.
- **Sleeping**: Tynemouth ›› p137.

A stretch of good quality, sandy beach, with nice peaks along its length and pretty clean water. Picks up northeasterly and southeasterly swells and works on all tides. Good for all surfers. Check to the south where you might find a couple of nice hidden spots.

6 Black Middens

- **Break type**: Rivermouth reef.
- **Conditions**: Big swells, offshore in westerly winds.
- **Hazards/tips**: Parking near Collingwood's Monument.
- **Sleeping**: Tynemouth ›› p137.

This left-hand reef break can produce some excellent waves in big easterly swells. The problem is that it breaks in the mouth of the industrial River Tyne. Water quality improving, but still very dire. For experienced and hardened surfers only.

7 Tynemouth

- **Break type**: Beach break.
- **Conditions**: All swells, offshore in westerly/southwesterly winds.
- **Hazards/tips**: Road parking near the beach.
- **Sleeping**: Tynemouth ›› p137.

Longsands is a spot popular with Newcastle surfers and offers decent waves on a northeasterly swell. This beach is where many of the city's surfers learnt their trade. Works on all tides. Was the venue for the 2004 British Champs. Nearby '**Eddies**' (King Edwards Bay) is also worth checking at low to mid tide.

8 Hartley Reef

- **Break type**: Reef break.
- **Conditions**: Medium to big swells, offshore in southwesterly winds.
- **Hazards/tips**: Crowds, experienced surfers.
- **Sleeping**: Tynemouth ›› p137.

Home break to many of the region's top surfers, this flat reef produces excellent quality lefts as well as some good rights. Hartley is a mid to high tide break and can hold decent-sized swell. Breaks up to 8 ft producing long, walling waves with hollow sections. Parking overlooking the break. Popular break that gets crowded when good. Access off the A193 at roundabout with B1325.

8 Hartley Reef

12 Guts, Seaton Point ›› p134

5 South Shields

9 Blyth

- ◑ **Break type**: Beach break.
- ◐ **Conditions**: Medium swells, offshore in southwesterly winds.
- ❶ **Hazards/tips**: Rips in big swells.
- ◓ **Sleeping**: Tynemouth ▸▸ *p137*.

Long, crescent-shaped sandy bay that can have good lefts and rights. Again, works in northeasterly and southeasterly swells. Access via the A193. Parking at the beach.

10 Druridge Bay and Creswell

- ◑ **Break type**: Beach break.
- ◐ **Conditions**: Medium swells, offshore in westerly winds.
- ❶ **Hazards/tips**: Suitable for all surfers.
- ◓ **Sleeping**: Tynemouth/Alnmouth/Alnwick ▸▸ *p137*.

Picturesque, dune-backed bay reminiscent of Les Landes in France. Facing east, this crescent-shaped bay picks up lots of swell, the northern end best in southeasterly swells and the southern end best in swells from the north. Works on all tides. Has great potential. Worth checking the reef at **Creswell** on the southern end of the bay. This is where the Northumberland Heritage Coastline ends so from here

11 Alnmouth peak

south the water quality deteriorates. Ellington Colliery marks the start of the industrial northeast. Coast road to Creswell liable to flooding.

11 Alnmouth

- ◑ **Break type**: Beach break.
- ◐ **Conditions**: All swells, offshore in westerly winds.
- ❶ **Hazards/tips**: Rips by the river.
- ◓ **Sleeping**: Alnmouth/Alnwick ▸▸ *p138*.

A long, flexible sandy beach that can have excellent waves in northeasterly and southeasterly swells. At the northern end, by the links golf course, Alnmouth rivermouth can be classic and produce some good banks depending on the flow of the river. On an outgoing tide there can be some strong currents so be aware, this part of the beach is not for inexperienced surfers. The rivermouth is offshore in northwesterly winds and parking is available through the golf course. The main beach, south of the river, is a long crescent with some great peaks. Watch out for rips in bigger swells. Park behind the sand dunes via a very bumpy track.

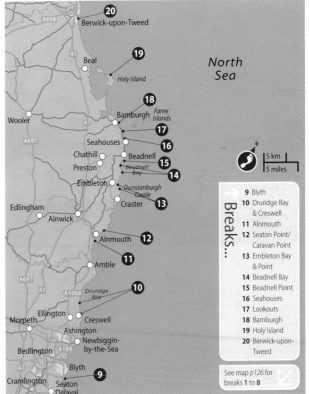

North Sea

20 Berwick-upon-Tweed

A698

A1

19 Beal

Holy Island

Wooler

A697

A1

18 Bamburgh · Farne Islands

17

Seahouses **16**

Chathill · Beadnell **15**

Preston · *Beadnell Bay* **14**

Embleton · *Dunstanburgh Castle*

Edlingham · Craster **13**

Alnwick

Alnmouth **12**

11

Amble

A697

A1 A1068 · *Druridge Bay* **10**

Ellington

Morpeth · Creswell

Ashington

Newbiggin-by-the-Sea

Bedlington A189

A1 · Blyth

Cramlington · Seaton · **9**

Delaval

N

5 km
5 miles

Breaks...

9 Blyth
10 Druridge Bay & Creswell
11 Alnmouth
12 Seaton Point/ Caravan Point
13 Embleton Bay & Point
14 Beadnell Bay
15 Beadnell Point
16 Seahouses
17 Lookouts
18 Bamburgh
19 Holy Island
20 Berwick-upon-Tweed

See map *p126* for breaks **1** to **8**

DEMI TAYLOR

12 Seaton Point/Caravan Point

- ◐ **Break type**: Left-hand point.
- ◑ **Conditions**: Big to huge swells, offshore in northerly winds.
- ❶ **Hazards/tips**: Shallow, rocky, experienced surfers.
- ◒ **Sleeping**: Alnmouth/Alnwick ⤍ *p138*.

This very sheltered bay works in massive swells. The beach breaks through the tides but the waves can be a bit weak as the banks aren't great. The Point needs a big northerly swell or decent southeasterly swell to get going, but produces nice long lefts, even in northerly winds. Good place to check in big winter storms. Best at low to mid tide. Park by the holiday chalets that overlook the break.

13 Embleton Bay and Point

- ◐ **Break type**: Beach break and rocky point.
- ◑ **Conditions**: All swells, offshore in westerly winds.
- ❶ **Hazards/tips**: Rips when big, rocky point.
- ◒ **Sleeping**: Alnmouth/Alnwick/ Beadnell ⤍ *p138*.

Embleton is a beautiful bay overlooked by the haunting ruins of Dunstanburgh Castle. It is home to some of the best beach break waves on this coastline, with hollow peaks producing nice barrels in 3 to 6 ft swells. Offshore in southwesterly or westerly winds and works on all tides. At the southern end is a point that comes to life in good swells when quality rights peel into the bay at mid to high tide. Beach can be powerful in bigger swells. Park and walk across the golf course.

14 Beadnell Bay

- ◐ **Break type**: Beach break.
- ◑ **Conditions**: Medium to big swells, offshore in westerly winds.
- ❶ **Hazards/tips**: Flexible spot, very quiet.
- ◒ **Sleeping**: Beadnell ⤍ *p139*.

This huge, crescent-shaped bay picks up swells from the south, east and north. Can have some nice waves all the way through the tides. At the south is a small bay called **Football Hole**, which is worth checking. Nice open beach with sand dunes. Parking at northern and southern (Newton) ends.

DEMI TAYLOR

17 Lookouts

15 Beadnell Point

- ⚙ **Break type**: Left-hand point break.
- 🌊 **Conditions**: Big to huge swells, offshore in northerly/northwesterly winds.
- ❶ **Hazards/tips**: Park near the sailing club, winter break.
- 🛏 **Sleeping**: Beadnell ▸▸ *p139*.

A walling left-hand point that breaks in front of the old lime kiln at Beadnell Harbour. The point is offshore in northwesterly or northerly winds because the waves wrap into the bay, but it needs a big northerly or northeasterly swell to get going. Great place to check when everywhere else is maxed out.

16 Seahouses

- ⚙ **Break type**: Right-hand reef breaks.
- 🌊 **Conditions**: Medium to big swells, offshore in southwesterly winds.
- ❶ **Hazards/tips**: Ledge is shallow and heavy. Experienced surfers only.
- 🛏 **Sleeping**: Beadnell ▸▸ *p139*.

A series of reefs in front of the houses on the coast road that heads north towards Bamburgh. Work best in a big southeasterly swell. There is also a dredging right-hander near the harbour mouth called the **Ledge**. Parking on seafront and in car park near harbour.

17 Lookouts

- ⚙ **Break type**: Right-hand point break.
- 🌊 **Conditions**: Big swell, offshore in southwesterly.
- ❶ **Hazards/tips**: Can have longshore rips in a big swell pushing north. Clean water.
- 🛏 **Sleeping**: Beadnell ▸▸ *p139*.

This good quality, sand-covered rocky point works in a big, clean, southeasterly or easterly swell. Works through the tides but is best from low to mid. In a good swell, long, walling rights peel along the reef. Just to the north, a sandbar peak offers good lefts and rights. Park on the road near the lifeguard tower.

18 Bamburgh

- ⚙ **Break type**: Beach break.
- 🌊 **Conditions**: Small to medium swells, offshore in southwesterly winds.
- ❶ **Hazards/tips**: Overlooked by Bamburgh Castle.
- 🛏 **Sleeping**: Beadnell ▸▸ *p139*.

Good quality beach break that picks up loads of swell. In a southeasterly the southern end of the beach picks up the most swell; and in a northeasterly the castle end is the place to go. Can have some good sandbars with lefts and rights and working through all tides. Parking available near castle end of beach behind the dunes. There is also a rocky

DEMI TAYLOR
13 Embleton Point

DEMI TAYLOR
16 Seahouses

DEMI TAYLOR
Secret left-hand reef

finger of reef that extends out towards the Farne Islands that has a right-hand point break in southeasterly swells.

19 Holy Island

- 🌀 **Break type**: Beach break.
- 🌊 **Conditions**: Medium swells, offshore in southwesterly winds.
- ❶ **Hazards/tips**: Quiet spot, access via low-tide causeway.
- 🛏 **Sleeping**: Beadnell ⤍ *p139*.

There is a low tide left-hand reef that breaks towards the northern end of the island. Although rarely surfed it can be classic on its day. Needs a good, clean north or northeasterly swell. To the west of the reef lies a stretch of low to mid tide beach break. Park in the car park and walk to the north coast of the island. There can also be a left point off the southern tip of the island in big swells. The wave wraps over a boulder reef into deep water. Access to Lindisfarne is only possible at low tide via a causeway that is submerged at high tide. Make sure you have your tide times or you may find your visit extended longer than you planned.

20 Berwick-upon-Tweed

- 🌀 **Break type**: Beach break.
- 🌊 **Conditions**: Medium swells, offshore in southwesterly winds .
- ❶ **Hazards/tips**: Beware of rips from the river, not for inexperienced surfers.
- 🛏 **Sleeping**: Beadnell ⤍ *p139*.

Peeling along a sandbar near the rivermouth is a left-hander that needs a good clean northeasterly swell but can produce excellent, long walls. Quiet line-up.

Secret reef

14 Football Hole ⤍ *p134*

Secret harbour reef

Listings

Saltburn

This is a very pleasant Victorian resort town complete with a water-balance cliff tram ferrying people to and from the seafront and the pier.

⬤ Sleeping

There are a couple of hotels and plenty of B&B options on the Victorian terraces running down to the cliff top. The most expensive are **B The Spa Hotel** on the hill above the beach, T01287 622544, and **B Queen Hotel** on Station St, T01287 625820. **Camping** In terms of camping try **Hazel Grove Caravan Park**, Milton St, T01287 622014, open Mar-Jan. **The Serenity Touring Caravan Park** on the A174 in Hinderwell, T01947 841122, is open Mar-Oct.

⬤ Eating/drinking

Gary Rogers of **Saltburn Surf Shop** recommends **Alessie's Italian** for an evening meal and **Vergo's Café** for good lunchtime food – both on Dundas St. A lot of the local crew drink in the **Victoria**, again on Dundas St. Local surfer Andy Cummins recommends **Windsor's** for a beer and **Signals Café** for a bite to eat.

⬤ Directory

Surf shops & facilities Saltburn Surf Shop and Hire, T01287 625321, www.saltburnsurf.co.uk, was opened in 1986 and is run by Gary Rogers and Nick Noble. As well as stocking hardware and clothing, they also hire boards and suits and run BSA-approved lessons. The shop is open year-round and you can ring their surf check line on T09068 545543 for a surf update (60p/min). The shop is in the seafront car park by the pier. **Tourist information** Railway station, T01287 622422.

Tynemouth

Head through the Tyne Tunnel and towards the coast to Tynemouth – the hosting grounds of the 2004 British Championships. The main focus here is Font St packed with places to eat, drink and sleep. This is not a wild or pretty town but it is a handy base for exploring the region.

Bamburgh Castle

DEMI TAYLOR

England Northeast Listings Saltburn to Tynemouth

137

Sleeping

A **Park Hotel**, Grand Parade, T0191 257106, www.parkhoteltynemouth.co.uk. Separated from Longsands by the road, the hotel has en suite rooms

Watch out for the tractor beam...

Teeside, teeing off

Secret spot, Northeast left

with beach views. B-C **Guesthouse**, Front St, T0191 2573687, looks out towards the mouth of the Tyne and has tearoom downstairs as well as a secure garage to store bikes and boards in. **Camping** Just north in Whitley Bay is the **Whitley Bay Holiday Park**, T0191 2531216, www.gbholidayparks.co.uk. This is a traditional family holiday camp taking families and mixed groups only. Statics are good value: 8 berth from £130 per week. Open end Mar-end Nov.

Directory
Surf shops & facilities
Tynemouth Surf Co, Grand Parade, T0191 2582496, www.tynemouthsurf.co.uk, overlooks Longsands Beach. Stephen Hudson opened up in 1995 and has been servicing the region's expanding surf scene with hardware, equipment hire, BSA surf school, ding repair services and now a surf report line, T09058 200177 (65p/min).

Alnmouth

This is a small, quiet coastal village with a couple of pricey B&Bs and hotels as well as a choice of golf courses. A-B **Beaches**, Northumberland St, T01665 830443, offers cosy B&B accommodation. A-B **The Hope and Anchor**, Northumberland St, T01665 830363, www.hopeandanchorholidays.co.uk. This pub is the village hot spot and as such can be a bit noisy. However the rooms are en suite, clean, and pretty. If you ask nicely they may even stash your boards for you. B-C **The Grange**, Northumberland St, T01665 830401, is set back from the road, considered the best and very popular so book ahead.

Eating/drinking
The Tea Cosy Tea Room offers typical café fare such as jacket potatoes and pretty average sandwiches.

Alnwick

Alnwick is a pretty walled town just inland from Alnmouth and is a good base for Northumberland trips. With easy access from the A1, it is close to the breaks and offers a good choice of amenities.

Sleeping
There are plenty of B&B options here. Try C **Bondgate House Hotel**, Bondgate Without, T01665 602025. Also try C **The Tea Pot**, Bondgate Without, T01665 604473. **Camping** Bizarrely you can camp at the **Alnwick Rugby Club** in Greensfield Park, T01665 510109. Other camping options are **Cherry Tree Campsite**, Edlington, Alnwick,

T01665 574635, or **Proctor Steads Caravan and Camping**, Craster, Alnwick, T01665 576613.

Eating/drinking
On the square on Bondgate Within is the pricy **Gate Bistro** where you can get a 3-course, candlelit meal. **The Grape Vine** offers basic, good value evening food and is on the same square. Opposite, **Chilli's** does good value, tasty Tex-Mex while up the road you can grab a cheap takeaway pizza.

Directory
Internet At Barter Books on Bondgate Without, www.barterbooks.co.uk. **Tourist information** On the Shambles, Market Pl, T01665 510665.

Beadnell

Beadnell makes for a good base to access Northumbria's northern breaks. Sitting just off the B1340 on a sheltered point break, it has great winter surf potential. There is a pretty 18th-century harbour with lime kilns at the head of 3 miles of sandy beach.

Sleeping
There are a couple of B&Bs in the village. **B Low Dover**, Harbour Rd, 30 seconds from the harbour, T01665 720291, is a quiet family-run B&B which also has a self catering option. For groups, **E Joiners Shop Bunkhouse**, slightly inland at Preston, Chathill, T01665 589245, offers beds from £9 per night. **Camping** There are also plenty of camping and caravan sites in the area. **Beadnell Camping and Caravaning Club** is on the B1340

Flat spells
Golf Saltburn by Sea G C, Hob Hill, Guisborough, T01287 622812, also has a snooker room. **Alnmouth GC**, T01665 850231, is an 18-hole course and one of the oldest in England. Handicap cert needed. **Alnmouth Village GC**, Marine Rd, T01665 830370, is a 9-hole course. **Dunstanburgh Castle GC** at Embleton Bay, T01665 576562, is a lovely 18-hole links course. **Seahouses GC**, T01665 720794, heading south out of Seahouses is another links course.

Sights This is officially castle country. **Alnwick Castle**, T01665 510777, is pretty impressive but at £7.50 entry is fairly pricey too. **Bamburgh Castle**, www.bamburghcastle.com, looks impressive as you approach, as it dominates the skyline and overlooks an amazing beach. Not quite so nice up close though. Open Apr-Oct. **Dunstanburgh Castle**, T016655 576231, is a spectacular ruin overlooking Embleton Bay and is

open daily, entry around £2.50. Like a backdrop to a horror film, the jagged keep towers over the crashing sea. **Hadrian's Wall** Heading west out of Newcastle on the B6318 this 73-mile long wall was erected by the Romans to mark the northern boundary of their empire (and keep the marauding Celts out). This is a World Heritage Site so stick to footpaths and be mindful of this delicate piece of history. **Holy Island** or **Lindisfarne** is separated from the mainland by a tidal causeway. Famous for its monastery founded in AD 634, it is well worth a visit, but check the tides as it is cut off for about 5 hrs a day.

Skating R-Kade Skatepark, Majuba Rd, Redcar, T01642 483520, www.r-kadeskatepark.com. This is an excellent indoor wooden park with everything a skater could ask for – banks, spined mini ramps, bowled corners etc, some of which has been masterminded by ramp-building legend, Snoz. Entry from £4.

between Beadnell and Seahouses, T01665 720586. **Dunstan Hill**, T01665 576310, is inland from Embleton and open Mar-Oct. **Newton Hall Caravan Park** sits to the southern end of Beadnell Bay in the grounds of Newton Hall, T01665 576239, www.newton holidays.co.uk. A couple of miles up the coast in Seahouses, the **Seafield Caravan Park**, T01665 720628, offers statics and views across to the Farne Islands open Apr-Nov.

Eating/drinking
There are 2 good pubs in the village.

The Craster Arms offers a selection of decent pub grub and is well known for its crab sandwiches. Nearby, **The Towers** offers bar meals and has a slightly more expensive restaurant. **The Village Pantry**, opposite the church, has a range of provisions as well as coffee and sandwiches.

Directory
Surf shops The Ledge Surf Shop is actually a corner of an arcade, opposite the Olde Ship Hotel in Seahouses, selling basics such as wax. **Tourist information** Seahouses car park.

The mighty Thurso East ▸▸ *p166*

DEMI TAYLOR

Scotland

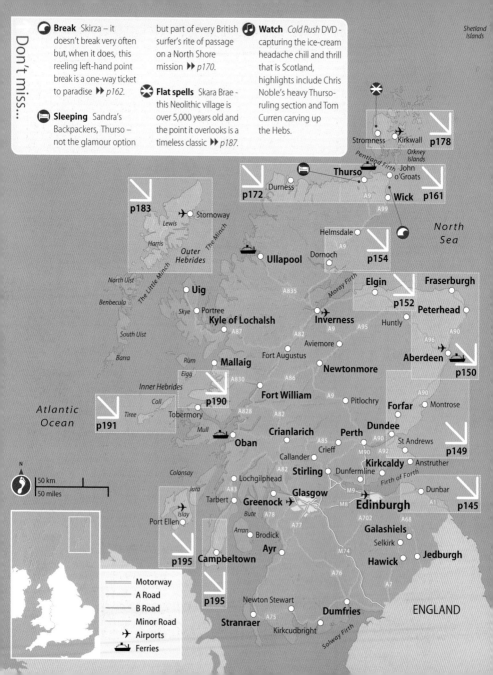

Don't miss...

Break Skirza – it doesn't break very often but, when it does, this reeling left-hand point break is a one-way ticket to paradise ▶▶ *p162*.

Sleeping Sandra's Backpackers, Thurso – not the glamour option but part of every British surfer's rite of passage on a North Shore mission ▶▶ *p170*.

Flat spells Skara Brae - this Neolithic village is over 5,000 years old and the point it overlooks is a timeless classic ▶▶ *p187*.

Watch *Cold Rush* DVD - capturing the ice-cream headache chill and thrill that is Scotland, highlights include Chris Noble's heavy Thurso-ruling section and Tom Curren carving up the Hebs.

p178
p172
p161
p183
p154
p152
p150
p149
p145
p190
p191
p195
p195

Stromness   Kirkwall
Orkney Islands
Pentland Firth
Thurso   John o'Groats
Durness   Wick
North Sea

Helmsdale
North Sea

Stornoway
Lewis
The Minch
Harris
Outer Hebrides
Dornoch
Ullapool
Moray Firth
Elgin   Fraserburgh
North Uist
The Little Minch
Uig   Peterhead
Benbecula
Skye   Portree
Kyle of Lochalsh
Inverness   Huntly
South Uist
Aviemore
Aberdeen
Barra   Rùm
Mallaig   Fort Augustus
Eigg
Newtonmore
Inner Hebrides
Fort William
Coll
Atlantic Ocean
Tiree   Tobermory
Pitlochry   Forfar   Montrose
Mull   Crianlarich   Perth   Dundee
Oban   Crieff   St Andrews
Callander   Kirkcaldy   Anstruther
Colonsay   Stirling   Dunfermline
Jura   Lochgilphead   Glasgow   Dunbar
Tarbert   Greenock   Edinburgh
Islay   Bute   Galashiels
Port Ellen   Arran   Brodick   Selkirk
Ayr   Hawick   Jedburgh
Campbeltown

Newton Stewart   Dumfries   ENGLAND
Stranraer   Kirkcudbright
Solway Firth

N
50 km
50 miles

Motorway
A Road
B Road
Minor Road
✈ Airports
⛴ Ferries

Firth of Forth
Firth of Forth

Introduction

Scotland seems to go against everything your average surf destination has to offer. It's cold, it's wet, the living is hard and the locals even harder. In the time it takes to drive from Cornwall to Thurso you could be exiting a 747, breathing in your first humid lungful of Indo air. But when you distil the essence of a surf trip, it boils down to one thing – the waves. Scotland, with its heady mix of fine sandy beaches, reeling rivermouths, tapering reefs and points hewn from awesome slabstone, has a landscape resembling the perfect surfing theme park. Subtly worked by time, it has the balance, maturity and weathered texture of the finest single malt. Add to that a dash of North Atlantic juice and you have something for the real aficionado.

After years of dodging the limelight, Scotland's key breaks have been thrust centre stage. Mundaka is so last year – Thurso is the new black. Yet tantalizingly close, pristine breaks patiently wait for the true connoisseur – those with discerning taste and a real spirit of adventure.

Scotland rating

Surf
★★★★

Cost of living
★★★

Nightlife
★★

Accommodation
★★★

Places to visit
★★★

Surfing the East Coast

The east coast of Scotland is a huge expanse of coastline with a massive variety of breaks. It is also home to probably Britain's hardiest bunch of surfers. Without the precious warmth from the remnants of the Gulf Stream enjoyed by the west and north coasts, winter water temperatures in the North Sea can drop to 4°C and the wind chill factor often hits -10°C. For the past couple of decades numbers were limited to a hardcore crew centred around Fraserburgh, Aberdeen and Pease Bay, but the surf boom of the late 1990s and advances in wetsuit technology has seen some line-ups take on a degree of crowding unimaginable just a few years ago. As Sam Christopherson from Coast 2 Coast Surf School says: "I rocked up at Pease Bay earlier this year and counted nearly a hundred and fifty people in the water. That's Cornwall numbers." And yet for every hotspot there are still many breaks where waveriders are few and far between. "I think this is one part of the UK where there really are some excellent breaks with only a small crew surfing them," says surf explorer Paul Gill, "and I think they'd like to keep it that way!"

Although the east coast doesn't enjoy the consistency of the Atlantic coastline, it does receive more swell than many people realise. As local surfer Mark Cox says, "Swells arrive from the north, northeast, east and southeast. Spots that sleep in a northeasterly can come to life in a nice southeasterly swell."

"Fraserburgh is a special surf destination for a number of reasons," says George Noble of Broch Surf Club. "It catches most of the swell on the east coast and it sits right on the northeast corner, so you only have to drive a few miles to find a spot that is offshore in most wind directions: 270° of flexibility ain't too bad! The water is very clean, especially at the beaches, and if you avoid the main spots you can still score good waves in solitude. Also it's the performance hub of Scottish surfing so the kids coming up are always challenged and inspired by decent surfers."

Coastline

The east coast of Scotland stretches from the border with England to the breaks of Caithness to the far north. With over 300 miles of surfable coastline, it offers a huge variety of wave riding potential. There are many excellent beaches such as Pease Bay, Broch and Brora all interspersed with some great points and intimidating reefs – mistakes at spots like Wiseman's can be punished harshly.

Localism

Pease Bay now draws on a huge surfing population in Edinburgh and the surrounding area and the

---

East coast board guide

Semi-gun
Shaper: Martin McQueenie, MCQ Surfboards

▸▸ 6'4" x 18⅛" x 2⅜" for Scratch.
▸▸ For average surfer 6'6" to 6'8".
▸▸ Squash tail for flexibility or rounded pin for reef board.
▸▸ Bonzer bottom with single to double concave.
▸▸ Good board for the beaches and reefs around Frazerburgh.
▸▸ Works well in clean, medium-sized powerful surf.

Fish
Shaper: Martin McQueenie, MCQ Surfboards

▸▸ 6'4" x 19½" x 2⅝".
▸▸ For average surfer 6'2" to 6'6".
▸▸ Swallow tail fish.
▸▸ Good all-round board for beaches when the waves are slacker.
▸▸ Flat bottom to reverse vee for speed and drive.
▸▸ Slightly extra volume for easy paddling and wave-catching.

Boards by **MCQ** Momentum Surf Shop
Factory: Dunbar, Scotland
T 01368 869810, M T 07796 752957
www.momentumsurfshop.com
post@momentumsurfshop.com

pressure is beginning to tell. This is pushing people out to explore new areas. Most other spots around the east coast are chilled, literally, and a good attitude will be rewarded.

With a hardcore crew of about 30 year-round surfers, swelling to nearly 100 in the warmer weather, Fraserburgh has always had a reputation as a bit of a tough town.

"In Fraserburgh guys don't sit around," says Chris Noble. "They are constantly paddling and trying to get waves, which keeps the line-up moving, meaning the next person gets his or her wave. This leads to less stress. My advice to anyone visiting Fraserburgh would be to keep it cool, again, give the guys some space and you'll get your waves and a warm welcome." The points are particularly sensitive. "If you're going to come to Fraserburgh I'd advise that you avoid the points at peak times like weekends. The take-off area is so small and the line-up is so competitive you'd struggle to get a wave," says Iain Masson of Point North East Surf Shop in Fraserburgh.

Top local surfers

Andy Bennetts is one of the pioneers of the Edinburgh coastline and Martin McQueenie is a respected surfer/shaper based in Dunbar. According to George Noble of Broch Surf Club: "The stand-out surfers include Scratch, Russell Cruickshank, Groover, Iain Masson, William Watson (big wave hellman) and James McKay." Mike McWatt of ESP in Elgin rates Chris Noble as the best surfer the area has produced.

> There are an amazing number of breaks along the Scottish east coast. Some are well known, some are still genuine secret spots...The growth in numbers is pushing people into exploring more and more.

Martin McQueenie, McQ Surfboards, Dunbar

Getting around

The east coast is well served by roads along its entire length. The A1 hugs the shore between Berwick and Edinburgh. The A90 serves the coastline north to Fraserburgh where it morphs into the A98 and then into the A96 to Inverness. The bridge over the Moray Firth and the football stadium are famous markers for those making the pilgrimage to Thurso – only a few more hours on the A9. Many secret points of excellent potential sit just off this road, as this leg of the trip usually sees a flat North Sea or is tackled under cover of darkness!

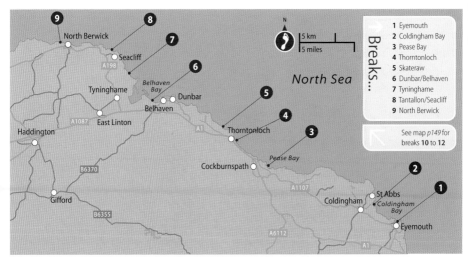

Breaks...

1 Eyemouth
2 Coldingham Bay
3 Pease Bay
4 Thorntonloch
5 Skateraw
6 Dunbar/Belhaven
7 Tyninghame
8 Tantallon/Seacliff
9 North Berwick

See map *p149* for breaks 10 to 12

North Sea

Breaks

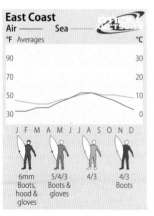

1 Eyemouth

- **Break type**: Beach break.
- **Conditions**: Big swell, offshore in southwesterly winds.
- **Hazards/tips**: Only worth checking in big, clean swells.
- **Sleeping**: Coldingham Bay ▸▸ p155.

This is a low to mid tide beach break which can have average lefts and rights, but needs a decent, clean northeasterly swell. High tide sees it transformed into a bit of a shore dump. Has protection from big, stormy northerlies. There can be pollution from the harbour. Access from the A1107 and park above the bay.

2 Coldingham Bay

- **Break type**: Beach break.
- **Conditions**: Medium to big swells, offshore in westerly winds.
- **Hazards/tips**: Check when Pease Bay big and crowded.
- **Sleeping**: Coldingham Bay ▸▸ p155.

This easterly facing beach picks up less than Pease Bay so is an ideal place to head in big swells. Works on all tides but is best from low to mid. Can have some quality waves and worth a check when Pease is busy. Follow the A1107 off the A1.

3 Pease Bay

- **Break type**: Beach break.
- **Conditions**: Medium to big swells, offshore in southwesterly winds.
- **Hazards/tips**: Gets very crowded.
- **Sleeping**: Pease Bay ▸▸ p155.

Pease Bay is usually crowded when it breaks due to its proximity to Edinburgh and the fact that it is one of the breaks on the Ceefax surfcheck pages. It is a sandy bay with peaks that work through the tides. A rocky reef towards the southern end gets very busy when it's working and a left breaks at the northern end. Check the breaks from the road down to the caravan park; access is through the camp. Safe for beginners.

4 Thorntonloch

- **Break type**: Beach with reef.
- **Conditions**: Medium to big swells, offshore in westerly winds.
- **Hazards/tips**: Torness Nuclear Powerstation.
- **Sleeping**: Pease Bay ▸▸ p155.

This spot is visible from the A1 but is overshadowed by the nearby rectangular box that is Torness Power Station. Worth checking as there can be some quality waves here and the crowd

East Coast

Air —— **Sea**

°F Averages   °C

90   30

70   20

50   10

30   0

J F M A M J J A S O N D

6mm Boots, hood & gloves	5/4/3 Boots & gloves	4/3	4/3 Boots

3 Pease Bay overview

www.c2adventure.com

factor is virtually zero. Can handle winds from the northwest in a big swell. The reef works best at low tide and the beach from mid to high. There is a small parking area.

5 Skateraw

- **Break type**: Left and right reef.
- **Conditions**: Big swells, offshore in southwesterly winds.
- **Hazards/tips**: Access via farmer's land, be respectful.
- **Sleeping**: Dunbar ⤍ *p156*.

This is an experts-only reef with serious lefts and rights. Best from mid to high tide in southwesterly or westerly winds. Access is via a farmer's land – right turn after power station and via some houses. Park respectfully.

6 Dunbar/Belhaven

- **Break type**: Beach.
- **Conditions**: Medium swells, offshore in southwesterly winds.
- **Hazards/tips**: Safe beach, good for beginners.
- **Sleeping**: Dunbar ⤍ *p156*.

Nice beginners' wave that works on most tides in clean swells. A very user-friendly spot. Popular with the local surf school.

7 Tyninghame

- **Break type**: Beach break.
- **Conditions**: Medium swells, offshore in southwesterly winds.
- **Hazards/tips**: Do not park in the farm.
- **Sleeping**: Dunbar ⤍ *p156*

The wave here is heavier than Belhaven and, with a 15-minute cross-country hike, is best left to intermediate and advanced surfers. This big beach is becoming more popular as spots like Pease become more crowded. Best at low tide. Due to its northeasterly aspect, Tyninghame will be bigger than Pease in a southeasterly swell, about the same in a northeasterly but smaller in a northerly. No access via the farm as the farmer is frustrated by inconsiderate parking.

8 Tantallon/Seacliff

- **Break type**: Beach.
- **Conditions**: Medium swells, offshore in southerly winds.
- **Hazards/tips**: Stunning location.
- **Sleeping**: Dunbar ⤍ *p156*.

A private, north-facing beach with a reef that is overlooked by Tantallon Castle. This wonderful beach works well up to head high but when bigger can suffer from rips. Just off the A198.

9 North Berwick

- **Break type**: Beach and reef.
- **Conditions**: Medium to big swells, offshore in southerly winds.
- **Hazards/tips**: Can have bad rips in big swells.
- **Sleeping**: Dunbar ⤍ *p156*.

On the town beach you'll find a mid to high tide left-hand beach/sand-covered reef. Works best in southerly winds and again needs a decent northeasterly swell to get going. There are beaches and reefs to the east and west worth checking. The west side of the harbour offers protection from big easterly swells and winds. The area is prone to rips when big and there are some rocks at low tide.

10 St Andrews

- **Break type**: Beach breaks.
- **Conditions**: Medium to big swells, offshore in southwesterly and westerly winds.
- **Hazards/tips**: Beach car parks.
- **Sleeping**: St Andrews ⤍ *p157*.

There are some fine sandy beaches around St Andrews, the spiritual home of Scottish golf. To the east is a huge open expanse of beach, which can have some quality peaks through the

Secret spot Seek and ye shall find...

6 Belhaven

DEMI TAYLOR

www.o2adventure.com

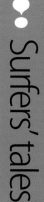

Thurso East ▶▶ p166

My First Barrel
By Martin McQueenie

It had been a very long day at Thurso, we'd been in about three times and there wasn't much light left. It was about half past four and I had one dry wetsuit left with holes in the shoulders, so I was determined not to get my shoulders wet. Surfing in Scotland is a matter of getting all the variables right and we'd been in the water since half past eight in the morning, making the most of the light of the short November day.

I paddled out and it was just getting on dusk – there was a kind of orange light coming over the town and the sets were coming in at about head high, head high and a half. I paddled out into the line-up, turned for a wave and paddled really hard. I took off and went along the face of the wave as it raced straight down the line, then the whole thing just barrelled over me. Some people have different visions of what happens, of what goes on – everyone is slightly different. I found that time stood still. There was so much to take in. All your senses are trying to work out what's going on. You've got the reef going below you really fast – you can see all the rocks underneath because it's so shallow and you've got light filtering through the back of the wave – it's very like a cathedral with all these different colours going on. As you travel on at Thurso East and get to the inside there's a peat river that feeds into the sea and changes the water into an Irn Bru orange colour. Going along, it's super blue and then suddenly it's orange. I knew there was a good chance that I could make it and luckily the board was trimming high enough and I got spat out the end.

Everybody on the beach started clapping and I didn't really realize what was going on – only that I'd managed to keep my shoulders dry. My hair was still dry and I looked at my friend and he knew from my reaction. I just waved and paddled into the shore.

Now, 15 years later, I've got a surf shop in Dunbar and I teach surfing but that is something that will always stay with me. Some people go through their whole surfing career without experiencing something like that. But it's something that I'll always remember.

tides, but best mid to high. Also worth trying are the beaches to the east heading out towards Kingsbarns on the A917, with parking at Cambo Sands.

11 Lunan Bay

- 🏄 **Break type**: Beach break.
- 🌀 **Conditions**: Medium to big swells, offshore in southwesterly to northwesterly winds.
- ❶ **Hazards/tips**: Access, isolated, rips.
- 🛌 **Sleeping**: Montrose ⇒ *p157*.

Turn off the A92 towards Lunan to access this quiet, dune-backed, 2-mile-long bay. At the north end of the bay a good quality left point breaks in clean northerly swells with winds from the southwest or west. The rest of the bay has a series of beach break peaks. Always worth checking are the banks near the rivermouth, but watch out for rips which can be bad on dropping tides and bigger swells. Red Castle, at the mouth of the stream, was once owned by Robert Bruce and this beautiful beach was a popular landing spot for raiding Vikings.

12 Stonehaven

- 🏄 **Break type**: Reef and beach.
- 🌀 **Conditions**: Medium to big swells, offshore in westerly winds.
- ❶ **Hazards/tips**: Rips.
- 🛌 **Sleeping**: Montrose/Aberdeen ⇒ *p157*.

This sheltered bay needs a decent swell from the north or south, or a clean easterly, to get going. There is a decent reef on the southern end of the bay and waves along the beach depending on

the banks. The harbour here used to be the only safe haven on this coast in northeasterly gales.

13 Nigg Bay

- 🏄 **Break type**: Beach and reef.
- 🌀 **Conditions**: Medium to big swells, offshore in westerly winds.
- ❶ **Hazards/tips**: Advanced surfers when big.
- 🛌 **Sleeping**: Aberdeen ⇒ *p157*.

To the south of Aberdeen, Nigg Bay is a haven for surfers when big northerly swells close out the town beaches to the north. Nigg has a few breaks that can work in very big swells, when the conditions are right – if not they too can become painful closeouts. The rocky right point works on all tides but can become sketchy at low tide. There is also a left and a peak that are all worth checking whether the swell comes from the northeast, east or southeast. Produces hollow and powerful waves.

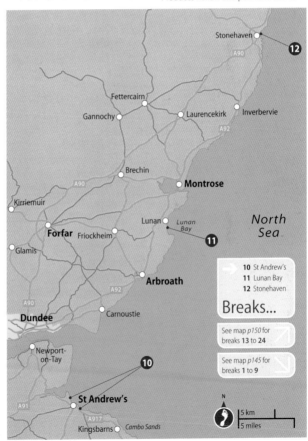

Breaks...

10 St Andrew's
11 Lunan Bay
12 Stonehaven

See map *p150* for breaks 13 to 24

See map *p145* for breaks 1 to 9

14 Aberdeen

- ◉ **Break type**: Beach break.
- ☁ **Conditions**: Medium to big swells, offshore in westerly and southwesterly winds.
- ❶ **Hazards/tips**: Groynes.
- ◔ **Sleeping**: Aberdeen ▸▸ p157.

This is a 3-mile stretch of beach to the north of the River Dee. It has a series of banks and works through the tides but has the obvious high tide impediment of a series of groynes to prevent beach erosion. Can have some great waves but isn't a classic beach. Picks up swell from northeast and southeast and is home to a large committed crew. The Don rivermouth can have good waves and it is worth searching to the north around Balmedie and Newburgh.

15 Cruden Bay

- ◉ **Break type**: Beach break.
- ☁ **Conditions**: Medium to big swells, offshore in westerly and northwesterly winds.
- ❶ **Hazards/tips**: Rips in big swells.
- ◔ **Sleeping**: Cruden Bay ▸▸ p158.

This picturesque, southeasterly-facing bay is lined with distinctive pink sand and can produce an excellent, hollow left near the harbour wall at the north end of the bay. To the south there is a small rivermouth that can have excellent banks at low to mid tide. In big swells there can be dangerous rips here so this is not a place for the inexperienced. Access to the southern end of the bay is via a golf course and farmer's field. Respect. The bay also picks up summer southerly swells.

16 Sandford Bay

- ◉ **Break type**: Point and beach.
- ☁ **Conditions**: Medium to big swells, offshore in westerly winds.
- ❶ **Hazards/tips**: Dangerous point wave, lots of seals.
- ◔ **Sleeping**: Cruden Bay ▸▸ p158.

Sandford sits in the shadow of Boddam Power Station and this conventional gas/oil generator uses the waters as coolant. The slight rise in temperature means the place is crowded with seals, and makes for good sea bass fishing, but it isn't warm enough to go without gloves and boots in the winter – as some guides

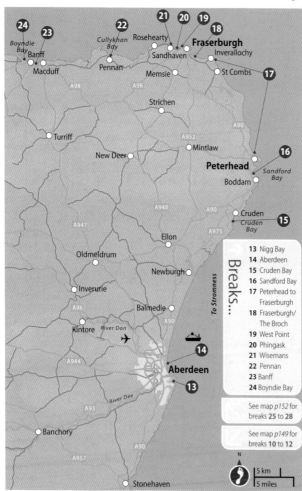

Breaks...

13 Nigg Bay
14 Aberdeen
15 Cruden Bay
16 Sandford Bay
17 Peterhead to Fraserburgh
18 Fraserburgh/ The Broch
19 West Point
20 Phingask
21 Wisemans
22 Pennan
23 Banff
24 Boyndie Bay

See map p152 for breaks 25 to 28

See map p149 for breaks 10 to 12

5 km
5 miles

have said. There is also an excellent right that breaks inside the bay from low to mid tide, with the slight inconvenience of two boulders to avoid on the inside. The outside left point is a dangerous beast that needs to be huge before it sits off the rocks enough to become surfable. But it is rideable in huge northeasterly swells with winds from the northwest.

17 Peterhead to Fraserburgh

- ⚐ **Break type**: Beach and reefs.
- 🌀 **Conditions**: All swells, offshore in winds from the S, SW,W and NW.
- ❶ **Hazards/tips**: Works in north, northeasterly, easterly and southeasterly swells.
- 🛏 **Sleeping**: Fraserburgh ⏵ *p158*.

This is a great area to explore, as there are many reef and beach breaks along this stretch of coast. From Peterhead the coast turns through a series of open beaches to face northeasterly. An amazingly flexible stretch of coastline with so many variations of wind and swell and often empty line-ups.

18 Fraserburgh/ The Broch

- ⚐ **Break type**: Beach break.
- 🌀 **Conditions**: All swells, offshore in southwesterly winds.
- ❶ **Hazards/tips**: Pollution, cold, crowds.
- 🛏 **Sleeping**: Fraserburgh ⏵ *p158*.

This crescent-shaped beach faces north to northeasterly, works on all tides and picks up the most swell on this coastline. The harbour (western) end picks up less swell but is home to a good quality left point breaking over boulders at high tide in a good north swell. Water quality can be poor. **Philorth** at the eastern end is a beach break with banks of various quality. Offshore in winds from the south.

Fraserburgh is the centre of the east coast surf scene and is home to a growing number of surfers. They are a committed and hardcore crew. Fraserburgh is also home to the Broch Surf Club who organize local events and contests. Check out their website www.brochsurfclub.com. It gets seriously cold here in the winter.

19 West Point

- ⚐ **Break type**: Point break.
- 🌀 **Conditions**: Medium to big swell, offshore in southerly winds.
- ❶ **Hazards/tips**: Poor water quality.
- 🛏 **Sleeping**: Fraserburgh ⏵ *p158*.

Right-hand point on the west side of town. This reef break works on all tides but best at mid to high, needs a good, clean northeasterly with southerly winds. Water quality is poor. This is a popular spot with local surfers so don't turn up by the bus load. Also surfable in an easterly swell.

20 Phingask

- ⚐ **Break type**: Reef break.
- 🌀 **Conditions**: Small to medium swells, offshore in southerly winds.
- ❶ **Hazards/tips**: Consistent, rocky reef.
- 🛏 **Sleeping**: Fraserburgh ⏵ *p158*.

A good quality reef that throws up long lefts and the occasional right. Works through the tides and is best in a southerly wind. Rocky reef so best left to exper-

East coast surfer Sam Christopherson gets slotted

ienced surfers. It's visible from the coast road heading west out of Fraserburgh.

21 Wisemans, Sandhaven

- **Break type**: Left reef.
- **Conditions**: Medium to big swells, southerly winds.
- **Hazards/tips**: Shallow, heavy wave, experienced surfers only.
- **Sleeping**: Fraserburgh ⇒ p158.

A heavy left that breaks near the harbour at Sandhaven. Popular wave but best left to experienced surfers. It's rocky, shallow, hollow and very heavy but can produce some nice, short barrels. The wave lunges up from deep water onto an unforgiving and sharp ledge. It is a jacking take-off but the rewards are big and hollow. Park by the break.

22 Pennan

- **Break type**: Reef breaks.
- **Conditions**: Medium swell, offshore in southerly winds.
- **Hazards/tips**: Rocky at high tide.
- **Sleeping**: Fraserburgh/Cullen ⇒ p158.

Looking out into Cullykhan Bay, the village of Pennan has a series of breaks that are worth checking in a good swell. A right breaks at the eastern end and a peak near the middle. There is backwash at high and it is difficult to exit the water. Works in a southerly wind. Access off the B9031.

23 Banff

- **Break type**: Rivermouth and beach.
- **Conditions**: Medium swells, offshore in southerly winds.
- **Hazards/tips**: Poor water quality and rips.
- **Sleeping**: Cullen ⇒ p158.

Where the River Deveron meets the North Sea, a sandbar is deposited and can produce lefts or rights depending on the swell and sandbar. Quality break in a clean northeasterly or northerly swell. Water quality isn't the best and rips can be problem. Not for inexperienced surfers. To the east is a fickle, but quality reef that can produce good right-handers in clean northeasterly swells. West of the river is a quality beach break with shifting

peaks. Can have hollow, powerful waves. Best from low to three-quarter tide. Access from next to Banff harbour. Further east at the picturesque village of **Gardenstown** is a reef that produces good right-handers at low tide. It is also worth checking neighbouring **Crovie** – a right-hand point that can fire in a northeasterly/easterly swell.

24 Boyndie Bay

- **Break type**: Point and beach.
- **Conditions**: Medium swells, offshore in southerly winds.
- **Hazards/tips**: Rips when big.
- **Sleeping**: Cullen ⇒ p158.

A good quality right-hand point that works from mid to high tide and a beach break with lefts and rights. Excellent waves on offer here in a clean northeasterly swell. Parking above the bay in town.

25 Sandend Bay

- **Break type**: Rocky point and beach.
- **Conditions**: Small to medium swells, offshore in southerly winds.
- **Hazards/tips**: Easy-going atmosphere.
- **Sleeping**: Cullen ⇒ p158.

A small bay with a harbour by the village at the western end. This pretty spot has a left that peels along a rocky reef by the harbour. Other quality peaks can be found in the bay. Works on all tides but is best at low and in a southerly wind. Car park close to the beach. It's also worth checking **Sunnyside Bay**, a quiet secluded spot overlooked by the 15th-century Findlater Castle.

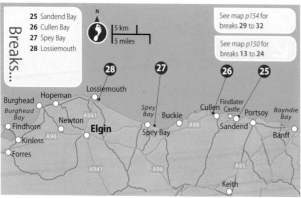

Breaks...

25 Sandend Bay
26 Cullen Bay
27 Spey Bay
28 Lossiemouth

N

5 km
5 miles

See map p154 for breaks 29 to 32

See map p150 for breaks 13 to 24

26 Cullen Bay

- 🌀 **Break type**: Beach break.
- 🌊 **Conditions**: Small to medium swells, offshore in a southerly wind.
- ❶ **Hazards/tips**: Quiet beach with good waves.
- 💤 **Sleeping**: Cullen ➤➤ p158.

Cullen produces good quality waves with peaks that work in northeasterly swells with southerly winds. Can be checked from the A98.

27 Spey Bay

- 🌀 **Break type**: Beach break.
- 🌊 **Conditions**: Small to medium swells, offshore in southerly winds.
- ❶ **Hazards/tips**: Rips when big.
- 💤 **Sleeping**: Lossiemouth/Elgin ➤➤ p158.

Again a fair beach break that works through the tides, with lefts and rights breaking on shifting sandbanks. Follow signs from the A96. There are a couple of reefs at Buckie also worth checking.

28 Lossiemouth

- 🌀 **Break type**: Beach break.
- 🌊 **Conditions**: Medium swells, offshore in southerly winds.
- ❶ **Hazards/tips**: ESP surf shop in nearby Elgin.
- 💤 **Sleeping**: Lossiemouth/Elgin ➤➤ p158.

A long, flat northeasterly facing beach with fair waves that work in a southerly wind. Best in a decent-sized northeasterly swell. Can have good lefts close to the harbour at low tide. It's worth checking **Burghead** as it is

sheltered in big northeasterly and easterly gales.

29 Wilkhaven

- 🌀 **Break type**: Rights and lefts.
- 🌊 **Conditions**: Medium to big swells, offshore in southwesterly winds.
- ❶ **Hazards/tips**: Open, sandy bay .
- 💤 **Sleeping**: Brora ➤➤ p159.

This peninsula works in a swell from the northeast, when waves can be found on either side with a little bit of exploring. Check the western side for right-handers and the eastern side for lefts. It's also worth checking Golspie for lefts at the north end of the beach in a big northeasterly. Dunrobin Castle Museum to the north houses a Hawaiian Ola board ridden by the Duchess of Sutherland in Hawaii during the 1930s.

Secret spot East coast

21 Wisemans

30 Brora rivermouth ➤➤ p153

30 Brora Beach ➤➤ p153

I find that the most memorable sessions are when I've been surfing with some of my friends and had some good waves with a good vibe in the water. Coming out and having a couple of beers... watching the waves with the last of the light slipping away is one of the best things for me.

Chris Noble

MARK LUMSDEN

Chris Noble

Helmsdale
Lothbeg
Dalchalm **31**
Brora **30**
Golspie
Dornoch
Wilkhaven **29**
32

5 km
5 miles

Breaks...

29 Wilkhaven
30 Brora
31 Lothbeg Point
32 Helmsdale

See map *p152* for breaks **25** to **28**

30 Brora

- **Break type**: Beach break and rivermouth.
- **Conditions**: Small to medium swells, offshore in westerly/northwesterly winds.
- **Hazards/tips**: Long beach with good peaks to suit all surfers.
- **Sleeping**: Brora ►► *p159*.

Good quality beach break that comes alive in good northeasterly or easterly swells. Works through the tides. Has some great sandbanks which can produce hollow peaks and long walling lefts and rights. There are lefts at the northern end close to the A9. The rivermouth at the southern end of the beach has a good right peeling into the peaty brown water. Water quality is excellent here. Access beach through golf course on footpath

154

and rivermouth via village. A good place to check if the north coast is blown out.

31 Lothbeg Point

- **Break type**: Left point.
- **Conditions**: Medium to big swells, offshore in northwesterly winds.
- **Hazards/tips**: Difficult access.
- **Sleeping**: Brora ▸▸ p159.

Excellent left point breaking over a flat reef. Works in good northeasterly and easterly swells. There is also a right breaking along the north side of the point in easterly swells. Offshore in a northerly and northwesterly wind. All tides. Access is pretty difficult. Turn off the A9 and drive under the railway bridge to the caravan park. Quality wave when it works but rarely surfed.

32 Helmsdale

- **Break type**: Left reef.
- **Conditions**: Medium swells, offshore in northwesterly winds.
- **Hazards/tips**: Rocky reef.
- **Sleeping**: Brora ▸▸ p159.

Left breaking in the bay near the mouth of the River Helmsdale. Works in a big, clean northeasterly, a clean easterly or a southeasterly swell. This is a sand and rocky break best left to experienced surfers. Water quality is excellent and the village is very picturesque. Visible from the A9. Home to an award-winning 'Land Clearances' visitors' centre.

Coldingham Bay

Crossing over from England to the Scottish Borders on the A1, Coldingham Bay is an easy detour off the more coastal A1107.

Sleeping

L-A **St Vedas Hotel**, T01890 771679, complete with a 'surfers bar', overlooks the beach at Coldingham, as does D **Dunlaverock Country House Hotel**, T01890 771450 – ideal for couples. E **Coldingham Sands Hostel**, T08700 041111, open Mar-Oct, is the budget alternative room with a view. Just up the road at St Abbs (renowned for its diving) is E **The Rockhouse**, T01890 771288, with excellent bunkhouse accommodation with storage and kitchen facilities. They also have slightly pricier B&B accommodation plus a cottage to let. **Camping Scoutscroft Holiday Centre**, T01890 771338, open Mar-Nov, has a cottage to let as well as camping facilities and a PADI Dive Centre in their grounds, about half a mile from the sea.

Directory

Surf shops St Vedas Surf Shop, T01890 771679, www.stvedas.co.uk, based at the hotel, hires and sells all basic hardware as well as running a handy surf cam.

Pease Bay

Due to the close proximity of an urban population and its mention on the daily Ceefax surf report, this pretty beach is quite possibly the most surfed spot in all of Scotland.

☺ Sleeping

B **The Anchorage B&B** on the roundabout overlooking Pease Bay, T01368 830254, is run by a surfing family. It has, as Martin McQueenie puts it, "conversation-stopping views". Recommended. They can even organize a packed lunch for around a fiver.

Camping Pease Bay Holiday Home Park, T01368 830206, www.peasebay.co.uk. With statics for hire and evening entertainers in the bar this is a real family park – closed Feb. A week for 2 in Mar costs from about £160. Their website has up-to-date tide tables for the area.

Dunbar

North of Torness Nuclear Power Station sits this elegant, north-facing seaside town with plenty of amenities and a growing surf community.

☺ Sleeping

Local surfer and entrepreneur Sam Christopherson runs a surfer-friendly B **B&B**, T07971 990361, sleeping up to 4, open Easter onwards.

Camping There are plenty of sites in the area including **Barns Ness**, T01368 836536 (Caravan & Camping Club site) to the south, open Mar-Nov. **Belhaven Bay Meadowhead Park**, T01368 865956, www.meadowhead.co.uk, 3 miles north of Dunbar, is open to campers and tourers as well as hiring out statics sleeping up to 8 for £190-450 per week, open Mar-Dec. Heading towards North Berwick on the A198 and perched on the cliffs is **Tantallon Meadowhead Park**, T01368 893348, offering similar facilities to its Belhaven sister site.

❷ Eating

Sam Christopherson recommends grabbing a bite to eat at the **Hillside Hotel**, Queens Rd, while Martin McQueenie recommends heading for **Umberto's** on the High St for traditional Italian or just a good value all-day breakfast.

❶ Directory

Surf shops Momentum Surf Shop, High St, T01368 869810, is fully stocked with hardware as well as being a base for their BSA surf school.

Owner Martin McQueenie has been shaping for nearly 10 years under the Pro Liberty and MCQ marks and makes boards for Scotland's top surfer Chris Noble, among others.

Coast 2 Coast, T07971 990361, www.c2cadventure.com, run by Sam Christopherson, is a BSA school operating daily Apr-Nov. For the hardy they run weekend-only extreme lessons Dec-Mar. The school also operates year-round surf trips for all standards to the Western Isles, east or north coast depending on conditions.

Edinburgh

Heading west from Dunbar on the A1, this beautiful city steeped in history and the spiritual home of Hogmanay is not a natural surf trip stopover, but if you are passing through there is plenty to distract you, from the castle that dominates the skyline to the festival that dominates the world of culture.

☺ Sleeping

East of the castle and to the south of Waverley station there is plenty of cheap hostel accommodation

Or, y'know, stay in a smelly old caravan when the rain's driving hard and the surf's flat...

No-one ever said it was gonna be easy...

including the small and friendly **E Brodie's Backpacker Hostel**, High St, T0131 556 6770. If you're after something a bit more lively try **E High Street Hostel**, Blackfriars St, T0131 5573984. There's also **E Royal Mile Backpackers**, High St, T0131 5576120. **Camping Edinburgh Caravan Club**, T0131 3126874, just north of the centre in Silverknowes, is a good bet and open year-round.

🍴 Eating

Momentum's Martin McQueenie suggests **China China**, opposite the Playhouse Theatre on Greenside Place, as a great place to grab an 'all you can eat' £5 buffet. Also worth trying is **Chiquito's** at the Fort Kinnaird Shopping Centre, for Mexican; all you can eat for around £7.50.

🕓 Directory

Internet There are plenty of places to get on-line, one of the cheapest being EasyEverything, Rose St, from £1/hr. **Surf shops** Animal, Rose St, T0131 2203156, has a full range of Animal products. **Boardwise**, Lady Lawson St, 08707 504420, caters for all your triple 's' needs.

Tourist information Princess St, T0131 473 3800, www.edinburgh.org, north of Waverley Station, open year-round.

St Andrews

Better known as a golfing Mecca than a surfing hot spot, this is a pretty university town.

💤 Sleeping

E Cairnsmill Caravan Park, T01334 473604, a mile out of town on the A915, offers statics for hire plus a bunkhouse.

Montrose

This pretty, bustling town is all but surrounded by water. Set on a spit, Montrose looks out to the North Sea while backed by a tidal basin and is a haven for wildlife.

💤 Sleeping

C Lunan Lodge, T01241 830267, south of Montrose on the A92, is a pretty B&B with views over Lunan Bay as well as a drying room facility.
C Oaklands Guest House, Rossie Island Rd, T01674 672018, a comfortable B&B with en-suite rooms run by a motorbike enthusiast. **Camping** There are a couple of good options in the area. Heading north on the A92, **East Bowships Caravan Park**, T01674 850328, a mile from the beach at St Cyrus, offers statics Apr-Oct. **South Links Caravan Park**, T01674 672105, set back from the beach at Montrose, is open Apr-Oct to campers. Further north at Stonehaven, **Queen Elizabeth Caravan Park**, T01569 764014, is set just back from the sea. Open Apr-Oct to vans and tents. **Wairds Park**, Beach Rd, Johnshaven, T01561 362395, statics Apr-Oct.

Aberdeen

Scotland's third largest city is straight-talking, hard-working and uncompromising. Hewn from great grey granite blocks, the harbour city of Aberdeen is hemmed in by the River Don to the north and the Dee to the south.

💤 Sleeping

E Aberdeen Youth Hostel (SYHA) Queens Rd, T08700 041100, is open year-round and offers decent

low-budget beds. Rivalling the hostel are **E Hillhead Flats**, T01224 274000, www.abdn.ac.uk/hospitality, just south of the river on Don St. Part of the University of Aberdeen's campus accommodation, B&B in a 4-person flat is from £12 a night during Easter and the summer break.
Camping Lower Deeside Holiday Park, 6 miles southwest of the city on South Deeside Rd, Marycutler, T01224 733860. Open year-round to tents and vans with statics and bungalows sleeping up to 6 from £195 per week.

🍴 Eating/drinking

Ashvale on Great Western Rd is the undefeated champion of Scottish fish'n'chips and serves up its award-winning grub to eat in or take away – both of which are really reasonable. If you're after some Tex-Mex fare, try **Chiquitos** on the beach or **La Bamba** on Crown Terr who serve up their fajitas with a bit of extra spice! **Carmine's** on Union Terr is a tiny, busy, unlicensed little pizzeria serving up cheap and good Italian fare until 1930 only. **The Lemon Tree** café inside the arts centre on West North St is a great place to grab a vegetarian lunchtime bite. **The Prince of Wales** on St Nicholas Lane is the place to head for a glass of ale and a spot of decent and cheap pub grub. On Sun nights they break out their fiddles and the place packs out.

🕓 Directory

Surf shops Granite Reef, The Green, T01224-252752, is the city's well-known surf, skate and snowboard shop selling clothes and hardware as well as operating surf hire.
Tourist Information Union St, T01224 650065, www.aberdeen-

grampian.com. Open year-round, also offers internet access.

Cruden Bay

Sidetracking from the A90 brings you to Cruden Bay, home to a harbour, golf course and, of course, a beach overlooked by the crumbling ruins of Slain Castle perched precariously on the cliff edge.

● Sleeping
Camping Try the year-round **Craighead Caravan Park**, T01779 812251, just off the Cruden Bay road for camping. Also statics available from £135 per week.

Peterhead

Poking fingers of land out into the North Sea, the busy, functional fishing town of Peterhead is the most easterly point on the Scottish mainland. North to St Combs stretches 10 miles of dune-backed beach.

● Sleeping
Camping Peterhead Caravan Park, T01779 473358, is council-run, open Jul-Aug only and based at the Lido.

Fraserburgh

A serious, austere, no-nonsense working fishing port which leaves tourism to the pretty towns and villages that surround it. There has been a local surf community here since the 1960s when local fisherman Willie Tait returned from California with a longboard. Fraserburgh is also home to the Broch Surf Club – with more than 50 members – who run the annual Winter League surf circuit.

● Sleeping
A **Heath-Hill Hotel**, T01346 541492, is in Memsie, a few minutes outside Fraserburgh on Muir Rd. This small, clean, modern family-run hotel is recommended by George Nobel of Broch Surf Club. C **Coral Haven B&B**, Saltoun Place, T01346 519187, is close to the bay and open year-round. **Camping Esplanade Caravan Park**, T01346 510041, is a small, basic site at the Broch overlooking the Esp and the beach, open Jul-Aug.

● Directory
Surf shops Point North East Surf Shop, Cross St, T01346 517403, run by Ian Masson, stocks a full range of hardware and accessories. As George Noble puts it: "Point North East was long overdue and is great for the local surfing community – saves having to drive 40 miles for a block of wax!"

Cullen

Just off the A98 lies this pretty fishing village and the home of Cullen Skink, a fish soup (poached haddock chowder in posh restuarants).

● Sleeping
Self catering There are plenty of self-catering cottages to rent here including **Needle Cottage**, T01542 841066. Just back from the seafront, Jackie Kersley's cottage sleeps 4-5, costing from £270 per week. **Camping Cullen Bay Caravan Park**, T01542 840766, is open Apr-Sep.

Lossiemouth/Elgin

Lossiemouth on the edge of the Moray Firth is separated from the lively, cobbled, medieval market town of Elgin by a 20-min drive inland along the A941.

● Sleeping
Mike McWatt at ESP recommends the C **Moraydale Guesthouse**, Elgin High St, T01343 546381. C **Station Hotel**, T01343 830258, at Hopeman is to the west of Lossiemouth along the coastal B9012. The rooms are reasonable and clean and the bar downstairs has a pool table.

Camping At the western edge of Burghead Bay is the **Findhorn Bay Caravan Park**, T01309 690203, which is also home to the **Findhorn Foundation**, a spiritual New Age community. The park has varying standards of caravans (from £130 per week) and beautiful eco-chalets (from £395 per week) to rent year-round except Nov. Campers are welcome 1 Apr-31 Oct. There are several campsites around Lossie including **Lossiemouth Bay Caravan Park**, T01343 813980. Back from East Beach statics sleeping 4-6 are available to rent from £180 per week Apr-Oct. On the beach to the west at Hopeman, **Station Caravan Park**, T01343 830880, opens 1 Mar-31 Oct. **Silver Sands Leisure Park**, West beach, T01343 813262, is open end Mar-end Oct to campers as well as offering statics to rent.

● Eating/drinking
Mike at ESP advises that the **Skerry Brae Hotel** in Lossie is a nice place to grab a snack and watch the waves.

You can get a steak and Guinness pie for around a fiver or a jacket potato for less than £3. The beer terrace overlooks the golf course backing onto the beach.

ⓘ Directory

Surf shops ESP, Moss St, Elgin, T01343 550129, is run by Mike McWatt and is well stocked with surfing hardware and accessories as well as skate and snowboard gear. You can swing by for a surf report or to hire out equipment. **Tourist information** Elgin High St, T01343 542666, open year-round.

Brora

This traditional east coast village is focused around a central high street with all the amenities from banks to cafés and pubs. The beautiful beach runs north of the rivermouth until it meets the A9, giving a good vantage point to check the surf.

ⓢ Sleeping

C **Selkie B&B**, T01408 621717, in Lower Brora provides views over the rivermouth and a good breakfast to get you going. Packed lunches can also be arranged. **Camping Dalchalm Caravan Club**, T01408 621479, just north of Brora off the A9. Although fairly pricey, this site has excellent access to the beach, just 300 yds away over the golf course, often grazed by cows, Mar-Oct.

ⓔ Eating/drinking

If you fancy something to match the chill in the air head to **Capaldi's**, Rosslyn St, purveyors of locally made (Italian-sounding) ice cream. **Fountain Café**, Rosslyn St, does a good range of reasonably priced takeaway food.

 Flat spells

Cinema UCI Cinema, Fort Kinnaird Shopping Centre, Edinburgh, T08700 102030, is just one of the big multiplexes. Aberdeen has several cinemas including UGC Cinema on Queenslink, T0871 2002000. Moray Playhouse, Elgin High St, T01343 542680, is small but services this stretch of coastline.

Diving St Abbs and Eyemouth are the home to some of the best diving in Scotland and the Voluntary Marine Reserve. Contact Scoutscroft Dive Centre for details, T018907 71669.

Golf This is golfing country with plenty of sites (mainly links) lining the coastline ranging from reasonable to regal in terms of green fees – here's a selection at the cheaper end: Eyemouth GC, T018907 50004, accessed via the B6355, with seaside, parkland and wooded areas. Winter fees from £15. St Andrews is crawling with courses but just north of Dundee on the A92 is the more reasonable Arbroath GC, T01241 875837, links course fees from £20. Aberdeen is again fairly pricey – try the links Newburgh GC to the north accessed off the A975, T01358 789058. Inverallochy GC, T01346 58200, links course is 3 miles south of Fraserburgh, fees from £15. Cullen GC, T01542 840685, accessed off the A98, links course, fees from £15. Buckpool GC at Buckie, T01542 832235, is a well priced links course as is Hopeman GC, T01343 830578, further west and accessed off the B9012. Brora GC, T014088 621417, accessed off the A9, north of the village. Although more pricey, this is a beautiful links course.

Skating Sighthill Skatepark off Broomhouse Rd, Edinburgh, is an outdoor park with something for everyone including a 6 ft mini ramp. **Livingstone Skatepark** Heading west of Edinburgh on the M8, this classic concrete park accessed off the A899 near the Almondvale Shoppping Centre is one of Britain's best-known and best-loved with a good local scene – do not miss this! North of Edinburgh on the M90 East Perth Skatepark, Lesser South Inch, is another great free outdoor concrete bowl – lights off at 2200. Factory Skatepark, Balunie Drive, Dundee, T01382 509586, is an indoor, pay to play park where helmets are compulsory. With ¼ pipe, fun box, flatbanks, grind rails, vert wall etc as well as a shop, café and showers. A 2-hr session is from £5, open all day weekends, weekdays 1600-2200. Arbroath, on the A92 is home to the indoor Flipz Skatepark, John St West, with ramps and rails etc. Helmets are compulsory, 2 hrs costs £3.50. There are a couple of skateparks around Aberdeen including Westhill Skatepark heading west on the A944 – it's small but has a few ¼ pipes, fun box and grind rails etc. Kemnay Skatepark is a concrete bowl in the local park on Bogbeth Rd, Kemnay.

Swimming Stonehaven's Olympic-sized, outdoor, art deco, saltwater heated pool is kept at a luxurious 29°C from Jun-Aug. Take a dip for £3.50 – they also do weekly midnight dips for the stargazers…

Snowboarding Sample some of the dry stuff at Midlothian Ski Centre, T0131 445 4433, Hillend to the south of Edinburgh on the A702.

Surfing Caithness

"Murkle Point actually means 'the point on the hill of death' – from *Morte Hill,*" the local landowner told us. "It was here that the invading Vikings were driven back into the sea. They still plough up bodies every now and again." Caithness is rich in ancient history. It's a shame then that the region's biggest tourist attraction is the cheap and tacky John O'Groats, for the area has something else to offer – incredible surf potential. Thurso East is one of the world's premier waves and since it was first surfed in 1972, has managed to avoid the fate of many other world-renowned spots; its distance from a large metropolis and the cold water has managed to keep the crowds at bay.

"Since the BPSA event at the end of 2004 and all the magazine coverage it received, there have been a lot more people coming up to surf," says local surfer Andy Bains. With a WQS event pencilled in for 2005, the fear is that the days of empty line-ups may have gone. "I think the advances in wetsuit technology have also helped bring more people north, as now you can surf for two hours comfortably twice a day in the depth of winter," says Jamie Blair of Clan. However, to put it into perspective, while a crowded day at Thurso currently means 10-12 people in the water, a busy day at Porthleven can see more than triple that number.

The opening of the Dounreay Nuclear Facility brought much-needed jobs to the area. Local surf legend Pat Kieran came north to work at Dounreay, but it was the region's surf that really lured him to Thurso. He moved into a house overlooking Thurso reef in 1977, where he shaped boards in his spare time for local riders. "I lived in a farmhouse cottage overlooking the surf," says Pat. "It was a brilliant spot. I was a single bloke surfing and shaping boards in the barn and the bedroom next door. Surfers from all over the country used to drop in and stay, even when I wasn't home. I never used to lock my door. When I moved out a few years later, I picked up the key to hand it back to the landlord and it left a key-shaped hole in the dust."

Coastline

Heading west from Duncansby Head, the most northeasterly point in mainland Britain, the coastline of Caithness unfolds into series of flat

Caithness board guide

Semi-gun
Shaper: Martin McQueenie, MCQ Surfboards

- 6'8" x 18¼" x 2⅜" for Chris Noble.
- Average surfer 6'6" to 6'10".
- Rounded pin or squash tail.
- Shaped for Chris to get barrelled at Thurso.
- Vee through the tail with concave before the fins for stability in the barrel.
- Gives good drive off the bottom turn.
- Nose kick and rocker for steep take-offs at reef breaks like Thurso East.
- Boards need extra volume because of the thicker wetsuits needed up here.

Thruster
Shaper: Martin McQueenie, MCQ Surfboards

- 6'4" x 18¾" x 2½".
- Average surfer 6'2" to 6'5".
- Squash or swallow tail for versatility in powerful waves.
- Moderate rocker for speed and manoeuvrability.
- Flat bottom to vee or reverse vee.
- Use larger fins in more powerful conditions.
- Good for fun days at point waves like Point of Ness or Zeppelins.

Boards by **MCQ** Momentum Surf Shop Factory: Dunbar, Scotland
T 01368 869810 M T 07796 752957
www.momentumsurfshop.com
post@momentumsurfshop.com

slabstone reefs, which eventually run into the towering cliffs of Dunnet Head, the mainland's most northerly point. The long, open sand of Dunnet Bay sits sheltered in its shadow and the protected dunes are a nature sanctuary and nesting site. From here the coastline opens out into flat slate again. Reef after reef leads into the seclusion of Thurso Bay and the natural harbour at Scrabster. Fittingly, the huge, slab reef at Brims Ness shows that even the Vikings recognized the potential of this spot when they named it Surf Point.

Localism

Caithness remains a place where you can truly escape the crowds. Many breaks remain relatively quiet, while the number of local surfers is still relatively low. However Thurso East is now suffering from the 'Mundaka factor' – it has become a world-famous break, it is the region's biggest draw and is the focal point for chart-watching travelling surfers. In a world of internet forecasting, locals who sit patiently through poor surf days can now be swamped just as a good

swell arrives. This change has taken place swiftly over the past couple of years and is leading to the first signs of strain in the line-up.

Top local surfers

While guys like Pat Kieran and Andy Bennetts helped pioneer surfing in Scotland, and Neil Harris oversaw many years' worth of swells rolling into Thurso Bay, the current top surfers any traveller is likely to run into in a Caithness line-up are Chris Noble and Andy Bains.

Getting around

The roads up here are of very good quality and rarely busy, even in the height of the tourist season. There is a brief rush hour, more like 20 minutes, at knocking-off time at Dounreay, but other than that it is quick and easy to get around by car. The A836 follows the coast and access roads run off it to most of the breaks. Some spots are only accessible via farms or over fields. Remember to be respectful and, if in doubt, ask first.

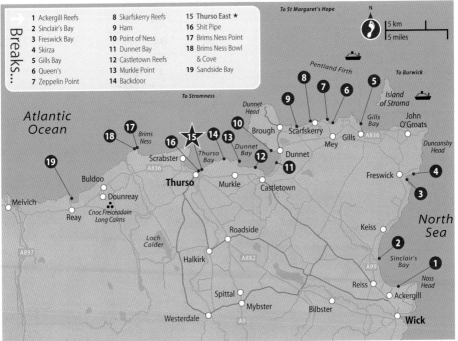

Breaks...

1 Ackergill Reefs	8 Skarfskerry Reefs	15 Thurso East ★
2 Sinclair's Bay	9 Ham	16 Shit Pipe
3 Freswick Bay	10 Point of Ness	17 Brims Ness Point
4 Skirza	11 Dunnet Bay	18 Brims Ness Bowl
5 Gills Bay	12 Castletown Reefs	& Cove
6 Queen's	13 Murkle Point	19 Sandside Bay
7 Zeppelin Point	14 Backdoor	

Breaks

1 Ackergill Reefs

- ⊙ **Break type**: Right reef.
- ☁ **Conditions**: Medium swells, offshore in westerly/southwesterly winds.
- ❶ **Hazards/tips**: Good waves in spectacular location.
- ⊜ **Sleeping**: John O' Groats/Dunnet Bay ➤➤ *p169*.

There are two right-hand reef breaks that sit at the southern end of Sinclair's Bay. These waves are set in a spectacular location overlooked by dark castle ruins. They break in northeasterly or big southeasterly swells with winds from the west. Access is via Ackergill off the A99. Park near the jetty.

2 Sinclair's Bay

- ⊙ **Break type**: Beach break.
- ☁ **Conditions**: Medium to big swells, offshore in westerly winds.
- ❶ **Hazards/tips**: Quiet spot, rarely surfed.
- ⊜ **Sleeping**: John O' Groats ➤➤ *p169*.

This huge, east-facing, crescent-shaped bay works in a big northeasterly as well as easterly swells. It is a good quality break that is rarely surfed. Park at the northern end of the bay at Stain or access via the dunes.

3 Freswick Bay

- ⊙ **Break type**: Beach break.
- ☁ **Conditions**: Medium to big swells, offshore in westerly winds.
- ❶ **Hazards/tips**: Quiet spot, pronounced 'Fresik'.
- ⊜ **Sleeping**: John O' Groats ➤➤ *p169*.

Freswick is a picturesque, small bay with sand and rocks forming lefts and rights in big northeasterly swells. Works through all tides. Great break but not really suitable for beginners.

4 Skirza

- ⊙ **Break type**: Classic left point.
- ☁ **Conditions**: Big to huge swells, offshore in westerly winds.
- ❶ **Hazards/tips**: Rocky, fast, heavy waves.
- ⊜ **Sleeping**: John O' Groats ➤➤ *p169*.

A wonderful, long, peeling, left-hand point, with waves reeling along the rocky headland in the biggest north or northeasterly swells. Skirza can be epic in the right conditions producing leg-numbing rides. Worth checking when the north shore is maxed out. Access from the A99 signposted Skirza. Follow road to harbour and park respectfully. Wave peels towards quay, over rocks and boulders.

Caithness

Air —— Sea ——

°F Averages °C

90												30
70												20
50												10
30												0

J F M A M J J A S O N D

6mm Boots, hood & gloves	5/4/3 Boots & gloves	4/3	4/3 Boots

THE GILL

4 Skirza

It used to drive me mad. When local people found out I was a surfer, they'd say 'There's no surf in Scotland.' You'd be coming out of the water and it would be perfect 6 ft barrels, and you'd meet someone on the beach and they'd say 'You're not surfing are you? There's no waves round here.'

Chris Gregory, ex-Scottish Surf Team

5 Gills Bay

- ⚐ **Break type**: Left point.
- ☁ **Conditions**: Big and huge swells, offshore in southwesterly winds.
- ❶ **Hazards/tips**: Big, heavy wave for experts
- ⬛ **Sleeping**: John O' Groats/Dunnet Bay ⇥ *p169*

In a big northwesterly swell this long point comes to life, and can produce huge, heavy barrelling waves that break over a slate reef. Holding waves of over 10 ft, it is one of the north shore's true quality waves. Can be checked from the pier at Gills Bay harbour. This is a wave for experienced surfers only. Northeast charger Del Boy surfed it and described it as "a Scottish G-Land".

6 Queen's

- ⚐ **Break type**: Left reef.
- ☁ **Conditions**: Small to medium swells, offshore in southerly winds.
- ❶ **Hazards/tips**: Overlooked by royal Castle of Mey.
- ⬛ **Sleeping**: John O' Groats/Dunnet Bay ⇥ *p169*.

A low to mid tide slate reef that produces walling lefthanders in clean northwesterly swells. Intermediate and experienced surfers. Access is via left at crossroads after Mey village.

7 Zeppelin Point

- ⚐ **Break type**: Left point.
- ☁ **Conditions**: Medium swells, offshore in southerly winds.
- ❶ **Hazards/tips**: Shallow and rocky.
- ⬛ **Sleeping**: John O' Groats/Dunnet Bay ⇥ *p169*.

Quality slate reef point break that produces long, shallow left-hand walls. Works best at mid tide. Walk along the point from the pier. Park at Harrow Pier, which, bizarrely, was officially opened by rock legend Jimmy Page.

THE GILL

7 Zeppelin Point

DEMI TAYLOR

5 Gills Bay

8 Skarfskerry Reefs

- ◑ **Break type**: Reef breaks.
- 🌊 **Conditions**: Small to medium swells, offshore in southerly/southeasterly winds.
- ❶ **Hazards/tips**: Rocky reefs, rarely surfed.
- 🍽 **Sleeping**: Dunnet Bay ⁍ *p169*.

Check these reefs from the coast road through Skarfskerry. These breaks need a clean northwesterly swell and south or southeasterly wind. Rarely surfed reefs but worth checking.

9 Ham

- ◑ **Break type**: Left reef.
- 🌊 **Conditions**: Big swells, offshore in westerly winds.
- ❶ **Hazards/tips**: Shallow reef, breaks in storms.
- 🍽 **Sleeping**: Dunnet Bay ⁍ *p169*.

This sheltered left reef can be the only wave working on the north shore in big, stormy surf and westerly winds. Swell wraps around the headland and into the sheltered bay. Best from low to three-quarter tide. Not an epic but a decent, if shallow, walling left. There is also a heavy, shallow left further out on the point definitely for experienced surfers only. Ham breaks in front of the remains of a massive, 200-year-old slate harbour.

10 Point of Ness

- ◑ **Break type**: Right point.
- 🌊 **Conditions**: Medium swell, offshore in southeasterly wind.
- ❶ **Hazards/tips**: Fun but rocky reef.
- 🍽 **Sleeping**: Dunnet Bay ⁍ *p169*.

This quality right point breaks over a slate reef. It needs a decent, clean northwesterly swell to work and is offshore in a southeasterly wind. Works best around mid tide and is best left to experienced surfers. Parking available at Dwarwick Pier. Access from the rocks.

11 Dunnet Bay

- ◑ **Break type**: Beach break.
- 🌊 **Conditions**: Small swells, offshore in southeasterly winds.
- ❶ **Hazards/tips**: Closes out in swells over 4 ft, looks better than it is.
- 🍽 **Sleeping**: Dunnet Bay ⁍ *p169*.

Disappointing beach break, which picks up northwesterly swells. Can be good fun in small swells but the lack of good banks means it tends to close out when the swell picks up. Works on all tides. The middle of the bay by the stream picks up the most swell and has the best banks. Great for beginners. There are three access points to the bay – via the campsite; through the dune path in the middle and at the Castletown end.

12 Castletown Reefs

- ◑ **Break type**: Reef breaks.
- 🌊 **Conditions**: Medium to big swells, offshore in south/southwesterly winds.
- ❶ **Hazards/tips**: Difficult access on foot, rarely surfed .
- 🍽 **Sleeping**: Dunnet Bay/Murkle Point ⁍ *p169*.

A series of excellent reefs, starting in the corner of Dunnet Bay with a sheltered A-frame reef. Past the harbour are more exposed, slate reefs that need a big, clean northwesterly swell and southwesterly winds. The reefs are visible from the main A836 Thurso road.

13 Murkle Point

- ◑ **Break type**: Point break.
- 🌊 **Conditions**: Medium to big swells, offshore in south, southwesterly winds.
- ❶ **Hazards/tips**: Rips, rocks.
- 🍽 **Sleeping**: Murkle Point ⁍ *p169*.

A pinwheel left point wrapping around the 'Spur' at Murkle Point. This can be an excellent wave but is exposed and susceptible to wind. Needs light winds from a southerly direction. Access is via farm tracks. Definitely a break for experienced

9 Ham

10 Point of Ness

14 Backdoor ⁍ *p166*

Surfers' tales

Castle Reef steps into the limelight

For many years the reef at Thurso East has managed to remain amazingly uncrowded. Three or four surfers sitting in the line-up of a wave dubbed 'the cold water Nias' would always be a welcome surprise whenever we rocked up after the long drive north. But have those days gone? On a trip in December 2004 we were greeted by 12 surfers, mid-week, mid-winter. Realm-sponsored rider Chris Noble, who lives overlooking the reef (and probably spends more time in the barrel than anyone else), has a theory as to why those empty line-ups may now be a thing of the past.

"A few different variables have impacted on the rise in popularity of Thurso over the past couple of years. These include the fact that the number of people surfing in Scotland and the UK is greater than ever before and the standard of surfing in Scotland and the UK is getting better all the time with people becoming more capable of surfing challenging waves. Wetsuit technology is now better than ever meaning it's not just the hardcore who can brave the winter waters now."

Chris also believes the coverage the wave has received over the past year has had a profound effect: "There has been heightened media attention over the last couple of years. The BPSA contest has brought the best surfers in the UK to Thurso and the wave has featured in a couple of DVDs lately."

He thinks that this may be just the beginning of Thurso's new-found popularity, "I don't feel that we have seen the full impact of any of the above yet. Numbers of people have increased even more this year. Five years ago I would surf alone a lot, however this year I didn't surf alone until late December; even then if the waves were good others were in the water."

Although the increased numbers in the water bring drawbacks, Chris tries to focus on some of the positives: "The flip side of this is that with more people it will push the level of surfing. When you surf alone it is hard to push yourself to do things differently because you do not have the visual impact of someone doing a big off the top or something while you are paddling out and you think to yourself 'I want to try that!' That is one of the biggest positives I have found from the BPSA coming up here. Also with more people in the water there will be more revenue coming into Thurso for local businesses. We even have a surf shop now whereas before people used to come up here fully stocked up for the worst."

Chris has some advice for anyone making the trek to the north: "There are lots of breaks with access through private property. As of yet there have only been minor incidents that have been smoothed over, but please remember to close gates behind you and park in sensible places. Common sense really. There are also a few locals who try to avoid the crowds and only get to surf on weekends. If you do meet or surf with them give them some space and be friendly, you will get your waves and have a laugh at the same time. Also try not to turn up in too big a group. Sure it saves on fuel money, but if three or four vans rock up with four or five people in them and only a small swell then it gets crowded – which will bring its own problems."

surfers only. Exposed, with rocks. Can be awesome though.

14 Backdoor/The Left

- ⦿ **Break type**: Right and left reefs.
- ⦿ **Conditions**: Medium swells, offshore in southerly winds.
- ⦿ **Hazards/tips**: Shallow, heavy, for experienced surfers only.
- ⦿ **Sleeping**: Murkle Point/Thurso ⇒ p169.

Shallow, hollow, ledging right-hander plus shallow left point. Needs southerly winds. An exposed spot that picks up loads of swell. Access via farm tracks.

15 Thurso East

- ⦿ **Break type**: Right-hand reef.
- ⦿ **Conditions**: Medium/large swells.
- ⦿ **Size**: 3-12 ft.
- ⦿ **Length**: 50-100 m.
- ⦿ **Swell**: Huge westerly, big north-westerly or any northerly swell.
- ⦿ **Wind**: Southeasterly.
- ⦿ **Tide**: All tides, best quarter to three-quarter tide on the push.
- ⦿ **Bottom**: Kelp-covered slate reef.
- ⦿ **Entry/exit**: Off the rocks, or via the river in big swells.
- ⦿ **Hazards**: Rocky bottom, can be heavy when big.
- ⦿ **Sleeping**: Thurso ⇒ p170.

Thurso East holds a unique place in European surf lore. For a spot that has been called anything from 'a cold water Nias' to 'the best right reef in the UK', it is amazingly uncrowded. It is also easy to make it out onto the peak, even on the biggest days. Thurso River feeds into the bay next to the break and the water will carry a surfer out to the peak and deposit

them, complete with dry hair, even in a thumping swell. It's once you are on the peak that fun really begins.

Big swells fresh out of the Arctic roll into Thurso Bay and are fanned by southeasterly winds. As a wave nears the reef it starts to rear up into a peak.

"The thing about Thurso is that the take-off is pretty straightforward," says Shaper/photographer Paul Gill, credited as the first person to surf the reef back in 1975. "It's what happens next that is interesting."

The simple take-off leads into either a long, fast perfect wall or a speeding barrel, depending on the swell direction – more east in the swell is more walling, more west is more barrelly. "I remember heading up for the British surfing championships," says James Hendy, "and we had it classic for a week before everyone else rolled in. It's such a great wave. Big walls with barrel sections." But the shallow reef is always just one little mistake away.

Catch Thurso perfect, and it is a dream (see Surfers' tales, p148). Driving down the track behind the castle, clouds can be seen rising from the shore as if great fires are burning to warn of Viking invaders on the horizon. Wind down the window and the rolling thunder of a B52 strike will reverberate inside the confines of a car. But to witness the beauty of a 10 ft swell exploding onto the flat reef at the mouth of Thor's River is to see the raw power of an Arctic storm condensed into a huge, perfect barrel.

A real Thurso trademark is the peaty brown water, fresh off the Caithness hills. In the winter, this influx of cold water also drops the temperature, testing even the hardiest surfer.

When it comes to crowds, although the locals are a tight-knit group, they are increasingly having to contend with

groups of travellers turning up and hassling on the peak. Stay chilled and respectful, and you find them a friendly lot. If not, your welcome will be as frosty as the water.

ⓘ *If you like Thurso East try Coxos in Portugal or Ireland's Easky Right.*

16 Shit Pipe

- ⦿ **Break type**: Right reef.
- ⦿ **Conditions**: Medium to big swells, offshore in southerly winds.
- ⦿ **Hazards/tips**: Excellent wave overshadowed by Thurso East.
- ⦿ **Sleeping**: Thurso ⇒ p170.

This is an excellent quality, right-hand reef that breaks in front of the pier at Thuso rivermouth. Picks up less swell than Thurso East but can hold a solid swell. Fast, walling waves with occasional barrels peel in southerly winds. Works on all tides except high. The peaty river run-off can make the waves brown and drops the water temperature in the winter. A good wave that is often overlooked due to its proximity to Thurso East. There is a car park on the seafront.

17 Brims Ness Point

- ⦿ **Break type**: Left point.
- ⦿ **Conditions**: All swells, offshore in southerly winds.
- ⦿ **Hazards/tips**: Heavy wave, dangerous rips, experts only.
- ⦿ **Sleeping**: Thurso ⇒ p170.

This left point peels along a flat slate reef producing excellent long walls. This exposed spot picks up plenty of

15 Chris Noble - Thurso East

18 Johnny James - Brims Bowl

The Bowl can be 4 ft when Thurso is flat. It is best left to experienced surfers as any mistake will be met by the barnacle-encrusted reef. Regulars wear helmets! Works from quarter to three-quarter tide and is offshore in southerly winds.

The Cove to the right of the Bowl is a short, hollow right-hand wave breaking onto a kelp-covered, slanting shelf. It is also offshore in a southerly wind and is a less heavy wave than the Bowl, but still for experienced surfers only.

Access is the same as the **Point**. This is an exposed spot so wind is important. These breaks can get really busy in the summer, when they may be the only surfable spot. Watch out for dive-bombing terns in the June nesting season.

swell but the direction of the wind is key. In light southerly winds it will work from low up to three-quarter tide. The point can hold big swells, and is best left to experienced surfers. Surf is visible from the A836, but as it is a couple of miles away, any sign of white water means that there are waves. Access is via a farm track with respectful parking in the farmers'

yard. Remember that you are on private land at the farmer's discretion. Access was nearly withdrawn a couple of years ago after an incident involving a visiting surfer. If there is no access to Brims, we all suffer.

18 Brims Ness Bowl and Cove

- 🌀 **Break type**: Right reefs.
- 🌊 **Conditions**: Small swells, offshore in southerly winds.
- ❗ **Hazards/tips**: Shallow, powerful and consistent.
- 💤 **Sleeping**: Thurso ⤥ *p170*.

These two right-hand reef breaks have salvaged many a trip to the north shore, as they hoover up any swell available. **The Bowl** is a fast, hollow, shallow, barrelling right that lunges out of deep water onto a slate shelf.

19 Sandside Bay

- 🌀 **Break type**: Reef break.
- 🌊 **Conditions**: Medium to big swells, offshore in a southwesterly wind.
- ❗ **Hazards/tips**: Quality break overshadowed by Dounreay.
- 💤 **Sleeping**: Thurso ⤥ *p170*.

A quality walling left that breaks over a shallow reef in front of a slate harbour. Works best when the tide has pushed in a bit, so from mid to high and, although it is offshore in a southwesterly wind, it can handle wind from the west. Sandside needs a big westerly swell or a medium northerly to work. It is overshadowed by Dounreay nuclear power plant. There have been leaks of material from the plant and a sign warns of particles found on the beach. It warns children not to play in the sand and advises owners not to let their dogs dig – so how safe is it to surf there?

19 Chris Nelson - Sandside

Listings

John O'Groats

Grubby, dreary, joyless place on the northwest edge of the mainland with rows of tat shops claiming to be 'The first and last'. Take your picture by the milemarker sign, get your souvenir piece of rock and get out!

🛏 Sleeping
Camping The best bet is **The Stroma View Caravan & Camping Site**, T01955 611313, about a mile west along the A836. Open Mar-Oct, the site also offers a 4-berth static caravan to rent as well as a great view across to Stroma Island. If you are stuck here you can camp at the basic (and joyless) **John O' Groats Caravan Site**, T01955 611329, Apr-Sep, who charge for showers. The plus point is that you can often see dolphins or orcas swimming off the coast in the Pentland Firth.

Dunnet Bay

Although John O'Groats takes all the glory, Dunnet Head is actually the most northerly point on the British mainland with awesome 300-ft cliffs topped by a lighthouse.

🛏 Sleeping
C Dunnet Head B&B, T01847 851774, on the B855 to Dunnet Head at Brough, can organize packed lunches or dinners and have a shed to store boards and bikes in.
Camping Dunnet Bay Campsite, T01847 8213129, is beautifully located in the dunes overlooking the eastern edge of the 2-mile crescent. It's a Caravan Club site open Apr-Sep so if you're planning a long stay, it may be worth joining for the discounts.

Murkle Point

Murkle was the scene of a great battle where the Celts rose up to defend their land, driving the Vikings back into the sea. Murkle, derived from *Morte Hill* or 'hill of death', certainly lives up to its name with the local farmers still ploughing up skeletons that have lain covered for thousands of years.

🛏 Sleeping
For spectacular seclusion and your own private access to a firing point and a sandy bay, stay at the lovely **C Murkle B&B**, T01847 896405, in west Murkle. If you're a Caravan Club member, they also run a certified site with running water for about £3 a night.

DEMI TAYLOR

5 Gills Bay overview ▶▶ *p163*

Thurso

Thurso takes its name from the Norse meaning 'Thor's River'. Straight up the A9 from Inverness, it is the most northerly town on the mainland and the only town on this coastline. Although fairly bleak, it is a good base for trips to the north shore, as well as a good jumping-off spot for the Orkneys with ferries leaving from Scrabster to the west, and Gills Bay to the east. Thurso has hosted a **European Surfing Championships** and has been the site of many a legendary surf trip – it is almost as famous for its beer and brawling as it is for its outstanding right-hand reef.

🛏 Sleeping
L-B The Royal Hotel, Traill St, T01847 893191, is the best of the bunch and if you want a quiet night get a room at the back. Off season, you may be

able to strike a deal for long stays. **B-C The Central**, Traill St, T01847 893129, has rooms above the legendary **Central Bar**, ensuring the sounds and smells from the weekend travel up to meet you. **B-C The Holborn Hotel**, Princes St, T01847 892771, offers a reasonable B&B. With a pool bar showing Sky Sports on the big screen downstairs, it can get noisy. **E Sandra's Backpackers**, Princes St, T01847 894575, is a popular and recommended choice for surfers offering good hostel accommodation (dorms and doubles) with no curfews. Open year-round, they provide a basic breakfast in with the price, free hot showers and cooking facilities as well as a lock-up for bikes and boards. If a big swell is predicted, book in advance. **E Thurso Hostel**, Ormlie Rd, T01847 896888, is also open year-round. **Camping Campbell Caravan Hire**, T01847 893524, is just

off the main road into Thurso, overlooking the bay. Open Apr/May-Sep, with up to 6-berth statics to rent, it's a good bet for groups as it can be one of the cheapest options around as well as providing prime views towards the reef. Next door is the council-run **Thurso Caravan & Camping Park**, T01847 894631, also open Apr/May-Sep. Thurso town is within stumbling distance but there is also a basic café on site. Opening times vary year to year so call ahead.

🍴 Eating/drinking
Le Bistro opposite the Central is moderately priced and not a bad choice for an evening meal that isn't fish and chips. It also does good cakes and coffee. **The Central** has had a facelift downstairs and has opened up the **Central Café** next door serving up cappuccinos, lattes,

Stoned again at Camster Long Cairn

homemade cakes and a whole variety of toasted paninis – Thurso's answer to café society. Upstairs, you can still grab good, basic pub grub for around £5. **Sandra's** and **Robin's** sit opposite each other on Princes St frying up 'with chips' combos. **Somerfield** has a café where you can get an all-day breakfast and pot of tea for less than a fiver. Swing by on your way back from the reef. **Tempest Surf Shop**, Thurso Harbour, T01847 892500, will have a café next door serving up post-surf grub from early 2005.

In Scrabster, Andy Bain recommends heading to **The Upper Deck** restaurant at the **Ferry Inn** for "the best steak in Scotland". A bit of prime Highland-reared beef may set you back around £15, but it's worth it. They also serve fish options. Andy also recommends **Charlie Chan** on Sinclair St if you're pining for a Chinese.

ⓘ Directory
Internet Try Sandra's, 75p for 15 min, or Tempest Surf Shop, below. **Surf shops** Thurso Surf, T01847 841300, www.thursosurf.com. Run by North Shore charger Andy Bain, this BSA school offers lessons to beginners and intermediates Mar-Oct. Andy also sells wetsuits and surfboards and offers a board repair service, T07748 362397. **Tempest Surf Shop**, Thurso Harbour, T01847 892500, www.tempestsurf. co.uk, is run by Rick Picken and is well stocked with clothes and hardware including custom boards and wetsuits. From the start of 2005 they will also offer internet access and a café next door serving up post-surf grub. **Tourist information** Riverside Rd, T01847 892371, fairly helpful, open Apr-Oct.

✪ Flat spells

Boat charter From Scrabster harbour you can charter boats for sea angling or dolphin-spotting. Try *Elana* with John and Malcom, T01847 891112.

Bowling and Cinema The All Star Factory, Ormlie Rd, Thurso, T01847 89080, has a 2-screen cinema complex. The factory is also home to the tenpin bowling arena **The Viking Bowl**, T01847 8905050, open 7 days a week and housing a bar-cum nightspot-cum-sports screening venue with eating options.

Cairns Cnoc Freiceadain Long Cairns overlooking the Dounreay Nuclear Power Station. Signposted from the A836 heading west, these neolithic ceremonial cairns are worth a visit and provide excellent views along the coast. There are many other cairns in the area accessed via the A99 south of Wick – the best is the partially reconstructed **Grey Cairns of Camster.**

Golf Following the B870 out of town, **Thurso's 18 hole course** is just southwest of the town, T01847 893807. Green fees £15.

The stanes massive...

Nuclear flower

14 The Left ▸▸ *p166*

Sutherland

Surfing Sutherland

Sutherland is as wild and open as any countryside you could imagine. Its rolling hills, open peatland and sheltered coves are home to some of Britain's rarest wildlife. Golden eagles soar overhead while brown hares dart for cover. In crystal-clear streams, otters chase young trout and dragonflies hover over the orchid-strewn blanket bogs. Huge open beaches like Torrisdale can have Mundaka-like rights peeling away from the rivermouth towards a beach where often there are no human footprints and the only locals in the line-up are seals waiting to ambush the salmon returning to spawn.

It's not that the beaches of Sutherland are particularly hard to access – many are visible from the A836. There just isn't the surfing population in the county. Visitors to Scotland's 'North Shore' are usually distracted by the breaks near Thurso, the legendary reef in Caithness. Those who stray across the border usually surf the beaches at either Melvich or Strathy, so the breaks further west can go unridden. Sutherland's most awesome beach can be found at the end of a 4-mile hike into Sandwood Bay. This huge stretch of sand boasts excellent waves from quality sandbanks to reefs, but is a true hardcore mission. The beach is so exposed that it picks up swell even when there appears to be no waves out there. It can also jump overnight into one of the UK's most powerful beach breaks when a good swell hits. It is truly one of European surfing's last great adventures.

"Sutherland is a true soul surfing experience," *says Aussie surfer Aaron Gray. "The water is* *crystal clear, there are dolphins and whales, you* *are lucky to see other surfers, and a big night out* *would be a couple of pints in a cosy local pub with* *a peat-burning fire."*

Coastline

Following the A836 into Sutherland from Caithness, the change in geography is immediately apparent. The flat sandstone reefs are left behind and an open countryside rolls down to a rocky coastline interspersed with

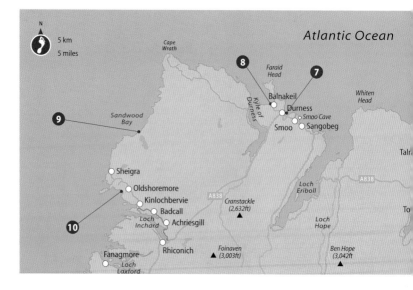

stunning sea cliffs and beautiful sandy beaches, usually cut by small rivermouths and backed by pristine grassy dunes. The cliffs provide breathtaking views of the north shore. Strathy Point looks east to the Orkneys and Dunnet Head and across to the storm-ravaged Cape Wrath to the west. The beauty of the bays is that as they all face different directions, so in theory there should always be a rideable wave when there is a swell running.

Localism

Find a local if you can. As Scottish surfing legend Pat Kieran says: "In Sutherland it's not so much a case of finding a quiet spot, it's more a case of finding someone to go surfing with."

Top local surfers

See above.

Getting around

The A836 follows the coast and access roads run off it to most of the breaks. Once past Melvich there are long stretches where it turns into a single track with passing places. Bear in mind that it takes a lot longer to get between breaks than you think when you look at a map. The A838 loop around Loch Eriboll in particular is a 40-minute detour.

CHRIS NELSON

5 Torrisdale ⇒ *p174*

Breaks...

1	Melvich	8	Balnakeil Bay
2	Strathy	9	Sandwood Bay
3	Armadale	10	Oldshoremore
4	Farr Bay		
5	Torrisdale		
6	Kyle of Tongue		
7	Sango Bay		

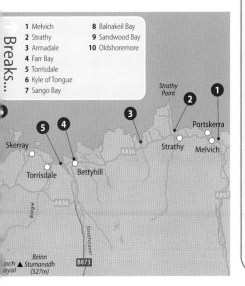

Sutherland board guide

Fish
Shaper: Martin McQueenie, MCQ Surfboards

- ▸▸ 6'4" x 19½" x 2⅝" for Chris Noble.
- ▸▸ Average surfer 6'2" to 6'6".
- ▸▸ Good for small days.
- ▸▸ Swallow tail for manoeuvrability
- ▸▸ Good width and volume for linking sections.
- ▸▸ Flat rocker for speed.
- ▸▸ Try 'Speeed Fins' for flex – as used by Mick Fanning.
- ▸▸ Forgiving board for beaches around Melvich and Strathy.

Thruster
Shaper: Martin McQueenie, MCQ Surfboards

- ▸▸ 6'3" x 18¼" x 2¼".
- ▸▸ Average surfer 6'3" to 6'5".
- ▸▸ Swallow or rounded pin.
- ▸▸ Performance thrusters to make most of good beach breaks up to 6 ft.
- ▸▸ Flat bottom to generate speed with vee in the tail.
- ▸▸ Single concave bottom if a more flexible board required.
- ▸▸ Medium rocker with nose kick for hollow days.
- ▸▸ For head-high Torrisdale.

(i) Boards by **MCQ** Momentum Surf Shop
Factory: Dunbar, Scotland
T 01368 869810, M T 07796 752957
www.momentumsurfshop.com
post@momentumsurfshop.com

Breaks

1 Melvich

- ◑ **Break type**: Rivermouth.
- ◍ **Conditions**: Small to medium swells, offshore in southerly winds.
- ❶ **Hazards/tips**: Rips when big.
- ◔ **Sleeping**: Melvich ▸▸ *p176*.

The brown, peaty river at the eastern end of the bay lays down a sandbar which produces some quality long, walling rights. Other peaks work in the bay in swells up to 6 ft. A great spot that's usually very quiet and works on all tides. Parking available at the western end behind the dunes, or at the eastern end near the Big House. Not suitable for beginners due to rips and isolation. Good water quality.

2 Strathy

- ◑ **Break type**: Beach break.
- ◍ **Conditions**: All swells, offshore in southerly winds.
- ❶ **Hazards/tips**: Beautiful spot, stunning location.
- ◔ **Sleeping**: Melvich ▸▸ *p176*.

Walling lefts peel from the rivermouth at the western end of this beautiful bay. The sheltering effect of Strathy Point means although this spot picks up less swell in northwesterly and westerly swells, it provides shelter from westerly winds. The beach produces lefts and rights, working on all tides. Park by the graveyard and walk down to the beach through the dunes. This is a wonderful, quiet spot. Suitable for beginners, as long as they are supervised by more experienced surfers.

3 Armadale

- ◑ **Break type**: Beach break.
- ◍ **Conditions**: Medium swells, offshore in a southerly wind.
- ❶ **Hazards/tips**: Quiet beach.
- ◔ **Sleeping**: Melvich/Bettyhill ▸▸ *p176*.

Quiet, north-facing beach, which can have good surf in a medium-sized northwesterly or northerly swell. Works on all tides but is rarely surfed. Another quiet beach that is a great spot to escape to. Surfed less than Strathy, and can be checked from the A836 coast road.

4 Farr Bay

- ◑ **Break type**: Beach break.
- ◍ **Conditions**: Medium swells, offshore in a southeasterly wind.
- ❶ **Hazards/tips**: Closes out in big swells.
- ◔ **Sleeping**: Bettyhill ▸▸ *p176*.

Farr picks up more swell than Armadale and Strathy due to its northwesterly orientation. It is a small bay that works on all tides, with shifting banks, but tends to close out in bigger swells. Access is via a path from Bettyhill, where parking is available.

5 Torrisdale

- ◑ **Break type**: Beach and rivermouth break.
- ◍ **Conditions**: All swells, offshore in southerly winds.
- ❶ **Hazards/tips**: Isolated spot with rips in big swells.
- ◔ **Sleeping**: Bettyhill ▸▸ *p176*.

A big bay that really feels part of the big country. Depending on how the sandbar is working, Torrisdale can produce some

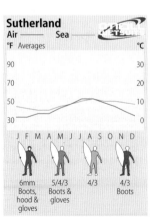

Sutherland

Air —— Sea

°F Averages

°C

90	30
70	20
50	10
30	0

J F M A M J J A S O N D

6mm Boots, hood & gloves	5/4/3 Boots & gloves	4/3	4/3 Boots

epic waves. When the bank is at its best, long hollow rights peel away from the river at the eastern end of the bay and long hollow lefts peel towards it. This is a very flexible spot as it works in small swells to well over head high and from low to three-quarter tide. There are many lefts and rights along the beach and there is another rivermouth at the western end that generally picks up less swell, but can also have some great waves. Access via Bettyhill village onto track to rivermouth at the eastern end. For the western end keep on the A836, then turn right to Torrisdale village. Can have big rips but the river can be useful for getting out back in big swells. Experienced surfers only.

6 Kyle of Tongue

- 🌀 **Break type**: Beach break.
- 🌊 **Conditions**: Big swells, offshore in southerly winds.
- ❶ **Hazards/tips**: Rips.
- ⬤ **Sleeping**: Tongue ⇥ *p176*.

Legend has it that on very big, clean, northerly swells, there are long, reeling waves on each side of the bay. Definitely a place to check, but watch out for rips on big tides. Check from the road either side of the inlet.

7 Sango Bay

- 🌀 **Break type**: Beach break.
- 🌊 **Conditions**: Medium swells, offshore in southwesterly winds.
- ❶ **Hazards/tips**: Quiet beach with average waves.
- ⬤ **Sleeping**: Durness ⇥ *p176*.

Sango is a very pretty beach that sits below the village of Durness. It works on all tides and although it faces

northeast, it does pick up plenty of swell. Not a renowned surfing beach but does have some OK waves. You can also visit Smoo Caves from Sango Bay.

8 Balnakeil Bay

- 🌀 **Break type**: Beach break.
- 🌊 **Conditions**: Medium swells, offshore in southeasterly winds.
- ❶ **Hazards/tips**: Very flexible spot.
- ⬤ **Sleeping**: Durness ⇥ *p176*.

An amazing, big U-shaped bay at the mouth of the Kyle of Durness that picks up northwesterly swell but is sheltered from northerly winds. Works through all tides and is best in an easterly wind. Follow road from Durness to Balnakeil. Watch out for rips – not for inexperienced surfers.

9 Sandwood Bay

- 🌀 **Break type**: Beach break.
- 🌊 **Conditions**: Small to medium swells, offshore in southeasterly winds.
- ❶ **Hazards/tips**: Very isolated spot, rips, no road access.
- ⬤ **Sleeping**: Kinlochbervie ⇥ *p177*.

Definitely not one for the beginner, this beach is very remote and picks up

the most swell in northern Scotland. If it's flat here, it's flat everywhere. This is a long, sandy beach set in a stunning location. The surf can be excellent with many peaks and a couple of reefs to choose from. Works on all tides. The only access to this bay is on foot so come prepared. It's a wonderful hike into the bay and a great place to camp for a few days. Check the chart before you make the hike as the last thing you want is to be pounded by a 20-ft swell closing out the beach, which does happen, or get drenched by days of endless rain.

10 Oldshoremore

- 🌀 **Break type**: Beach break.
- 🌊 **Conditions**: Medium to big swells, offshore in northeasterly winds.
- ❶ **Hazards/tips**: Sheltered break with great views.
- ⬤ **Sleeping**: Kinlochbervie ⇥ *p177*.

The small, southwesterly-facing bay at Oldshoremore works on all states of tide. Needs a good westerly or northwesterly swell to wrap in around the offshore island. Parking overlooking the break. Stunning location looking across to the Isle of Lewis. A good indictor spot for Sandwood Bay.

DEMI TAYLOR

1 Melvich

Listings

DEMI TAYLOR

2 Strathy ►► p174

Melvich

Crossing over into Sutherland via the A836, Melvich is an unassuming first stop.

🛌 Sleeping

B The Melvich Hotel, T01641 531206, is on the headland overlooking the bay complete with bar, pool table and eating options. To the west Strathy Point is a stunning location and home to **C Sharvedda**, T01641 541311. As well as a B&B, it's a working croft, so no dogs, but it does have the bonus of a storage area for boards or bikes and a shed for hanging up wetsuits. **Camping The Halladale Inn Caravan Park**, T01641 531282, is a small site with basic camping facilities and good showers. It's only a short walk to Melvich Bay and a stroll next door to the Halladale Inn where you can grab a pint. Pick up provisions at the **West End Store**, Portskerra.

Bettyhill

Following the A836, the road narrows to stretches of single track with passing places. Bettyhill, named after Elizabeth, Duchess of Sutherland, was created following the clearances of the 19th century. The Duchess evicted her tenants or crofters who managed small-holdings in the valley to make way for a more profitable option – sheep.

🛌 Sleeping

C The Bettyhill Hotel, T01641 521352, in the village, offers B&B as well as negotiable rates for longer stays. **C Dunveaden House B&B**, T01641 521273, also manage the **Craig'dhu Caravan Camping Site**, a pretty average place just off the main A836.

🍴 Eating/drinking

The Bettyhill Hotel does a range of food from good all-day breakfasts to bar snacks and full 3-course meals. **Elizabeth's Café and Crafts** on the main road overlooking Farr Bay is open Fri and Sat only during the winter season from 1700-2000 serving up cheap, basic grub – burgers, pizzas and chips to eat in/take away. Summer sees the café open 1200-2000, Mon-Sat, serving up good home cooking as well as afternoon teas. **The Far Bay Inn**, on the road into Bettyhill, does reasonable bar food.

🛌 Directory

Internet Get online at the Teleservice Centre.
Tourist information Available seasonally at **Elizabeth's Café**.

Tongue

🛌 Sleeping

C Rhian Guest House, T01847 611257. From Tongue head south on the single track route towards Ben Hope for this pretty, former gamekeeper's cottage. They have storage for boards/bikes and can also organize packed lunches and evening meals, plus they're fully licensed. **Camping Kincraig Camping & Caravan Site**, T01847 611218, just south of the village is open Apr-Oct. Take the causeway across the Kyle of Tongue and head north to **Talmine**, T01847 601255, and another, smaller, beachfront site.

Durness

Durness is the most northwesterly village on the mainland and one of the most spectacularly located, nestled between coves of blindingly white sand and awesome limestone cliffs.

Sleeping
As a fashionable spot for ecotourism, there are plenty of sleeping options. **C Smoo Falls**, T01971 511228, opposite Smoo Caves is popular. Slightly cheaper is **C-D Orcadia**, T01971 511336, a bungalow to the east of Smoo Caves. **F The Lazy Crofter Bunkhouse**, T01971 511209, is a good bet. It has kitchen facilities, is close to the village store, has bike/board storage and no curfew. **Self catering** A good option for groups is **Cranstackie**, T01732 882320, www.norsehaven.com. A short walk from Sango Bay, the cottage sleeps 4 people for £195-360 per week. **Camping Sango Sands Oasis Campsite**, T01971 511761, on the road into Durness, has statics as well as bar and restaurant facilities.

Eating/drinking
Just north, Balnakeil is home to a hippy craft village with a couple of cafés – **Balnakeil Bistro** is only open Easter-Sep while the **Loch Croispol Bookshop & Restaurant** is a bizarre-looking affair, serving up good food year-round. Summer opening until 2030, winter until 1730.

Directory
Tourist information Just off the A383, www.visithighlands.com.

Kinlochbervie

On the northwest coast of Sutherland sits the large fishing port and small village of Kinlochbervie. It's not very pretty but is a handy place to stop off before trekking to Sandwood Bay.

✪ Flat spells

Cape Wrath May-Sep take the ferry across the Kyle of Durness from Keodale, just south of Durness, T01971 511376. From here you can take a minibus, T01971 511287, along the 12 miles of rough road to the cape – the most northwesterly tip on the Scottish mainland and one of the most dramatic. Despite the number of ships claimed by this coastline, the cape actually takes it name from the Norse for 'turning place' – the Vikings used the cliffs as a navigation point during their raids on the Highlands. The cliffs, topped by a lighthouse, are still used for navigation.

Fishing Buy permits for trout and salmon fishing at **Kinlochbervie Hotel** or **Rhiconich Hotel** and catch your own supper.

Golf Get a round in at the 18-hole seaside course at **Reay**, T01847 811288, green fees around £20. Further along the coast **The Durness GC**, T01971 511364, west of the town has a 9-hole course.

Sandwood Bay Park up at Blairmore and make the 4-mile trek to this secluded bay. Makesure you've got good footwear as the track follows an old peat road across exposed and oftendamp moorland. As it's a crofting estate with grazing, no dogs are allowed on the track.

Smoo Caves Just east of Durness, these awesome limestone, beachfront caves are the area's biggest draw. The caves are 200-ft long and home to a stunning 80-ft waterfall which bursts through the cave's roof and can be seen from the entrance. Take a walk or take the boat trip but be careful after heavy rains.

Swimming North Coast Leisure Pool in Bettyhill, T01641 521400, has a sauna and jacuzzi to help chill out after a heavy session.

Sleeping
A-B The Old School Hotel & Restaurant, T01971 521383, is on the B801 between Rhiconich and Kinlochbervie and serves up great lunch and dinner at reasonable prices. **C Braeside B&B**, T01971 521325, is fair but unremarkable, as is **C Clashview**, T01971 521733. **Camping** Camp to the north at **Oldshoremore**, T01971 521281, a basic and fairly ugly site with showers open Apr-Sep. Heading further north to **Sheigra** along a single track you can camp overlooking the beach for a daylight-robbing £5 for no facilities except a tap.

Eating/drinking
The **Fisherman's Mission** on the harbourside is a good place to grab a mug of tea and a bite to eat, while **The Kinlochbervie Hotel** has a bar and does reasonable bistro-style meals.

Directory
Banks The mobile bank visits on a Mon and Thu. **Supermarkets London Stores** just south in Badcall sells all the basics, but if you want to pick up some fish get down to the port in the evening.

Orkney & Hebrides

Surfing Orkney & Hebrides

"As you come down the road to Bru, the coastline opens out in front of you. You don't have to confuse the issue with break names. The points – the best of them are of Peruvian quality, 500-600 yds long – are walling when small, a real challenge when the surf hits 6-8 ft. One year at 'Gunshots', it was 15 ft hell barrels and Derek Hynd laid down the gauntlet to some of the best surfers in the world. Even Tom Curren said he didn't have the right equipment with him. There are few places in Europe that have waves to match the pure power and energy of the waves here." Derek McCloud, Hebridean Surf.

There is a path that leads from the modern, angular visitor centre at Skara Brae on Orkney's mainland down to the white, sandy beachfront. Subtle plaques mark out relative history as you journey back in time towards the Neolithic village, nestled

in the wind-scoured sand dunes 200 yds away. Within a few steps you are past the discovery of the 'New World', the Dark Ages arrive all too quickly and at the halfway mark the pyramids are being built by one of the world's most renowned civilizations. Yet there, 100 yds away, sits a village of warm, stone-built residences, a sewage system

Breaks...

1 Skara Brae
2 Skaill Point ★
3 Marwick Reefs
4 Marwick Bay
5 Brough of Birsay

Orkney & Hebrides board guide

Thruster
Shaper: Martin McQueenie, MCQ Surfboards

- ▸▸ 6'4" x 18¾" x 2½"
- ▸▸ Average surfer 6'2" to 6'5".
- ▸▸ Squash or swallow tail for versatility in powerful waves.
- ▸▸ Moderate rocker for speed and manoeuvrability.
- ▸▸ Flat bottom to vee or reverse vee.
- ▸▸ Use larger fins in more powerful conditions.
- ▸▸ Good for fun days at beaches like Europie.

Semi-gun
Shaper: Martin McQueenie, MCQ Surfboards

- ▸▸ 6'8" x 18¼" x 2⅜".
- ▸▸ Average surfer 6'6" to 6'10".
- ▸▸ Rounded pin or squash tail.
- ▸▸ Vee through the tail with concave before the fins for stability in the barrel.
- ▸▸ Gives good drive off the bottom turn.
- ▸▸ Nose kick and rocker for steep take offs.
- ▸▸ Boards need extra volume because of the thicker wetsuits needed up here.
- ▸▸ Good for when the big swells hit the Hebrides reefs and points.

(i) Boards by **MCQ** Momentum Surf Shop
Factory: Dunbar, Scotland
T01368 869810, M T07796 752957
www.momentumsurfshop.com
post@momentumsurfshop.com

runs under their paths and stone sideboards sit decorated with precious ornaments. Within this short journey, 5000 years have melted away and you find yourself transported to an ancient place. Standing stones and ceremonial circles erupt from the pastureland while Viking graffiti, left deep in burial mounds raided for treasure, bears witness to an altogether more violent era in Orkadian history. If there is an overwhelming feeling in these Scottish islands, it is the relentless pressure of time, weighing heavy on the landscape and the relics of lost civilizations that litter the countryside.

And yet, if you look up from the amazing archaeological site at Skara Brae, you will see that the landscape has conspired to produce two wonderful point breaks, unnoticed by the scientists and birdwatchers drawn to these shores. The surf breaks of Orkney and the Hebrides are some of the most unspoilt and pristine in the whole of Britain, offering consistency, quality and, in the summer, near 24-hour daylight. The question is, why have you never been?

Coastline

The **Hebrides** are composed of grey Lewisian Gneiss, some of the oldest exposed rock in the world, sitting at the far northwestern corner of Britain. Their exposed position means that their reefs and beach breaks pick up swell from every low pressure system out in the Atlantic. The islands are home to every conceivable type of wave from firing rocky pointbreaks to sheltered white-sand beaches that produce Hossegor-type waves. The rugged coastline and winding roads mean that a week-long trip won't even begin to open up the surf potential of this magical place. However the islands are also renowned for the storms that come lashing through and for the severe, unforgiving winter winds. The east coast of the islands can offer some wonderfully sheltered little gems when the westerlies kick in.

Lying off the northeastern tip of Britain are the Orkney Isles, an extension of the wonderful slabstone geography of the Caithness region and a world-renowned danger to shipping since humans first took to the sea. Add to this the fact that the islands pick up more swell than the mainland and you have a place of amazing surf potential. Mainland Orkney has some excellent slab and boulder reefs and points that go unridden every day, a big call in the era of boats queuing up to surf reefs deep in the backwaters of the Indonesian archipelago.

66 99

The Hebrides is an instruction in atmosphere. Low, steel grey skies look down on barren landscapes and Byzantine coastal rock formations. Whilst looking for a surf on the sabbath you may be stared at disapprovingly by stern-looking men in black suits and their wives in pastel twinsets and chintzy hats going to chapel.

Mike Fordham, Editor, Adrenalin

Localism

The Hebridean Islands of Lewis and Harris have a local waveriding population of about 20 but the line-up is now regularly peppered with visiting surfers. This is not the place to breach surf etiquette – it wouldn't be tolerated. Plus the waves here are powerful and the rips can be dangerous, so if you do get into trouble, it will be the locals who bail you out. In the Orkneys, surfers rarely make the journey across the waters.

Top local surfers

Former fisherman **Derek McCloud** and his Surf Camp have championed Hebridean surfing since 1996. In 2001 the camp played host to some of the world's most respected surfers including **Tom Curren** and **Derek Hynd**. The surf community on Orkney is either very underground or non-existent.

Getting around

The road networks on the Scottish islands are of pretty good quality but are long and winding and can get clogged with tourists in the summer, particularly coaches on Orkney. Always allow way more time to get somewhere than you think. In the Hebrides, the Lewis breaks (from Port Nis to Dalmore) are quickly navigable. The trek south to the Harris breaks is more of a mission – Dalmore to Valtos can take around 45 minutes.

Breaks

Orkney

1 Skara Brae

- 🌊 **Break type**: Left point.
- ☁ **Conditions**: All swells, offshore in easterly winds.
- ❶ **Hazards/tips**: Shallow when small, very quiet spot.
- 💬 **Sleeping**: Westcoast Mainland Orkney ▸▸ *p187*.

This is a wonderful, pinwheel, left-hand point that breaks over a shallow boulder reef into the calm waters of Skaill Bay. The point sits in front of the awesome Neolithic site at Skara Brae and one look at the postcard selection will show you how consistent this point is. Works in any northwesterly or westerly swell; the wind needs to be from an easterly direction.

1 Scara Brae left

2 Skaill Point

- 🌊 **Break type**: Right-hand point.
- ☁ **Conditions**: All swells.
- ⊕ **Size**: 3-10 ft.
- ⟷ **Length**: 50-200 m.
- 🌀 **Swell**: W to NW.
- 🌬 **Wind**: Easterly.
- 🌊 **Tide**: Mid to low tide.
- 😎 **Bottom**: Flat reef.
- ✪ **Entry/exit**: Off rocks/from beach.
- ❶ **Hazards/tips**: Long walls breaking over rocky reef.
- 💬 **Sleeping**: Westcoast Mainland Orkney ▸▸ *p187*.

Skaill Point is a long, walling right-hand point on the northern edge of the bay. In perfect conditions, swell unloads onto flat slabstone reef sending waves reeling through to the beach. The wave can be hollow on the outside, but as it hits the inside section it lines up into a long, long wall perfect for carving turns and cutbacks. In big swells with little wind, this place is a wonderful, empty, crystal blue, picture-book wave, the likes of which are very rare in the surfing world these days. At a time when the remotest corners of the globe have surfers scrambling over them, the Orkneys must be one of the few areas where quality surf really does go unridden.

Orkney & Hebrides

Air ——— Sea
Averages

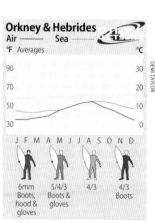

6mm Boots, hood & gloves	5/4/3 Boots & gloves	4/3	4/3 Boots

2 Skaill ride

4 Marwick Point

There are good reasons of course. The coastline around Thurso, where the ferry leaves for the Orkneys, is wave-rich and uncrowded, meaning there has always been little incentive to splash out on the expensive ferry tickets to the islands. Also conditions in Scotland are notoriously fickle. It really is the land of 'four seasons in one day' and a chart that looks perfect for the Orkneys can quickly change into a week of onshore rain.

However, Skaill Bay is a consistent swell catcher. Get it with light easterly winds and you should hopefully be treated to the sight of two quality point breaks reeling in each side of this bay, home to a world famous 5000-year-old Neolithic settlement. Skara Brae is probably the only break in the world where surfers are outnumbered by archaeologists.

ⓘ *If you like Skaill Point, try Lafitenia in France, Anchor Point in Morocco or Ribeira d'Ilhas in Portugal.*

3 Marwick Reefs

- 🌀 **Break type**: Reef breaks.
- 🌊 **Conditions**: Small to medium swells, offshore in easterly winds.
- ❶ **Hazards/tips**: Shallow, very quiet bay, experienced surfers only.
- 💤 **Sleeping**: Westcoast Mainland Orkney ⇢ *p187*.

A series of reefs to the south of the bay where waves come out of deep water and break onto a series of flat slab reefs through the tides. Those who have surfed Brims Ness will know exactly what to expect. These reefs throw up power- ful, shallow, barrelling waves in even small swells. Experienced surfers only.

4 Marwick Bay

- 🌀 **Break type**: Right reef.
- 🌊 **Conditions**: Small to medium swells, offshore in easterly winds.
- ❶ **Hazards/tips**: Quiet bay, boulder reef.
- 💤 **Sleeping**: Westcoast Mainland Orkney ⇢ *p187*.

Marwick is a beautiful, quiet bay popular with birdwatchers. It is also home to a nice mid to high tide right-hand reef that breaks over boulders in the middle of the bay. It throws up a quality, walling right that can produce the occasional barrel. Best in small to medium swells. In bigger swells a right will appear under the cliffs at the northern end of the bay. Rarely surfed spot, so not ideal for inexperienced surfers.

5 Brough of Birsay

- 🌀 **Break type**: Reefs.
- 🌊 **Conditions**: Medium to big swells.
- ❶ **Hazards/tips**: Rocks, access, shallow, big colony of seals.
- 💤 **Sleeping**: Westcoast Mainland Orkney ⇢ *p187*.

The Brough (pronounced Brock) of Birsay is a small offshore island which is attached to the mainland by a low tide causeway. There are a number of reefs in Birsay Bay that break at different tides and in different swell sizes. Offshore in easterly and southeasterly winds. There are three main reefs, the inner of which is the most sheltered but also the best quality. It worth exploring the east coast of the island in westerly winds.

3 Marwick Reefs

2 Skaill Point

DEMI TAYLOR

Hebrides

1 Tolsta

- **Break type**: Beach break.
- **Conditions**: Medium swells, offshore in southwesterly winds.
- **Hazards/tips**: Powerful, hollow waves.
- **Sleeping**: Stornoway ⇢ *p188*.

A mile-long stretch of beach that picks up northerly swell. Some quality sandbanks produce hollow peaks. Faces northeast and works through all the tides. Follow the B895 from Stornoway.

2 Port of Ness (Port Nis)

- **Break type**: Beach break.
- **Conditions**: Small and medium swells, offshore in southwesterly winds.
- **Hazards/tips**: Small bay with some rocks.
- **Sleeping**: Stornoway/West Coast Lewis ⇢ *p188*.

Port Nis is a sandy bay with rocks that has some excellent low tide rights. There are rocks at mid tide in the middle of the bay and a right breaking at the southern end, which picks up the most swell. There is also a left peeling off the broken pier. Can have bad rips.

3 Europie (Eòropaidh)

- **Break type**: Beach break.
- **Conditions**: All swells, offshore in southeasterly winds.
- **Hazards/tips**: Best beach break, big rips.
- **Sleeping**: Stornoway/West Coast Lewis ⇢ *p188*.

"Europie is a challenging, A-grade beach break and the most northwesterly break in Britain," says Derek McCloud. *"It's very powerful – like a big Hossegor. It's board-breaking and neck-breaking."*

The best-known break on the Hebrides and a very good beach with hollow, powerful sandbanks. At the southern end there is a sand-covered rocky bank that has some great, hollow waves at low tide. In the middle of the beach are some excellent barrelling rights which break into a channel and work best from low to near high tide. There are also big rights to be had at the northern end of the beach. Parking available near the cemetery. "It works on all swells. We had Tom Curren and the guys surfing it over 12 ft," adds Derek. Cars need to watch out for sinking sands at the north end of the bay.

4 Swain Bost Sands

- **Break type**: Beach break.
- **Conditions**: Small to medium swells, offshore in southeasterly winds.
- **Hazards/tips**: Rocks and rips.
- **Sleeping**: Stornoway/West Coast Lewis ⇢ *p188*.

Part of the same stretch of beach as Europie. Low tide rocky sandbanks that lie in a double bay, divided by a rocky reef. **Gunshots** is a massive, heavy left-hand tube for the hardcore. Breaks like Teahupoo when big and is a big paddle.

5 Barvas (Barabhas)

- **Break type**: Reefs and points.
- **Conditions**: All swells, offshore in south/southeasterly/southwesterly winds.
- **Hazards/tips**: A selection of excellent breaks, popular spots.
- **Sleeping**: Stornoway/West Coast Lewis ⇢ *p188*.

Barvas is a big, right-hand boulder reef that can hold swells up to 10 ft. Works like a reverse Easky Left, breaking through the tides and on all swell sizes. It produces long, walling quality rides

Eugene Tollemache, cold rush

10 Jason Duffy, Dalmore ⇢ *p184*

MARK LUMSDEN

182

and has sections that can combine in the right swell. A south or southeasterly wind is offshore.

Bru is a long left-hand point that has quality walling waves breaking over boulders. Best in a southerly or southwesterly wind. It is one of the islands' most recognizable waves due to the large green bus, hence the name **Bus Stops**. Long, walling waves.

According to Derek McCloud, "Bru is like a Peruvian point break that can peel for 500 yds on its day. When it gets big it is very heavy and challenging with big hold-downs and a hard reef."

Outer Lefts is a left point at on the western end of the rocks. It is a rock and boulder reef that is always bigger than the other breaks and can hold a big swell up to 10 ft. Offshore in southerly/

MARK LUMSDEN

Tom Anderson, tucking in

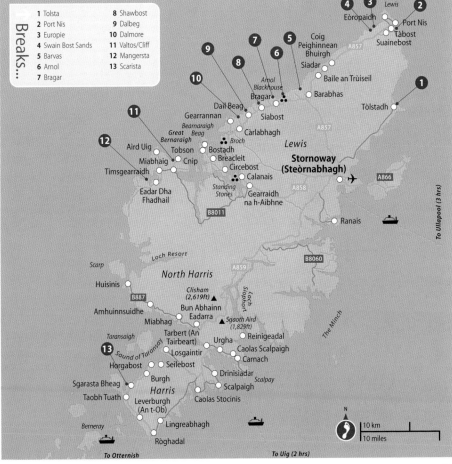

Breaks...

1 Tolsta	**8** Shawbost
2 Port Nis	**9** Dalbeg
3 Europie	**10** Dalmore
4 Swain Bost Sands	**11** Valtos/Cliff
5 Barvas	**12** Mangersta
6 Arnol	**13** Scarista
7 Bragar	

Butt of Lewis

Eòròpaidh
Port Nis
Tàbost
Suainebost

Coig Peighinnean Bhuirgh
Siadar
Baile an Trùiseil
Barabhas
Tòlstadh

Arnol
Blackhouse
Bragar
Dail Beag
Siabost
Gearrannan
Bearnaraigh
Great Beag
Bernaraigh
Broch
Càrlabhagh
Aird Uig
Tobson
Bostadh
Lewis
Miabhaig
Cnip
Breacleit
Timsgearraidh
Circebost
Calanais
Stornoway (Steòrnabhagh)
Eadar Dha Fhadhail
Standing Stones
Gearraidh na h-Aibhne
Ranais

Loch Resort
Scarp
North Harris
Huisinis
Clisham (2,619ft) ▲
Bun Abhainn
Amhuinnsuidhe
Eadarra
Miabhag
Sgaoth Aird (1,829ft) ▲
Reinigeadal
Tarbert (An Tairbeart)
Urgha
Caolas Scalpaigh
Taransaigh
Losgaintir
Carnach
Hòrgabost
Seilebost
Drinisiadar
Sgarasta Bheag
Burgh
Scalpaigh
Scalpay
Harris
Taobh Tuath
Leverburgh (An t-Ob)
Caolas Stocinis
Berneray
Lingreabhagh
Ròghadal

To Otternish
To Uig (2 hrs)
To Ullapool (3 hrs)
The Minch
Loch Seaforth
Sound of Taransay

N
10 km
10 miles

southwesterly winds. "Follow the road to Bru and you'll see all the breaks open out in front of you," says Derek.

yds are possible on good quality walling waves. Entry and exit from the water can be difficult over boulders and rocks.

small, sheltered bay with a strong rip at the right end. The wave here is powerful and hollow but closes out on the end section.

6 Arnol

- ◉ **Break type**: Reef.
- ◉ **Conditions**: Big swells, offshore in southwesterly winds.
- ◉ **Hazards/tips**: Big wave spot for experienced surfers.
- ◉ **Sleeping**: Stornoway/West Coast Lewis ▸▸ p188.

This is a big wave peak that breaks over a boulder and rock reef in the middle of the bay. It is best at low tide when it breaks up to 15 ft plus and there are strong rips. For hellmen only.

7 Bragar

- ◉ **Break type**: Rocky left point.
- ◉ **Conditions**: Medium swells, offshore in westerly winds.
- ◉ **Hazards/tips**: Difficult exit from water in big swells.
- ◉ **Sleeping**: Stornoway/West Coast Lewis ▸▸ p188.

A long, left-hand point break that fires along a rocky, bouldery reef. The tide depends on the swell size but in the right conditions rides of up to 300

8 Shawbost (Siabost)

- ◉ **Break type**: Rocky left point.
- ◉ **Conditions**: Big swell, offshore in westerly winds.
- ◉ **Hazards/tips**: Rocky wave, difficult access.
- ◉ **Sleeping**: Stornoway/West Coast Lewis ▸▸ p188.

This point needs a big southwesterly swell to get going due to the rocky nature of the line-up. Best at about 6 to 8 ft, access can be tricky due to boulders and rocks.

9 Dalbeg

- ◉ **Break type**: Beach break.
- ◉ **Conditions**: Small to medium swells, offshore in southeasterly wind.
- ◉ **Hazards/tips**: Powerful, hollow lefts.
- ◉ **Sleeping**: Stornoway/West Coast Lewis ▸▸ p188.

This beach has a low tide left breaking off a quality sandbank. Dalbeg is a

10 Dalmore

- ◉ **Break type**: Beach break.
- ◉ **Conditions**: Small to medium swells, offshore in southeasterly winds.
- ◉ **Hazards/tips**: Powerful peak.
- ◉ **Sleeping**: Stornoway/West Coast Lewis ▸▸ p188.

The next bay to Dalbeg, this spot has a low tide hollow peak, which produces punchy lefts and rights. As the swell picks up there is a dredging left-hand point. Once you step in the water you have to be committed due to the powerful nature of the waves and the rips.

11 Valtos (Bhaltos)/Cliff

- ◉ **Break type**: Beach break.
- ◉ **Conditions**: Medium swells, offshore in southeasterly winds.
- ◉ **Hazards/tips**: Rips.
- ◉ **Sleeping**: Stornoway/West Coast Lewis ▸▸ p188.

It's a one-hour drive inland and then out along the B8011 to get to the small

Sam Lamiroy 'Hebs' for cover

J Duffy soul

bay at Valtos. Here there are two peaks to choose from, both producing excellent hollow and powerful waves. The break works on all tides, but better at low to mid. There is parking overlooking the break. "Every year people get into trouble on the western breaks due to the powerful rips," says Derek, "and there are no lifeguards here. We have to bail them out ourselves."

12 Mangersta

- ⚙ **Break type**: Beach break.
- ☁ **Conditions**: Small swells, offshore in southeasterly winds.
- ⚠ **Hazards/tips**: Beautiful, white sand bay.
- ⛺ **Sleeping**: Stornoway/West Coast Lewis ⇥ *p188*.

Crystal clear water and white sand make this pretty beach an excellent destination; it just so happens that it also has an excellent low tide peak producing hollow lefts and rights. Best in small swells when it produces great barrels. Gets nasty when the swell picks up and is exposed to the wind.

13 Scarista

- ⚙ **Break type**: Beach break.
- ☁ **Conditions**: All swells, offshore in southeasterly winds.
- ⚠ **Hazards/tips**: Beautiful, exposed spot.
- ⛺ **Sleeping**: Tarbert ⇥ *p189*.

This is a big stretch of beach exposed to the wind. There are peaks along the length, with powerful waves from northwesterly and southwesterly swells. A beautiful spot that looks across to Taransay, home of the reality TV show, *Castaway*.

Listings

West Coast

MARK LUMSDEN

Orkney

The Orkney Isles take their name from the orca whales that make their migratory journey through the waters surrounding the islands. There are about 70 islands within the Orkney archipelago, the largest of which is Mainland. Although only a short hop across the water from the tacky John O'Groats, Orkney – with its Neolithic village and standing stones – is worlds apart.

⊙ Getting there

Air British Airways, T0870 8509850, operate direct flights to Kirkwall Mon-Sat from Aberdeen, Edinburgh, Glasgow and Inverness with connections from London Heathrow, Gatwick, Birmingham, Manchester and Belfast. Flights are pricey, ring ahead to make sure there will be room for your board especially during busy summer months. **Ferries** Northlink Ferries, T01856 885500, www.northlinkferries.co.uk, operate year-round between Scrabster near Thurso and the old fishing port of Stromness on the Mainland's west coast. Taking in the Old Man of Hoy along the way, a 450-ft sea stack, the journey takes about 1½ hrs and runs twice daily Mon-Fri with weekend services. Return from £26 foot passenger and £78 van. **Northlink** also operate ferries year round from Aberdeen on Scotland's east coast to Stromness. Taking 8 hrs, it costs about double the Scrabster service. **Pentland Ferries**, T01856 831226, www.pentland ferries.co.uk, run between Gills Bay, just off the A836 west of John O'Groats, and St Margaret's Hope on South Ronaldsay. Foot passengers from £24 return, vans from £56 return. **John O'Groats Ferries,**

www.jogferry.co.uk, T01955 611353, run a summer passenger service between John O'Groats to Burwick on South Ronaldsay or Kirkwall with returns from £24. Buses connect with the Burwick ferry and run to Kirkwall. They also run the **Orkney Bus** between Inverness and Kirkwall 1 May-2 Sep. The 5-hr door-to-door journey costs from £42 return inclusive of the ferry.

Stromness

Stromness is a pretty fishing town with cobbled streets and a strong sea-faring tradition – many of the Atlantic's whaling crews set out from here.

😴 Sleeping

C **Bea House B&B**, Back Rd, T01856 851043, is within walking distance of the ferry port and overlooks the town. C **Mrs Worthington's B&B**, 2 South End, T01856 850215, is open Apr–Oct with views over Scapa Flow and easy access to the town. E **Browns Hostel**, T01856 850661, is independent, popular, open year-round and well placed on Victoria St, beds from about £10. E **SYHA Stromness Hostel**,

Hellihole Rd, T01856 850589, is another cheap option May-Sep. **Self catering** There is plenty of self-catering accommodation which can often be the cheapest and easiest option for groups. On Dundas St, with good town access, is another stone property sleeping up to 4 people for under £200 a week from Apr-Oct. Contact **Mrs Boyes**, T01856 850120. **Mr & Mrs Seater's** traditional stone house also on Dundas St, T01856 850415, overlooks the harbour and sleeps up to 6 from £200. **Camping** The **Point of Ness Caravan and Camping site**, T01856 873535, is a short walk from the town, open May-Sep, and has great views across the water to neighbouring Hoy; can be a bit windy. Responsible **free camping** is permitted on the island but ask the landowner's permission first.

🍴 Eating/drinking

The Ferry Inn, again near the terminal, is a popular spot and does reasonably priced pub grub for lunch and dinner. If you feel like splashing out head to the **Hamnavoe Restaurant**, Graham Place, T01856 850606. Eat the catch of

the day, straight off the boats at this Egon Ronay restaurant Apr-Sep. **Julia's Café** opposite the ferry terminal does a good range of reasonably priced food at lunch – soup, sandwiches, salads, jackets etc.

❶ Directory

Car hire Norman Brass Car Hire, North End Rd, T01856 850850, is based at the Blue Star Filling Station; or try **Stromness Self Drive Cars**, 75 John St, T01856 850973. Both are within walking distance of the ferry. **Tourist information** At the Scrabster ferry port, open year-round, T01856 850716, www.visitorkney.com.

Kirkwall

Founded in 1035, Kirkwall is the capital of Orkney and a busy working town. Although lacking the natural charm of Stromness, it does offer basic amenities of chemists, banks, supermarkets etc.

😴 Sleeping

A-B **The Albert Hotel**, Mounthoolie Lane, T01856 876000, is centrally located and home to an OK restaurant and a couple of busy bars. C-D **Cumliebank B&B**, Cromwell Rd, T01856 873160, is about a 5-min walk into town. There are several other B&Bs around Cromwell Rd. E **Peedie Hostel**, Ayre Rd, T01856 875477, by the seafront, is basic and not particularly spacious with beds from £10. **SYHA**, Old Skapa Rd, T01856 872243, open Apr-Oct, is basic, about a 15-min walk into town and with a midnight curfew. **Self catering** Mrs **Sinclair's** house and flat on Tankerness are about as central as you can get. The house sleeps up to 7

Ring of Brodgar

Flat spells

Bike hire Orkney Cycle Hire on Dundas St, Stromness, T01856 850255, hires bikes by the day/week as does Bobby's Cycle Centre, Tankerness Lane, Kirkwall, T01856 875777.

Cinema and gym Pickaquoy Centre, Pickaquoy Rd, Kirkwall, T01856 879900, is home to the **New Phoenix Cinema** while **The Zone** fitness studio has a sauna, jacuzzi and steam room to help you chill out after a heavy session. Plus café and bar with pool tables and Sky TV.

Diving Scapa Flow, hemmed in by Mainland, South Ronaldsay and Hoy, attracts divers from all over the world to explore the wrecks of the scuttled WWII German fleet in crystal clear waters. **Scapa Scuba**, Ness Rd, T01856 851218, offers lessons, dives and equipment hire to novices and experienced divers.

Golf The Orkney GC is just west of Kirkwall on Grainbank with an 18-hole course, T01856 872457. Fees from £15.

Sights The Italian Chapel Built by Italian POWs based on the island during WWII, this beautifully detailed chapel started life as 2 Nissen huts, while the ornate decorations were crafted from salvaged scrap metal and old pieces of concrete. The prisoners built this in their spare time; their day job was to construct the nearby **Churchill Barriers**, protecting the British Navy based in Scapa Flow from enemy submarine invasion. Follow the A961 south from Kirkwall.

Maes Howe It may look like a hill from the outside but this is one of the most impressive chambered tombs in Western Europe made even more interesting by the fact it was raided by the Vikings in the 12th century. The plundering Norsemen took time to carve runic graffiti into the walls boasting of their conquests both in battle and with the ladies.

Skara Brae If you only see one thing while you're here, make sure it is this 5000-year-old village and World Heritage Site. It's 2000 years older than the pyramids, it even predates Stonehenge, but neolithic man still wanted to utilize the latest technology in his village. Skara Brae has a sewage system while individual dwellings boast stone sideboards for displaying treasures and even cool boxes. Open year round with an excellent visitors centre, entry about £5. Access via the B9056.

Standing Stones The Stones of Stenness and the bigger **Ring of Brodgar** are both spectacular ceremonial stone circles dating from the time of Skara Brae. Unlike Stonehenge, you're allowed to walk freely and actually touch the stones. Accessed via the B9055 running northwesterly off the A965, the circles and nearby standing stones run along powerful ley lines.

people with prices up to about £300, T01856 872035. **Camping The Pickaquoy Centre**, Pickaquoy Rd, T01856 879900, is about a 10-min walk into town and offers basic camping facilities May-Sep with pay showers (get a good haul of 20p coins).

Eating/drinking

The Bothy Bar at The Albert Hotel occasionally has live bands and serves a full range of real ales including **Dark Island** – an award-winning, Orcadian-style Guinness – as well as OK bar food. **Busters Diner** on Mounthoolie offers fairly cheap pizzas, pastas, and burgers, open lunch/dinner Mon-Sat, dinner only

Sun. **Empire Chinese Restaurant**, Junction Rd, is pretty good and offers reasonably priced eat in or take away food. **St Magnus Café** at the community centre is a good and cheap place to grab a sandwich and a cup of tea, as is **The Mustard Seed** on Victoria St who also do home baking.

Directory

Airport T01856 872421, 3 miles out of town along the A960. **Car hire** Due to a captive audience, car hire is pricey, about £150-plus per week. Plenty of options offering similar services: **James Peace & Co**, Junction Rd, T01856 872866; **WR Tullock** (Fords) with offices on Castle St,

T01856 87626, and the airport, T01856 875000; **John Shearer & Sons** (Vauxhalls), T01856 872950; **Ayre service station and Scarth Hire**, Great Western Rd, T01856 872125, also rent vans. **Medical facilities** Balfour Hospital and Health Centre, New Scapa Rd running south out of town. **Tourist information** Broad St, T01856 872856.

Westcoast Mainland

The west coast is home to the major breaks on Orkney and, if you don't mind being away from the pubs and shops, can be a good base for those wanting to escape the tourists. Sandwick is a short hop to Skaill Bay with its 2 point breaks while heading north from Skaill, Marwick Bay in Birsay has some excellent reefs and a good point.

🛌 Sleeping
Sandwick D Hyval Farm, T01856 841522, a family-run beef farm in a coastal location near Skaill Bay, B&B Apr-Oct. **D Netherstove**, T01856 841625, a working farm overlooking Skaill Bay, offers B&B May-Oct and year-round self-catering accommodation from £120/week for 2 people.

Birsay C Primrose Cottage, T01856 721384, views over Marwick Bay and comfortable B&B accommodation. **Self catering** There are plenty of self-catering facilities in Birsay including **Quoylonga Farm**, T01856 721225, open Apr-Oct, sleeps 4 people from £150 per week.

Hebrides

This 130-mile-long chain of islands sitting 30 miles off the coast of Scotland is home to Britain's most northwesterly beach, Europie, as well as puffins, golden eagles, dolphins, whales and basking sharks. As well as Europie, there are numerous sandy beaches in this very attractive area. Tradition has a strong foothold on the islands where Gaelic is still spoken and Sundays really are a day of rest.

🛬 Getting there
Air British Airways, T0870 8509850, operates regular flights Mon-Sat from Glasgow, Edinburgh and Inverness to Stornoway Airport, just to the east of the town.
Ferries CalMac, T01475 650100, www.calmac.co.uk, run regular services year round between Ullapool on Scotland's northwest coast and Stornoway on Lewis. Crossings run 2-3 times daily and take approximately 2 hrs 40 mins. Expect to pay from £150 return for a car and 2 passengers.

Lewis (Leodhas)

Stornoway (Steòrnabhagh)
Lewis makes up the top two-thirds of the most northerly island in the chain. The town of Stornoway on the east coast is the focal point for island life and the only major town servicing the islands.

🛌 Sleeping
E Laxdale Holiday Park, T01851 706966, www.laxdaleholiday park.com, is about 1½ miles outside Stornoway with camping facilities plus caravans for hire Mar-Oct. Year-round bunkhouse with beds from £10 per night.

E Stornoway Surf House, Keith St, T01851 705862 (day), T0151 701869 (evening), www.hebrideansurf.co.uk, is run by Derek McCloud and is the best option for visiting surfers. A former fisherman and hardy surfer, Derek's knowledge of this coastline is second to none. Ten pounds will buy you a bed in a dorm and access to a self-catering kitchen. Alternatively you can pay a bit more and have the cooking done for you and be taken to the best breaks every day.

🍴 Eating/drinking
The Crown Hotel on Castle St is a nice place to grab a pint and a bite to eat but there are also plenty of other pubs around the quay. **The Heb** is *the*

MARK LUMSDEN

Jump off

nightclub for the islands, so get down there Thu-Sat nights. Remember Sat night finishes early – before midnight – so as not to cross over into Sun. **Sunsets Restaurant** near the surf camp serves up tasty and healthy meals using local produce and fresh fish straight from the boats. **The Thai Café** on Church St is surprisingly decent and good value.

Directory
Car hire Lewis Car Rentals, Bayhead St, T01851 703760, and **Lochs Motors** on Southbeach, T01851 705857, can offer good rates on daily and weekly hire. **Internet** Get online at the library, Cromwell St. Connection is expensive, from £3.50 per hour. Or try **Captions** on Church St. **Surf shops** Derek runs a fully stocked surf shop off Keith St. **Tourist information** Cromwell St, www.visithebrides.co.uk, open year-round.

West Coast
Sleeping
Port Nis (Ness) sits at the Northwest tip of the Butt of Lewis, a 45-min drive from Stornoway. **L-A The Cross Inn**, T01851 810152, also have a bar serving food. **C Galson Farm Guest House**, T01851 850492, 8 miles south of Port Nis off the A857, an 18th-century converted farmhouse.

    Barvas (Barabhas) lies on the junction with A857 and A858 and gives good scope to explore the coastline – try **C Rockvilla B&B**, T01851 840286.

    Shawbost (Siabost) **B-C Airigh B&B**, T01851 710478, South Siabost. **Camping Eilean Fraoich Campsite**, T01851 710504, off the A858, open May-Oct.

    Garenin, the former crofting

village, sits on the coast road running from Carloway (Carlabhagh). **F Garenin Gatliff hostel** (non-profit) is open year-round with beds in the restored blackhouse from £8. You can't book ahead and it is heated by coal fire but it is a great place to stay and well located for Dalbeg and Dalmore Bays.

Eating/drinking
Try **The Copper Kettle** at Dalbeg bay for cheap lunchtime snacks and jacket potatoes.

Harris (Na Hearadh)

Tarbert (An Tairbeart)
Harris is actually not a separate island but shares a piece of rock with Lewis to the north and is famous for its tweed. The Port of Tarbert, lying in a sheltered bay, is the main settlement on the island with shops, bank etc joining north and south Harris.

Sleeping
B-C MacLeod Motel, T01859 502364, near the ferry pier, offers rooms as well as cottages to rent. **E Drinishader Hostel**, T01859 511255, is about 5 miles south of Tarbert with a roaring coal fire. **E Rockview Bunkhouse**, Main St, T01859 502626, is a cheap, well-placed option with kitchen facilities.

Eating/drinking
Try **Big D's**, Harbour St, for snacks, takeaway and dinner. **First Fruits Teahouse**, Harbour St, Apr-Sep, is a nice place to grab a lunchtime snack. **The Harris Hotel** near the ferry terminal does good value bar food as well as a comprehensive dinner menu

and serves on Sun.

    Although not the most lively of places, there are a few pubs on Harbour St including **Tarbert Hotel**, **Anchor Hotel** and **Corner House**.

Directory
Tourist information Harbour St, open Apr-Oct.

Leverburgh (An T-Ob)
Sleeping
Continuing south along the A859, Leverburgh has a shop and a few basic facilities including the **E Am Bothan Bunkhouse**, Ferry Rd, T01859 520251. An ordinary exterior gives way to a great interior with a drying room and beds from about £12.

Flat spells
Bike hire Alex Dan's Cycle Centre, Kenneth St, Stornoway, T01851 704025, hire bikes by the hr, day or week.

Golf Stornoway GC, Lady Lever Park, just east of Stornoway, T01851 702249, 18-hole course set in the grounds of Lews Castle. On Harris, get a round in at the 9-hole Scarista GC, T01859 502331, except Sun.

Sights Calanais (Callanish) Standing Stones, Lewis Forming a Celtic cross overlooking Loch Roag, these stones are the most spectacular Neolithic monument on the island. Clach an Truiseil near Barabhas is the largest monolith in Europe standing 20 ft tall.

East Coast Harris This is worth exploring for the bizarre lunar-style landscape alone.

Surfing the West Coast

The west coast of Scotland is a complex and convoluted coastline with myriad islands and inlets buffering the mainland from the raw power of the north Atlantic. This region offers stunning landscapes, dressed in a confusion of Celtic heathers and semi-tropical plants lovingly warmed by the last vestiges of the Gulf Stream. The islands of the Inner Hebrides offer a mind-blowing number of possibilities that open up when a travelling surfer scans a map of the region. "Tiree is a beautiful and consistent spot," says Suds from Wild Diamond Surf School, based on the island. "When the wind is from the south or east – it's on!" But surfing here is not for the impatient or faint-hearted. Many breaks are reached by a maze of B roads, winding single-track tarmac or island-hopping ferries. Even the closest breaks can be a mission. "On a good day it's about two and a half hours for the run up to the mainland breaks around Machrihanish from the city," says Jamie Blair from Clan in Glasgow.

Over the past couple of years more and more surfers are waking up to the fact that the west coast, with its stunning scenery, white sand beaches and twisting roads, is within reach of the major urban areas of Glasgow and even Edinburgh. "There are between 100 and 200 surfers in Glasgow," says Jamie. "The University surf club has about 90 members. The explosion in numbers has only really occurred recently. We used to drive up to the west coast and there would only be us and a couple of other guys. Now, on a really good summer weekend there can be 30 to 50 people around." Beaches like this area's best-known, Machrihanish, are drawing in more and more enthusiastic surfers from all over the west of Scotland. "The waves are a bit weak. Even when they look really good they seem to lack a real punch," says Scottish shaper Martin McQueenie. "But there are a few reefs hidden away that the locals will never tell you about."

West coast board guide

Fish
Shaper: Martin McQueenie, MCQ Surfboards

▸▸ 6'4" x 19½" x 2⅝" for Chris Noble.
▸▸ Average surfer 6'2" to 6'6".
▸▸ Good for when a nice swell hits Mull or Tiree.
▸▸ Swallow tail for manoeuvrability.
▸▸ Good width and volume for linking sections when the surf is a bit weaker.
▸▸ Flat rocker for speed.
▸▸ Try larger fins in 4-6 ft swells for better drive and stability.
▸▸ Versatile board.

Fun Board
Shaper: Martin McQueenie, MCQ Surfboards

▸▸ 7'0" x 20½" x 2⅝".
▸▸ Good for small, weak days.
▸▸ Square or wider squash tail for more drive.
▸▸ Good width and volume for catching waves.
▸▸ Double concave for lift.
▸▸ Wave-catching machine.
▸▸ Fun for average conditions at Machrihanish.

(i) Boards by **MCQ** Momentum Surf Shop
Factory: Dunbar, Scotland
T 01368 869810, M T 07796 752957
www.momentumsurfshop.com
post@momentumsurfshop.com

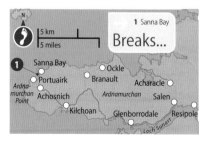

Breaks...

1 Sanna Bay

5 km
5 miles

1 Sanna Bay
Ockle
Portuairk   Branault   Acharacle
Ardna-murchan Point   Achosnich   Ardnamurchan   Salen
Kilchoan   Glenborrodale   Resipole
Loch Sunart

Coastline

The jigsaw of islands and lochs means that certain breaks on the west coast are incredibly fickle and will only work when swell passes directly through a narrow window. Local knowledge pays dividends here but can take years to accumulate as certain reefs may only work a couple of times each winter. There is also the effect of tides moving around between the Irish Sea, the various sounds and the Atlantic.

"I went to one of the local harbours to try to get some tide tables and they said that because there are three bodies of water moving around, the tides are pretty fickle and unpredictable. They don't get massive tides but they are affected by swell, winds and pressure systems," explains Martin McQueenie.

Localism

This whole region is pretty chilled and friendly in the water. Just bring a friendly attitude with you and it will pay dividends.

Top local surfers

"There are one or two surfers in each of the surrounding villages, maybe four or five in Campbeltown – but the number is growing all the time," says west coast regular **Jamie Blair** of Clan Surf. On Tiree, the number of year-round surfers is about five, including Wild Diamond surf instructor **Suds**. This number swells to anywhere near 30 in the summer.

Getting around

Patience is the key word here. Roads can be narrow or winding or narrow and winding. Tiree and Islay are accessed by ferry so make sure you check the charts before committing. Tiree benefits from a good road network left behind from the MOD and signifies its strategic importance.

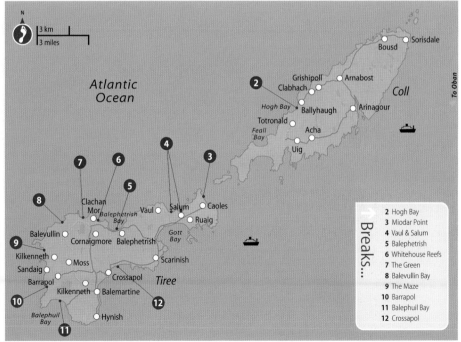

Breaks...

2 Hogh Bay
3 Miodar Point
4 Vaul & Salum
5 Balephetrish
6 Whitehouse Reefs
7 The Green
8 Balevullin Bay
9 The Maze
10 Barrapol
11 Balephuil Bay
12 Crossapol

Breaks

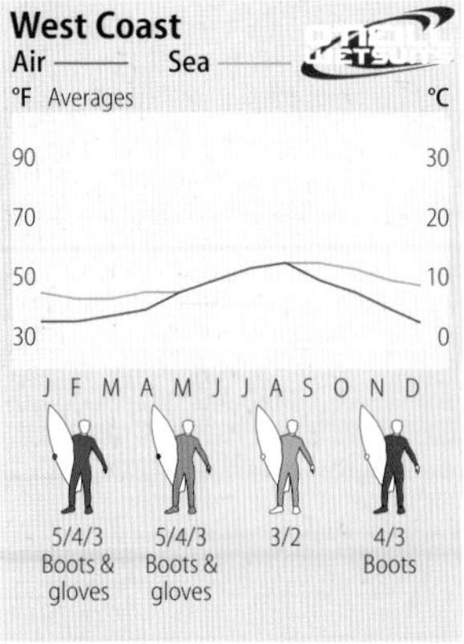
West Coast
Air
Sea
°F Averages
°C
90
70
50
30
30
20
10
0
J F M A M J J A S O N D
5/4/3 Boots & gloves
5/4/3 Boots & gloves
3/2
4/3 Boots

1 Sanna Bay

- **Break type**: Rocky beach break.
- **Conditions**: Westerly swells, offshore in easterly winds.
- **Hazards/tips**: Stunning bay, isolated.
- **Sleeping**: Ardnamurchan Peninsula » *p196*.

This picture-perfect white sand bay looks out at the Inner Hebrides and picks up westerly swell through a narrow window between Coll and Barra, or wrapping big northwesterly swells. There are a series of bays here as well as a couple of reefs. Not for the inexperienced due to its isolated location but an awesome spot to explore on a good chart. Mainland Britain's most westerly point.

2 Hogh Bay

- **Break type**: Beach break.
- **Conditions**: All swell, offshore in easterly/southeasterly winds.
- **Hazards/tips**: Exposed sandy bay.
- **Sleeping**: Coll » *p196*.

The west coast of the island of Coll has a series of sandy bays such as Hogh, which pick up plenty of swell but are also exposed to the predominant westerly winds. Feall Bay to the south offers a degree of protection at the southern end of the bay when westerly and southwesterlies blow. It is backed by huge sand dunes, some of which top 100 ft and are an RSPB reserve.

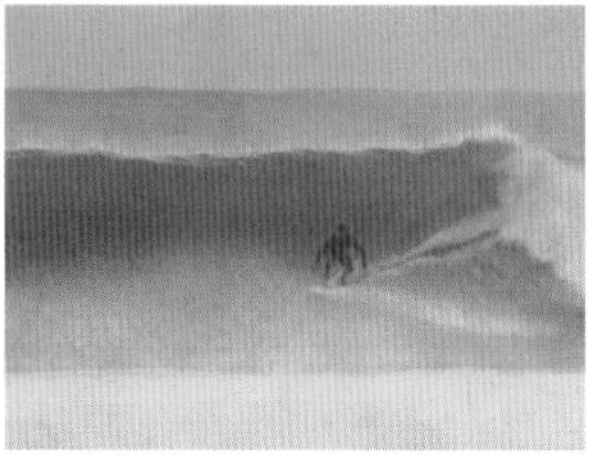

WILD DIAMOND SURF

8 Balevullin

3 Miodar Point

- **Break type**: Left point and right-hander.
- **Conditions**: Medium/big swells, offshore in southerly/southwesterly winds.
- **Hazards/tips**: Nasty rips in big swells.
- **Sleeping**: Tiree » *p197*.

The first of the breaks on the island of Tiree, this is a nice set-up that is rarely surfed. The point can have good quality waves but is best on a medium swell on a pushing tide. There is an offshore island that channels the rip so watch your position – a break for experienced surfers only. There are other reefs worth checking in the area.

4 Vaul and Salum

- **Break type**: Reef breaks.
- **Conditions**: Medium swells, offshore in southwest to southeasterly winds.
- **Hazards/tips**: Rocky break for advanced surfers.
- **Sleeping**: Tiree » *p197*.

These are fairly inconsistent rocky beach breaks that have a number of reefs working for short periods through the tides. As Suds of White Diamond Surf School says: "Unlike places like Caithness where you have a nice sloping ledge of rock that works through the tide, here they are more like clusters which can work for an hour or so, then another will start working."

5 Balephetrish

- **Break type**: Reef breaks and beach.
- **Conditions**: Medium to big swells.
- **Hazards/tips**: Heavy, offshore reefs plus beginners' beach.
- **Sleeping**: Tiree ▸▸ *p197*.

At the edges of Balephetrish sit a series of offshore reefs with intriguing potential. As yet unsurfed, some hold the potential for big, hollow waves. For advanced surfers only due to the paddle out and size. Best on light winds from a southerly direction. Enough swell does get through for beginners to surf the beach.

6 Whitehouse Reefs

- **Break type**: Reef break.
- **Conditions**: Medium to big swells, offshore in a southerly wind.
- **Hazards/tips**: Picks up lots of swell.
- **Sleeping**: Tiree ▸▸ *p197*.

Excellent potential here. A series of reefs that have been windsurfed but have yet to be surfed. These swell magnets can be checked from the comfort of your car, but it is a bit of a paddle out to them.

7 The Green

- **Break type**: Beach break.
- **Conditions**: Big swells, offshore in southwesterly to southeasterly winds.
- **Hazards/tips**: Good quality banks.
- **Sleeping**: Tiree ▸▸ *p197*.

The Green needs a decent-sized swell to get going, but with winds from any southerly direction, there should be decent waves here. At mid to high tide

the waves tend to be more hollow with plenty of punch. It's a reasonable-sized bay with the western end usually the smallest and the waves increasing in size as you travel east.

8 Balevullin Bay

- **Break type**: Beach break.
- **Conditions**: All swells, offshore in south to easterly winds.
- **Hazards/tips**: Most consistent break on Tiree.
- **Sleeping**: Tiree ▸▸ *p197*.

This is the island's most consistent spot and also a beach that can hold a decent-sized swell. When the prevailing westerly winds turn to the south or east, this place will be on. At low tide the waves are hollow and powerful, the most hollow beach waves on the island. On a southwesterly swell it produces predominantly lefts, on a northwesterly it is mainly rights. The most consistent banks are about halfway down the beach, working virtually through to high when it gets more mellow. There can be bad rips here in a big swell so

bear this in mind. There is a rock in the line-up about a third of the way along.

9 The Maze

- **Break type**: Beach break.
- **Conditions**: All swells, offshore in easterly winds.
- **Hazards/tips**: Beautiful spot.
- **Sleeping**: Tiree ▸▸ *p197*.

This picturesque beach picks up a reasonable amount of swell and works on all tides. At low it is punchy and hollow but off low it is a more mellow spot, ideal for longboarders. East and northeasterly winds are offshore and it picks up swell from most directions.

10 Barrapol

- **Break type**: Beach break
- **Conditions**: All swells, offshore in easterly winds
- **Hazards/tips**: Very rocky
- **Sleeping**: Tiree ▸▸ *p197*

This beach break has extensive rocky outcrops along the bay. Surf the area

TONY MARSH

8 Balevullin, Suds cutting back

TONY MARSH

8 Balevullin ⤵ *p193*

WILD DIAMOND SURF

West Coast, Suds

without rocks about two-thirds along. Watch out for the rock on the inside though. This bay is a swell magnet working best from low to mid tide.

11 Balephuil Bay

- ◉ **Break type**: Beach break.
- ☁ **Conditions**: All swells, offshore in easterly/northeasterly winds.
- ❶ **Hazards/tips**: Pretty consistent spot. Southerly facing
- ◉ **Sleeping**: Tiree ⤵ *p197*.

This beach works through the tides, with low producing better quality waves and high more mellow. Check the southeast end of the bay at low tide. It can hold a decent-sized swell but the paddle out can be hard work due to a lack of channels. This bay can be the only spot working in a northerly or northwesterly wind.

12 Crossapol

- ◉ **Break type**: Beach break.
- ☁ **Conditions**: Big swells, offshore in northerly winds.
- ❶ **Hazards/tips**: Check here in big swells.
- ◉ **Sleeping**: Tiree ⤵ *p197*.

When the swells are really pumping and the wind is from the north, this bay produces waves that look excellent, but ultimately fail to live up to the promise. As Suds explains, "It lacks power here so although the waves peel for ages, it's a real longboarders wave. They can get good, long rides but it doesn't have that punch you get on the west coast." If the breaks on the west coast are 6 to 8 ft it will be 2 to 3 ft here. This is a good winter spot and popular when big winter storms are closing out the north shore.

Tucking into Tiree tube

13 Islay

- **Break type**: Beach breaks.
- **Conditions**: All swells, easterly winds.
- **Hazards/tips**: Excellent potential.
- **Sleeping**: Islay ▶ p198.

Islay is an island that juts out a bit further into the swell window than Kintyre, and consequently helps block out swell bound for the beaches there. There are many spots to check including Saligo, Machir and Laggan.

14 Caravans

- **Break type**: Beach break.
- **Conditions**: Medium swells, offshore in easterly winds.
- **Hazards/tips**: Access near the caravan park.
- **Sleeping**: Kintyre ▶ p199.

Back on the mainland, Caravans is just off the A83. This beach break with rocks breaks through the tides, but picks up less swell than the spots further south. Works best from low on the push but can be disappointingly gutless. Check the banks near the rivermouth for a bit more consistency. As the name suggests, this break is close to the caravan park.

15 Graveyards

- **Break type**: Beach break.
- **Conditions**: Medium swells, offshore in easterly winds.
- **Hazards/tips**: Access by the graveyard.
- **Sleeping**: Kintyre ▶ p199.

A beach break with more rocks that picks up a bit more swell than Caravans. Just one of many spots along this stretch of beach that have shifting banks and work through the tides. These breaks like swell from a westerly direction or a big, clean northwesterly swell. Check the charts well before committing to the journey.

16 Westport

- **Break type**: Beach break.
- **Conditions**: Medium swells, offshore in easterly winds.
- **Hazards/tips**: Most consistent break in area.
- **Sleeping**: Kintyre ▶ p199.

At the northern end of Machrihanish beach sits an area of beach break that seems to be the most consistent swell catcher in the area. A fickle break that ranges from horrible to cranking. Catch it good and it's the perfect reward for

Floater, Western Scotland

West Scotland, Cotton Club

Orchid orchard

the drive, catch it gutless and dribbling and you'll pull your hair out. Can handle a decent-sized, clean swell though.

17 Machrihanish

- ⊙ **Break type**: Beach break.
- ⊙ **Conditions**: Medium westerly swells, offshore in easterly winds.
- ⊙ **Hazards/tips**: Schizophrenic beach ranging from gutless to cranking.
- ⊙ **Sleeping**: Kintyre ▸▸ *p199*.

Probably the best known of the west coast breaks, Machrihanish has exploded in popularity over the past few years. There is a growing crew of local surfers in the surrounding villages, which means there will pretty much be guys in the water whenever it gets good. This big expanse of beach looks like it should pick up plenty of swell but in reality the swell direction is critical. Jamie from Clan in Glasgow sums it up like this: "It's a mini-mal kind of wave with occasional sparks of brilliance every 15-20 trips." Scotland's only shaper Martin McQueenie agrees: "It's quite a weak wave, often looks better than it turns out to be." On the rare occasions when there is a massive swell running, check out Dunaverty to the south.

Dune reclamation...watch your step

Ardnamurchan Peninsula

The most westerly point of mainland Britain, this is a wild and rugged peninsula accessed by winding, single track meaning progress is slow. Kilchoan, the main village, is home to a post office, shop, petrol station and seasonal TIC.

⊙ Sleeping

C-D Sonachan Hotel, T01971 510211, 3 miles from the Ardnamurchan Point and set in 1000 acres of land, it really is in the middle of nowhere. As well as reasonable B&B they have a self catering, bedsit-style facility sleeping up to 6 from £60 a night.
Camping Glenview Caravan Park, further east along the A861, T01967 402123, is open to campers year-round. **Resipole Farm Caravan Park**, between the A861 and the Sunart Loch, T01967 431235, is open to campers Mar-Oct with statics to hire from £235 per week. Year-round they have wooden lodges to rent sleeping 4 from £275 per week. **Self catering Tigh na Cladach**, T01972 510285. This former croft house is just back from the seafront at Portuairk and well positioned to access Sanna Bay by foot. Sleeps 6 from £260 per week, open year-round.

Coll

The beautiful beaches and giant sand dunes of Coll are the first stop on the ferry from Oban to Tiree (see Tiree Getting there, opposite). The port and village of Arinagour is home to half the island's residents plus the village's main stores, hotel and amenities.

DEMI TAYLOR

Sleeping

L-A Coll Hotel, Arinagour, T01879 230334, is a relaxed small hotel with great views over the harbour. Good food available from great steak and onion baguettes for a fiver to sumptuous Coll lobster at £20 plus.
B First Port of Coll, Arinagour, T01879 230262, have B&B facilities from £25 and self-catering accommodation sleeping 5-6 from £200 per week Mar-Oct. They are also a café and restaurant dishing up good quality snacks and meals from curry to steaks to pasta.

Tiree

Regularly blasted by strong winds, Tiree has fast become a favourite with windsurfers who flock to the island every Oct for the **Wave Classic**. Despite this, the island, warmed by the Gulf Stream, enjoys a mild climate and holds Scotland's sunshine record. The main village Scarinish has everything you need including a post office, toilets, Co-op, bank as well as cafés and restaurants.

Getting there

Air Although **British Airways**, T0870 8509850, operate a Glasgow-Tiree service Mon-Sat on behalf of Logan Air, no Logan Air flights will accept surfboards.
Ferries CalMac, T08705 6500000, www.calmac.co.uk, operates a good ferry service from Oban on the western mainland, via Coll, to Tiree (around 3 hrs). Oct-Mar they run 3 services a week with singles costing from around £10 per foot passenger and £60 for a van. Mar-Oct they have a daily service from £12.50 per foot passenger, £75 for a van. Services between Coll and Tiree cost from £3.50 per person and from £18.50 for a van. If you need to overnight in Oban, **F Jeremy Inglis Hostel**, Airds Cres near the station,

Flat spells

Tiree

Bike A great way to explore the island is by bike. **Millhouse Hostel**, Cornaigmore, T01879 220435, hire bikes out from £8 a day as does **The Lodge**, Gott Bay, T01879 220368.
Golf Get 9 holes in at **Vaul GC**, T01879 220729. **The Lodge** (see above) hires out clubs.
Horse riding Tiree on Horseback, T01879 220881, run treks for novices and experts.
Windsurfing If the wind won't stop, don't fight it. Try your hand at kitesurfing or windsurfing, whatever your level, Mar-Dec, with **Wild Diamond Windsurf**, T01879 220399.

Islay

Bike hire Bowmore Post Office, 01496 850488, and **Mountain Bike Hire**, Port Charlotte, T01496 810366.

Kintyre

Bike hire The Bike Shop, Longrow in Campbeltown.
Cinema The Picture House, Hall St, T01586 553657, has been around since 1913 and shows current releases every night except Fri.
Golf Get a round (or just 9 holes) in at the **Machrihanish GC**, T01586 810213 or the **Dunaverty GC**, Southend, T01586 830677.
Skating North of Tarbert on the A83 at Ardrishaig is a skate park with ¼ pipe, mini ramp, fun box and grind rail.

17 Machrihanish

Beachwalk, Western Scotland

T01631 565065, is open year-round, a great stop over with personal, off-the-wall touches and extremely cheap from around £8.

🛏 Sleeping

B Scarinish Hotel, by the harbour, T01879 220308, runs a decent B&B with a residents' lounge kitted out with books and games and a restaurant and bar downstairs. **D-E Millhouse Hostel**, Cornaigmore, T01879 220435, is a self-catering facility with a large open-plan kitchen. Open year-round, they have dorm beds from £12, doubles from £15 and a wetsuit drying room. Within walking distance from the beaches, it comes recommended. **Self catering Mackays Cottage**, T01301 702425, on the southwest of the island overlooks the mile long Balephuil Bay. Open year-round, the traditional cottage sleeps 5-6 in 2 rooms from £150 per

week. **Camping** There are no official campsites on the island but responsible **free camping** is tolerated. Ask the landowner's permission first.

🍴 Eating

The Cobbled Cow in Crossapol is a lovely café specializing in reasonably priced, seriously good home cooking and is a good lunchtime stop. Despite looking fairly bizarre, **The Glassary** in Sandaig on the western coast serves up good, moderately-priced lunches and dinners in a large restaurant and conservatory. Suds at **Wild Diamond** recommends the **Scarinish Hotel** for decent portions of well-priced bar food – from £5 – plus **The Lodge** at Gott Bay.

🅾 Directory

Internet Get online at the High School Library, Cornaigmore. **Surf shops** Wild Diamond Surf, T07793

063849, www.surfschool scotland.com, is a BSA-registered surf school based at Ballevulin, open Mar-Dec and run by Scottish surfer 'Suds'. Wild Diamond also hire out reasonably priced basic surf equipment including wetsuits and boards. **Wild Diamond Windsurf**, Gott Bay, T01879 220399, run a windsurf shop which also stocks surf basics including wax, leashes etc. Open Mar-Oct and Nov-Feb by arrangement, T07712159205.
Transport Tiree airport, T01879 220309.

Islay

The most southerly of the Inner Hebrides, Islay (pronounced *eye-la*) is all about birds and booze – wintering geese and 7 whisky distilleries to be exact. Port Ellen at the south of the island is the main village while

Bowmore, north of Laggan Bay on the A846, the administrative centre, is home to the TIC, post office and leisure centre.

Getting there
Air Although British Airways, T0870 8509850, operate a Glasgow-Islay service taking 45 mins Mon-Sat on behalf of Logan Air, no Logan Air flights will accept surfboards.
Ferries CalMac, T08705 6500000, www.calmac.co.uk, operate a daily service between Kennacraig on Kintyre and Port Askaig on the east and Port Ellen on the south coast. The journey takes just over 2 hrs and costs around £8 per passenger and from £42 for a van. Kennacraig is basically a ferry port so the fishing town of Tarbert, at the northern end of Kintyre, makes a handy stopover on your way to Islay. **C-D Springside B&B**, Pier Rd, T01880 820413, is a traditional fishing cottage serving breakfast to fit with ferry times.

Sleeping
B Kintra Farm, Kintra Beach, Port Ellen, T01496 302051, has a B&B, self-catering cottages as well as beachside camping facilities Apr-Sept. **D Abbotsford Guest House**, Bruichladdich, T01496 850587, is small but charming and one of the cheapest B&Bs on the island. **E Islay Youth Hostel**, Port Charlotte, T0870 0041128, is part of the SYA and housed above the wildlife centre, off the A847, open Mar-Sep. **Self catering** The smart **Machrie Hotel**, T01496 302310, above Laggan Bay, has a series of 'lodges' sleeping up to 6 people year-round (2 twins and a sofa bed) from £50 per night – reductions for longer stays. The hotel also has a bar and restaurant serving up a range of food.

Directory
Tourist information Bowmore, T01496 810254, is friendly, helpful and open year-round. **Transport** Islay airport, T01496 302022.

Kintyre

This peninsula, attached to the rest of mainland Scotland by a thread, is practically an island in terms of geography and feel. The A83 connects the 2 main towns of Tarbert to the north and Campbeltown to the south; below lies the Mull of Kintyre, immortalized by Paul, Linda and Wings.

Sleeping
B-C Springfield House, Campbeltown High St, T01586 552080, is a pretty B&B with shared bathroom facilities. **C-D Glen Mhairi**, Craigowan Rd, T01586 552952, overlooks Campbeltown and is one of the cheapest B&Bs in the area. **Camping Machrihanish Caravan & Camping Park**, T01586 816366, is in a prime location overlooking both the golf course and the bay at Machrihanish. Open Mar-Oct, they also have 2 wooden wigwams to rent, sleeping 5 or 3 on foam mattresses.

Large wigwam from £35 per night for 4 people. It is within walking distance to the **Beachcomber Bar and Restaurant** overlooking the bay. **Musadale Holiday Park**, T01583 421207, on the main A83, is open 1 Apr-mid Oct to tourers. It also has statics to hire from £220 per week for 6 but does not allow single sex groups.
Self catering Carraig, T01706 827767, is a 4-bedroom bungalow with fantastic access to Machrihanish Bay – the garden backs onto it. Great option for groups from around £450 per week.

Directory
Surf shops Clan Surf Shop, Hyndland St, T0141 3396523, www.clanskates.co.uk, might be all the way over in Glasgow (about a 2½-hr drive) but it is one of the closest surf shops to this stretch of coastline stocking all the essentials as well as offering equipment hire and repair. Jamie Blair of Clan also runs a BSA surf school with regular trips to the west coast.
Tourist information Campbeltown Pier, T08707 200609, open year-round.

MARK LUMSDEN

Northern lights

North Wales gold

TURTLE

Don't miss...

Break Freshwater West - this is one of the most consistent spots in Wales and has something for everyone from dredging barrels to mellow peaks ▶▶ *p217*.

Sleeping Langland Cove Guest House - run by shaper/photographer/legend The Gill, his B&B overlooking Langland Bay is second to none ▶▶ *p232*.

Flat Spells Snowdonia National Park - Yr Wyddfa, Wales' highest peak, offers awesome views across the Llyn Peninsula ▶▶ *p212*.

Watch *All Day Breakfast* DVD with classic Wales footage featuring Guts - freesurf action to find out what you've been missing.

Irish Sea

Atlantic Ocean

Cardigan Bay

Bristol Channel

ENGLAND

Holyhead, Anglesey, Bangor, Llandudno, Conwy, Rhyl, Prestatyn, Colwyn Bay, Denbigh, Mold, Caernarfon, Ruthin, Wrexham, Yr Wyddfa (Snowdon), Betws-y-Coed, Y Bala, Llangollen, Llyn Peninsula, Barmouth, Dolgellau, Welshpool, Machynlleth, Newtown, Aberystwyth, Cambrian Mountains, New Quay, Llandrindod Wells, Cardigan, Builth Wells, Fishguard, Llandovery, St David's, Carmarthen, Brecon, Haverfordwest, St Brides Bay, Merthyr Tydfil, Abergavenny, Milford Haven, Ammanford, Tenby, Carmarthen Bay, Llanelli, Swansea, Newport, Porthcawl, Bridgend, Cardiff

p204, p209, p215, p222

Motorway, A Road, B Road, Minor Road, Airports, Ferries

20 km / 20 miles

Whether it's a secret point hidden somewhere in lush scenery on the western coastline or a thundering breakwater overlooked by an ominous, towering black industrial plant, you will find hard-charging committed surfers at every stop on this Celtic coastline.

To say that the Welsh are a proud people would be like saying the French enjoy the odd glass of wine. Nowhere is their patriotism better demonstrated than in the national sport of rugby. It's as if all the years of struggle were distilled into this one activity, a way to put one over on the old enemy, the English. In surfing too, the Welsh are equally driven. They have produced some of Europe's best surfers, guys like Carwyn Williams, Pete Jones, Chris 'Guts' Griffiths, Swinno, Frenchie, and Matt Stephens.

When the surfing is over, the Welsh will give any nationality a run for its money in the partying stakes. As legendary party king Carwyn says, "When it comes to the social scene, Mumbles is madder than anywhere in the world!" And at any international gathering, it won't be long before a rousing rendition of *Land of My Fathers* is heard from the Welsh corner.

Introduction

Wales

Wales rating

Surf
★★★

Cost of living
★★★

Nightlife
★★★★

Accommodation
★★★★

Places to visit
★★★★

Surfing North and West Wales

Come home to a real fire – buy a holiday cottage in Wales. An old joke that harks back to an era in the 1970s when fierce Welsh nationalism and the problem of second homes was the hot topic in the rural villages of North Wales. Today the lack of affordable housing is a problem faced by many of Britain's coastal communities.

The north of Wales has a solid core of Welsh language speakers and although 'The Valleys' of the south were the engine of the Welsh economy, those trading links also brought the south closer to the old enemy – the English. The northern counties, with their rural communities, seemed to take pride in their isolation from their neighbour across the border.

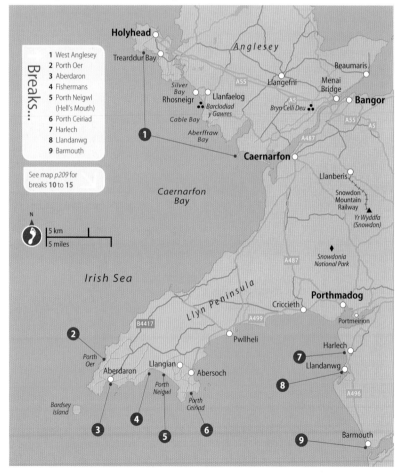

Breaks...

1 West Anglesey
2 Porth Oer
3 Aberdaron
4 Fishermans
5 Porth Neigwl
   (Hell's Mouth)
6 Porth Ceiriad
7 Harlech
8 Llandanwg
9 Barmouth

See map p209 for
breaks **10** to **15**

In surfing terms, North and West Wales are regions that can have great wave-riding potential. The beaches around Porth Neigwl, with its ready-made surf population in neighbouring Abersoch, are popular as are the breaks around university town Aberystwyth. The points inbetween remain relatively quiet. But sitting on their doorstep are the large metropolitan areas of Liverpool, Manchester and the Midlands, whose hordes of wave-hungry city surfers descend on the region with the advent of every new swell. Like the surfers of Northeast England, locals have become excellent meteorologists and with a similarly narrow swell window, they constantly scan the charts for those tell-tale low pressures that push precious southwesterly swells up the Irish Sea.

"What's so special about surfing in North Wales is the fickleness of it all. When it's good it's like everywhere else, but it doesn't get good very often. When it gets good, it's appreciated. Everyone drops everything. Work comes second." Spout, The West Coast Surf Shop.

Coastline

West Wales is a series of long, westerly-facing beaches interspersed with points. As swells come mainly from the southwest, the points tend to predominantly produce lefts – some of which can be very high quality. In the north, the Llyn Peninsula reaches out across the top of Cardigan Bay and sits waiting for the swell to hit. Its sandy beaches are exposed to the southwest trade winds, but when conditions combine and the wind switches, can have excellent waves.

Localism

Numbers in North Wales are still surprisingly small. But, as Spout explains: "There is a certain resentment about the influx of surfers, especially amongst the Anglesey people. There is an underlying anti-English thing anyway, and the graffiti on the walls is mostly anti-English as opposed to anti-surfer. Some of the local Welsh surfers use that as part of their general anti-English thoughts about people coming in to surf here. Obviously with the greater numbers comes more strain. It's going to happen everywhere but we seem to be less affected than other areas because most of our surf spots are so fickle." On the west coast, these points naturally become the focus of much attention when the conditions combine.

Top local surfers

In North Wales Kieran Evans is sponsored by local surf brand O'Shea. Brothers Chris and Leigh Hookes can be found surfing the Llyn, and the west coast is home territory for surf photographer Roger Sharp, as well as established local surfers like Steve Baxter and Tony Jeff.

Getting around

North Wales is well-serviced by A roads such as the A55 and A5 which feed Anglesey, or the A487 that hugs this length of coastline and feeds into a tangle of B roads on the Llyn Peninsula. Friday afternoon and evening commuter traffic can be heavy.

North and West Wales board guide

Longboard
Shaper: The Gill, ODD Surfboards

» 9'1" x 22½" x 2⅜" for Dan Harris.
» Flexible longboard for three times Welsh Longboard Champion.
» Helps make the most out of the inconsistent west and north coast surf.
» Rounded pin makes it a great board for when the west coast points are firing. Light, modern template for ease of turning.

Modern Fish
Shaper: The Gill, ODD Surfboards

» 6'2" x 19" x 2⅜".
» Average surfer 6'4" x 19½" x 2⅜".
» Flat bottomed with a fuller nose to help wave catching and give a neutral feel.
» Double concave through the swallowtail for drive, designed for average surf on the beaches of North Wales.
» When the surf picks up, use bigger fins to create a loose board in good surf.

(i) Boards by **ODD Boards**
Factory: Freelap Surfboards, Porthcawl, Wales
T 01656 744691
www.oddsurfboards.co.uk
gill@eurotelemail.net

Breaks

1 West Anglesey

- **Break type**: Beach break with rocks.
- **Conditions**: Big southwesterly swells, offshore in northeasterly winds.
- **Hazards/tips**: Rips, windblown, popular with windsurfers.
- **Sleeping**: Anglesey ▸▸ *p211*

The west coast of Anglesey allows plenty of opportunity for exploration when the right combination of wind and swell occurs. Trearddur Bay, Silver Bay, Rhosneigr, Cable Bay and Aberffraw Bay are all worth checking in huge swells but don't expect too much and you might be pleasantly surprised.

2 Porth Oer

- **Break type**: Sheltered beach break.
- **Conditions**: Big southwesterly storms, westerly winds.
- **Hazards/tips**: Very inconsistent, rocks on inside.
- **Sleeping**: Llyn Peninsula ▸▸ *p211*.

On the north coast of the Llyn Peninsula, this is the one of the spots that's worth checking when Porth Neigwl is maxed out. Chances are there will be a crowd on the rights and lefts, which can be wedgy and are popular with mat-riders. Watch out for rocks on the inside.

3 Aberdaron

- **Break type**: Beach break.
- **Conditions**: Southwesterly swell, offshore in northerly winds.
- **Hazards/tips**: Also has right point over boulders.
- **Sleeping**: Llyn Peninsula ▸▸ *p211*.

An open, sandy bay facing southwesterly with beach break peaks and a right-hander that breaks off rocks at the western end of the bay. Works on all tides and can have some excellent waves in the right conditions. Check on a similar swell to Porth Neigwl.

4 Fishermans

- **Break type**: Right-hand reef.
- **Conditions**: Southwesterly swell, offshore in northeasterly winds.
- **Hazards/tips**: Crowds, difficult access.
- **Sleeping**: Llyn Peninsula ▸▸ *p211*.

A good quality wave that is also fairly consistent and so tends to draw a regular local crew. Doesn't hold a crowd well. Access can be tricky which means it's probably best left to experienced surfers. Has a reputation for being the area's most 'local' wave.

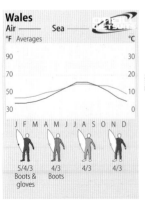

Wales
Air ——— Sea
°F Averages °C

90			30
70			20
50			10
30			0

J F M A M J J A S O N D

| 5/4/3 Boots & gloves | 4/3 Boots | 4/3 | 4/3 |

TURTLE

2 Porth Oer

Surfers' tales

Tommo Jones, Secret Spot, West Wales

Coming Home in a Body Bag

By Dan Harris, three-times Welsh Longboard Champion

The thing about Welsh surfing is that you have to have a sense of humour. One year we went on a trip to Ireland with the Aberavon surf club, and with us was Splinter, a bodyboarder, who was about 17 at the time. It was his first trip to Ireland and one of the guys noticed that after he'd got on the ferry back home to Fishguard, he'd thrown away his boarding card. So they started winding him up about needing your boarding card to get back into the country. Splinter piped up and said: "But I've lost mine, boys, what do I do?" All the older guys were saying to him: "Oh you've blown it now. With this IRA stuff – they're going to send you back to Ireland."

"Oh I can't," he said. "I've got college on Monday. What shall I do? I've got my passport." Everyone's pulling his leg and pretending to be dead serious, saying that a passport wasn't enough. Then someone said: "I've got an idea."

"What we should do is take one of the longboards out of one of the bags, and you'll have to hide in there and pretend to be a board. That's the only way you'll get through, Splint."

So they convinced him to get into the bag. He slides inside and he even had his hands up trying to be the middle fin of a longboard. While Splinter was lying in the bag, getting into character, one of the lads had gone off to find the customs official, and told him about the wind-up. So the official comes over and says: "What's going on here then? We've had reports that people are being smuggled in from Ireland in board bags." The board bag starts twitching and the fin sticks up even higher. The official starts poking the bag with a stick and suddenly there are all these muffled cries. The bag starts shaking and someone goes: "Oh Splint, what did you do that for? You've given the game away." He replied: "He just poked me in the eye." So the customs guy gets him out of the bag and pretends to be all official, marching him down the long line of traffic towards the office. Splinter has visions of being sent back to Ireland and pulls out his passport saying: "But I'm a British citizen!" In the end the guy couldn't hold out any longer and started laughing. So did everyone else. Splinter realised it was a wind up and was cursing and swearing. That's the thing about the Welsh scene – it's character building. And there certainly lot of characters.

5 Porth Neigwl (Hell's Mouth)

- **Break type**: Beach break with reef.
- **Conditions**: Southwesterly swell, off-shore in northeasterly winds.
- **Hazards/tips**: Always draws a crowd.
- **Sleeping**: Llyn Peninsula ›› *p211*.

This sandy bay is North Wales' most famous spot and the main indicator beach. Porth Neigwl has a series of peaks of various quality, depending on the sandbars. The **Corner** is a left-hander found at the far southern end of the beach. This break peaks and peels along the rocky bottom, finishing on sand. The **Reef** is to the north of the corner and is a decent quality right that always attracts a crowd.

6 Porth Ceiriad

- **Break type**: Beach break.
- **Conditions**: Southwesterly swell, offshore in northeasterly winds.
- **Hazards/tips**: Crowds, wedgy waves.
- **Sleeping**: Llyn Peninsula ›› *p211*.

This is a popular, high tide break with a series of peaks to choose from. Swell also bounces back off the cliff and meets in a sudden, wedging, barrelling left near the eastern end of the bay. This is a heavy wave that is a regular board breaker. "With waves along the length of the bay, it's probably best to leave the wedge for the locals, " advises surf photographer The Gill. Works best on the push.

7 Harlech

- **Break type**: Beach break.
- **Conditions**: Southwest swell, offshore in easterly winds.
- **Hazards/tips**: Inconsistent beach.
- **Sleeping**: Llyn Peninsula/ Aberystwyth ›› *p211/213*.

On the edge of the Snowdonia National Park, this long stretch of beach is a fairly average, fairly inconsistent spot. It needs a big swell to work with winds from the east, but even then it will be quiet as there are better spots worth searching out.

8 Llandanwg

- **Break type**: Beach break.
- **Conditions**: Southwesterly swell, offshore in east/south-easterly winds.
- **Hazards/tips**: Quiet beach.
- **Sleeping**: Llyn Peninsula/ Aberystwyth ›› *p211/213*.

Worth checking if the strong southwesterlies swing round to the southeast. A series of sandbanks of variable quality work through all tides. The rivermouth can have good waves but is best left to experienced surfers due to currents.

5 Porth Neigwl

3 Aberdaron ›› *p206*

6 Porth Ceiriad

9 Barmouth

- **Break type**: Beach break.
- **Conditions**: Southwesterly swell, offshore in easterly winds.
- **Hazards/tips**: Quiet beach, currents in rivermouth.
- **Sleeping**: Llyn Peninsula/ Aberystwyth ▸▸ *p211/213*.

Travelling south on the A4968, this series of sandbanks around the rivermouth can produce some good waves. Banks tend to shift around and inexperienced surfers should beware of the currents. Also worth checking the beach to the north of the rivermouth.

10 Llwyngwril

- **Break type**: Left point break.
- **Conditions**: Southwesterly swell, offshore in southeasterly winds.
- **Hazards/tips**: Advanced surfers only.
- **Sleeping**: Llyn Peninsula/ Aberystwyth ▸▸ *p211/213*.

Good quality lefts over boulders that fires in big southwesterly swells. Mainly two peaks out in front of the caravan park. Best at high tide. Walling long rides.

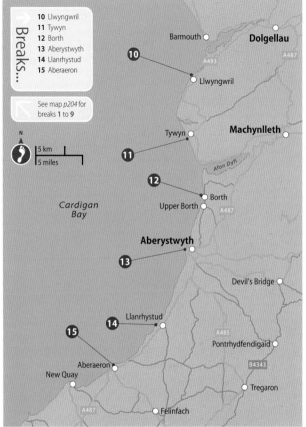

Breaks...

10 Llwyngwril
11 Tywyn
12 Borth
13 Aberystwyth
14 Llanrhystud
15 Aberaeron

See map *p204* for breaks **1** to **9**

N

5 km
5 miles

Cardigan Bay

Barmouth
Dolgellau
A493
A487
Llwyngwril

Tywyn
Machynlleth
Afon Dyfi

Borth
Upper Borth
A487

Aberystwyth

Devil's Bridge

Llanrhystud
A485
Pontrhydfendigaid
B4343

Aberaeron
New Quay
Tregaron

A487
Felinfach

Secret spot Welsh rivermouth

Secret point Harry Cromwell, West Wales

4 Fishermans ▶▶ *p206*

11 Tywyn

- **Break type**: Beach break.
- **Conditions**: Southwest swell, offshore in easterly/northeasterly winds.
- **Hazards/tips**: Long, quiet beach.
- **Sleeping**: Aberystwyth ▶▶ *p213*.

Just off the coastal A493 this long, open beach runs south to the Afon Dyff (River Dovey). It is normally pretty quiet and has plenty of room to spread out – not that it ever gets that crowded. A fairly average series of peaks that work through all tides.

12 Borth

- **Break type**: Beach break.
- **Conditions**: Southwesterly swells, offshore in easterly winds.
- **Hazards/tips**: Big, mellow beach.
- **Sleeping**: Aberystwyth ▶▶ *p213*.

A long stretch of shifting peaks that produce pretty mellow waves. The wave on the point to the south offers some shelter from the prevailing southerly winds. The beach is rarely busy so a good spot for learners. Works on all tides, but because it tends to be a bit weak, a pushing tide helps.

13 Aberystwyth

- **Break type**: Reef break, peak.
- **Conditions**: Big swells, offshore in easterly/southeasterly winds.
- **Hazards/tips**: Crowds, backwash at high.
- **Sleeping**: Aberystwyth ▶▶ *p213*.

Harbour Trap is a peak with hollow rights at low tide and long lefts at mid tide. This flat reef works from low to three-quarter tide. **Castle reef** produces a right-hander opposite the Trap at mid tide. **Queens** beach break works best from mid to low tide. **Bath Rocks** is a hollow reef for advanced surfers only, worth trying at high. It needs to be 6 ft on the south coast to work here and it's always busy when it does. Parking on the promenade. Big student surf club.

14 Llanrhystud

- ⚑ **Break type**: Left-hand point.
- ☁ **Conditions**: Southwesterly swell, offshore in southeasterly winds.
- ❶ **Hazards/tips**: Not for beginners.
- ☐ **Sleeping**: Aberystwyth/Aberaeron ⏵ *p213*.

A left point breaking over sand and rocks that works best from mid to high tide. Worth checking if southwesterlies switch to southeasterlies. Turn off from A487.

15 Aberaeron

- ⚑ **Break type**: Left point.
- ☁ **Conditions**: Big swells, offshore in southeasterly winds.
- ❶ **Hazards/tips**: Crowds, popular with longboarders.
- ☐ **Sleeping**: Aberaeron ⏵ *p213*

Boulder point that breaks about six times a year. Long walling lefthanders break on all tides, good for longboards. Busy when it's on. Only gets to about 4-5 ft. Needs to be 6 ft plus on the south coast before it starts breaking. Outside village but visible from the road. Right peaks on inside.

THE GILL

Secret point West Wales

Listings

Anglesey

Historically known as the breadbasket of Wales for its fertile and lush lands (read pretty wet and rainy), the isle of Anglesey is often overlooked by the cars that burn over the picturesque bridges and up the A55 to Holyhead and the ferry to Dublin. As a result, Holyhead is packed with cafes and pubs. However, the island has always been a popular holiday spot and today wakeboarders, windsurfers and jetskiers flock here.

☐ Sleeping

There are plenty of good sleeping options across the island. Close to the main break at Rhosneigr **C-D Fferam Fawr**, T01407 810026, in Llanfaelog offers year round B&B with access to a drying room as well as a games room and self-catering options in the grounds of the working Pensieri Farm. **Camping** For a swanky camping site try **Ty Hen** on Station Rd which also offers static caravans. Ten minutes from the village, open end Mar-Oct, it comes complete with a sauna and pool and prices to reflect the facilities.

Llyn Peninsula

Designated an Area of Outstanding Natural Beauty, this remote, rugged, fluent-Welsh peninsula reaches out towards Bardsey Island or Ynys Enlli – the island of currents. Abersoch, with surf shops, bars and eateries, is the centre of the peninsula for surfers but quieter, more secluded areas can be sought towards the toe and Aberdaron.

☐ Sleeping

For a B&B right on the seafront in **Aberdaron**, try **A-C Ty Newydd**

✳ Snowdonia National Park

Covering more than 2171 sq km in peaks and valleys, Snowdonia National Park is a climber's and walker's haven as well as the home of the highest mountain in Wales. **Yr Wyddfa** (Snowdon) at 3560 ft tall sits on the knuckle of the Llyn Peninsula, and on a clear day offers excellent views.

The best way to tackle Snowdon is via the village of **Llanberis** – take the A487 to Caernarfon and follow the A4068 to the village. From here you have plenty of choice ranging from the serious to the sedentary depending on ability. If walking isn't your thing, the easiest way to travel is on the Snowdon Mountain Railway, which has been carrying the weary uphill for more than 100 years, T0870 4580033, www.snowdonrailway.co.uk. Operating Mar-Oct (weather permitting), Britain's only rack and pinion railway takes the weight off your feet for about an hour, covering the 5-mile journey to the summit and offering breathtaking views (again weather permitting) for £20 return.

The **Llanberis Path** is the most popular route by foot. Following the railway line it takes about three hours on the way up (quicker on the way down). Although considered a fairly easy option, it is a mistake to underestimate the mountain and the unpredictable weather conditions. Boots are a necessity, as are warm clothes and waterproofs, year round, plus food and water. Whatever way you choose to travel, from May-Oct there is an open café at the summit. Check the weather conditions before heading out at the Llanberis Tourist Office or www.metoffice.com.

Stay at the popular The Heights on Llanberis High Street, T01286 871179, with dorms, B&B accommodation and a climbing wall facility. Chow down at the hearty Pete's Eats, also on the High Street, where serious portions of wholesome grub – casserole, chilli, pies – at fair prices will warm up even the coldest of climbers.

Hotel, T01758 760207, which does excellent off-peak deals and has a beach terrace bar to chill out in.

Camping   Aberdaron is home to several campsites including **Caerau Fferm**, T01758 760481, a basic site on a working farm – showers charged at 20p. **Dwyros**, T01758 760295, open Mar-Oct, overlooks the bay, as does

Marfa Mawr, T01758 760264, half a mile outside the village.

Within easy reach of **Porth Neigwl**, there are several good sleeping options. A good choice in Llangian is **C Rhydolion**, T01758 712342. A wing of the farmhouse can be rented for self-catering groups of up to 6 people (good deals can be had off season).

Limited camping is also available. Also in Llangian, **G** Tanralt, www.tanralt.com, with its comfortable bunkhouse-style accommodation, has always been a popular pit-stop with surfers. From £13 per person, including breakfast and free showers, it's easy to understand why.

❷ Eating/drinking

Spout recommends heading to **The Abersoch Power Boat Club**, just back from the seafront on the north side of town, if you want to catch a band. **Mañana** on Lôn Pen Cei in Abersoch is seasonal but popular surf/salsa/pizza kind of place run by a couple of surfers, the Hookes brothers. Don't miss the fajitas. **The Sandpiper** is a fairly pricey, yet busy traditional Italian – but they do serve up some good pizzas.

❶ Directory

Surf shops   There are several surf shops in Abersoch servicing the local and visiting surf communities. **Abersoch Water Sports,** Lon Pont Morgan, T01758 712483, stocks a good range of hardware and clothing. **Offaxis,** Glanafon Garage, T01758 713407, www.offaxis.co.uk, runs a BSA surf school as well as a wakeboarding centre and bike hire facilities. **West Coast Surf Shop** on Lôn Pen Cei sells and hires hardware as well as running a BSA accredited surf school. They also provide a couple of handy surf resources including the Hell's Mouth webcam, updated daily, and 'Spout's prospects for surf', updated by the owner every Thu morning for the weekend crew – check out www.westcoastsurf.co.uk. There's also **Abersoch Surf Shop** on Lôn Engan and **The Boardrider** on the high street.

If you need some inspiration head

to **The Craft Centre,** T01758 713641, www.turtlephotography.co.uk, where northwest Wales photographer **Turtle** has an excellent gallery with images of epic days, classic swells and beautiful landscapes of the Llyn Peninsula.
Tourist information Abersoch Tourist Information, Lôn Pen Cei, T01758 712483, www.abersochtourist info.co.uk, opens seasonally and during weekends throughout the year.

Aberystwyth

Sitting on the west coast on the A487, Welsh nationalism and the Welsh language is alive and kicking in this Victorian resort town, appropriated by students during term time.

🛌 Sleeping

C Yr Hafod, South Marine Terr, T01970 617579, just back from the seafront and the **C-D B&B** on Bridge St, T01970 612550, run by Mrs Williams. Five miles north in the village of Borth, the **E Borth Youth Hostel,** T01970 871498, overlooks the bay and opens Apr-Oct. The **F University,** T01970 621960, rents out single rooms in self-catering student flats outside term time.
Camping There are plenty of sites scattered around the area. You can camp next to the river at **Aberystwyth Holiday Village,** Penparcau Rd, T01970 624211, open Mar-Oct. They also rent static caravans. **Oceanview Caravan Park,** T01970 828425, overlooks North Bay and is open Mar-Oct, also with statics. **Borth** has a couple of camping options: **Brynrodyn Caravan and Leisure Park,** T01970 871472, in Upper Borth, open Jan-Oct, and **Swn-y-Mor Holiday Park,** T01970 871233, off the B4345, open Apr-Oct. Both also have statics available.

Ynys Fergi, T01907 871344, www.camping-ynysfergi-borth.com, on a working farm is basic, cheap and friendly with camping from a fiver.

🍴 Eating/drinking

As a student town there are plenty of cheap places to grab a bite to eat. **Gannets Bistro** on St James Sq is more expensive than some, but is a relaxed place serving up good home cooking using local fish and meat – the steak is very good. **The Treehouse** on Baker St combines an organic shop with a lovely lunchtime café. You can get a bowl of soup and a roll for about £3.50 or something more filling for about £6; it can get packed out but is worth waiting for.
In terms of cafés, **The Dolphin** on Great Darkgate is a winner for bacon and eggs combos, while **The Blue Creek Café** on Princess St has good veggie and more 'exotic' café food. There is no shortage of pubs here and many enjoy extended summer licensing hours including **Rummers** with a beer garden next to the river on Bridge St.

ⓘ Directory

Internet Pricey connection at **Biognosis** on Pier St or head to the library just off Corporation St.
Surf shops The Stormriders Surf Shop, Alexandra Rd, T01970 623363, www.storm-riders.co.uk, near the train station is well stocked with hardware and kit.
Tourist Information Terrace Rd running up towards North Beach, T01970 612125, open year round.

Aberaeron

Heading south on the A487, the port

✪ Flat spells

Ancient Monuments Anglesey is home to Wales's largest chambered tomb **Barclodiad y Gawres,** just south of Rhosneigr. Otherwise known as 'The Giantess's Apronful,' it was constructed around 3000 BC. **Bryn Celli Ddu** just off the A55, with its tomb and burial mound, is also worth a visit.
Bikes Hire a mountain bike from **Offaxis** in Abersoch, T01758 712483, and explore the wild, wet Llyn Peninsula.
Cinema Catch a movie at the **Commodore** on Bath St, Aberystwyth.
Golf Get a round in at the 18 hole **Abersoch GC,** Golf Rd, T01758 712622, www.abersochgolf.co.uk, with fees from £25; **Borth & Ynyslas GC** in Borth, T01970 871202; or **Aberystwuth GC,** Bryn-y-Mor, T01970 615104.
Portmeirion Just off the A487 to Porthmadog, T01766 770000. This kitsch, eccentric village created and designed in a swathe of architectural styles by Clough Williams-Ellis was also the set for the cult 1960s TV programme *The Prisoner*. Entry £5.50.
Skate Head south to New Quay and the skate park on Church Rd with mini-ramp, fun box and free entry.

of Aberaeron is home to the **Aeron Coast Caravan Park,** Norton Rd, T017974 202247. It's a bit more pricey than other sites in the area, offers statics and is open Mar-Oct.

Surfing Southwest Wales

The southwest of Wales is a land of rolling greenery and beautiful rugged coastline in the finest Celtic tradition. Tourists are drawn here from all over the world to sample the stunning scenery and crystal clear waters of the Pembrokeshire National Park. Its jagged coastline provides an immense area to explore for waves, the lure of uncrowded spots to be found just around the next bend in the road. The sandy expanses of St Brides Bay and Freshwater West are home to excellent beach break waves for surfers of all abilities, and there are always hidden reefs for those who like a real challenge.

Heading out to Fresh West with the dawn of a new swell, the red flags on the military firing range promising an offshore day, you know that surfers from the whole of south Wales will be drawn here. As three-times Welsh longboard champion Dan Harris says: "Fresh West is where I started surfing. My parents headed down there every summer – there are plenty of places to camp and it's a nice open beach. Everyone surfs their own areas in Wales but seem to meet up at Fresh West – everyone heads there in the summer. There are loads of different waves, it's pretty consistent, pretty popular. It can get crowded but there's no localism, no hassle."

Coastline

The Pembrokeshire coastline was designated a national park in 1952 and has been a huge tourist draw ever since the days the Victorians descended on Tenby. The wild coast, with sheltered bays and windswept cliffs, is a perfect place to explore when the swells kick in. It has the advantage of bays facing virtually all points of the compass meaning that as long as the swell is big enough, you can usually find a sheltered spot somewhere. The huge beach at Freshwater West is Southwest Wales's most consistent swell catcher.

Southwest Wales board guide

Thruster
Shaper: The Gill, ODD Surfboards

- ➤➤ 6' x 18¼" x 2¼" for Harry Cromwell.
- ➤➤ For average surfer 6'4" x 19" x 2¼".
- ➤➤ Good all-round, everyday board for typical Welsh beaches and reefs.
- ➤➤ Squash tail with more width and nose.
- ➤➤ Performs in good surf but with enough area to ride out any slow sections on the beach breaks.

Semi-gun
Shaper: The Gill, ODD Surfboards

- ➤➤ 6'7" x 18½" x 2⅜" for Isaac Kibblewhite.
- ➤➤ Narrow screwdriver or rounded pintail.
- ➤➤ Double concave bottom for rail to rail, down the line speed and stability.
- ➤➤ Designed for 6-8ft hollow waves when the Pembrokeshire reefs are firing.

(i) Boards by **ODD Boards**
Factory: Freelap Surfboards, Porthcawl, Wales. T01656 744691
www.oddsurfboards.co.uk
gill@eurotelemail.net

Localism

Pembrokeshire has some of the best-known spots in Wales and numbers have been steadily rising over the last few years to a point where uncrowded sessions are getting rare. Freshwater West is a large bay with plenty of room to spread out, as is St Brides Bay. Peaks like Broadhaven South and reefs like Manorbier are becoming increasingly competitive, but the likelihood of outright localism is low. Don't push it – follow the usual rules and there should be no problems.

Top local surfers

Pete Bounds is a former Welsh champion and Welsh team coach. Luke and Harry Cromwell are promising up-and-coming surfers while other top locals include Dave Jones, Dean Gough, Toby and Sam Bradley, plus former *Surf* magazine editor Alf Alderson and longboarder Bob Rogers.

Getting around

There seems to be a boundary line between the breaks to the south of Pembroke, such as Fresh West, Manorbier and Bosherton and those to the north such as Marloes and St Brides Bay. The A40 into Haverfordwest leads out to the breaks north of Pembroke, and the A477 from St Clear makes a beeline for the southwesterly breaks.

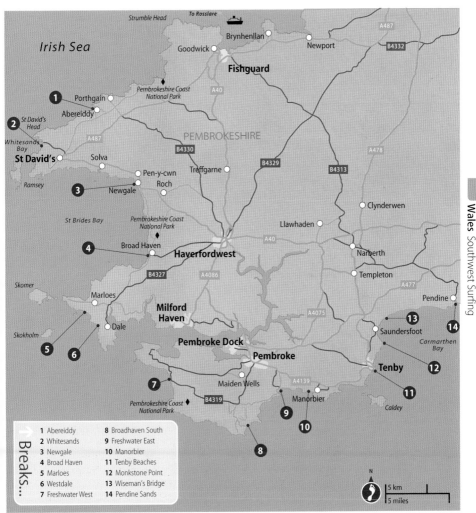

Breaks...

1 Abereiddy	8 Broadhaven South
2 Whitesands	9 Freshwater East
3 Newgale	10 Manorbier
4 Broad Haven	11 Tenby Beaches
5 Marloes	12 Monkstone Point
6 Westdale	13 Wiseman's Bridge
7 Freshwater West	14 Pendine Sands

Breaks

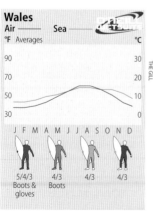

1 Abereiddy

- **Break type**: Slab reef.
- **Conditions**: Big swells, offshore in a southeasterly/southerly wind.
- **Hazards/tips**: Shallow reef. Beach car park.
- **Sleeping**: St David's ▸▸ *p220*.

When Whitesands is too big, check this left-hand reef – it's shallow, wedgy, breaks at mid tide and is really best left to advanced surfers. Found on the south side of the bay.

2 Whitesands

- **Break type**: Beach break.
- **Conditions**: Medium swells, offshore in southeasterly/easterly winds.
- **Hazards/tips**: Crowds. Parking near beach.
- **Sleeping**: St David's ▸▸ *p220*.

Whitesands is a popular and flexible break that works through the tides. There are peaks from sandbanks along the beach and at low tide to the north of the bay is the **Elevator**, a hollow right. There are crowds at the Elevator and surf schools and kayakers on the beach. Picks up less swell than Freshwater West.

3 Newgale

- **Break type**: Beach break.
- **Conditions**: Small to medium swells, offshore in easterly winds.
- **Hazards/tips**: Good for beginners, large uncrowded beach.
- **Sleeping**: St Brides Bay ▸▸ *p220*.

At the northern edge of St Brides Bay, Newgale is part of the Pembrokeshire Coast National Park so enjoys good water quality, and has plenty of room to spread out. It is a good spot for beginners when waves are small. Faces west, so picks up plenty of swell. Beach parking, easy access.

4 Broad Haven

- **Break type**: Beach break.
- **Conditions**: Medium swells, offshore in south/southeasterly winds.
- **Hazards/tips**: Not crowded, flexible beaches. Good for beginners.
- **Sleeping**: St Brides Bay ▸▸ *p220*.

When Newgale gets big, try Broad Haven and Little Haven at the southern end of St Brides Bay. They are good beach breaks with more protection from the wind. They work on all tides and have plenty of parking.

Wales

Air ——— Sea ———

°F Averages °C

90 — 30
70 — 20
50 — 10
30 — 0

J F M A M J J A S O N D

5/4/3 | 4/3 | 4/3 | 4/3
Boots & gloves | Boots | |

THE GILL

Secret spot Southwest left

216

5 Marloes

- 🌐 **Break type**: Beach break.
- 🌊 **Conditions**: Small to medium swells, offshore in northerlies.
- ❶ **Hazards/tips**: Quiet beach, walk from National Trust car park.
- 💤 **Sleeping**: Marloes ▸▸ p221.

A peaky beach break that picks up lots of swell and works up to three-quarters tide. Watch out for scattered rocks on the beach. Walk from car park down track. NB Car crime can be a problem here.

6 Westdale

- 🌐 **Break type**: Beach break.
- 🌊 **Conditions**: Small to medium swells, offshore in easterly wind.
- ❶ **Hazards/tips**: Quiet bay, not suitable for beginners.
- 💤 **Sleeping**: Marloes ▸▸ p221.

Westdale is a bay just north of Milford Haven inlet. It has a left at south and right at north. Best from low to three-quarter tide, as it is a bit rocky at high tide. Walk from the village car park. There is also a surf school based here.

66 99

What's special about surfing in South Wales? Nothing! No, we've got a great choice of waves where you can surf all winter. I think in Cornwall, they have fewer options when the big southwest swells kick in. We're lucky in that there are hidden spots where, no matter what the size of the swell, you can get a surf in the winter.

Frenchie

7 Freshwater West

- 🌐 **Break type**: Beach break.
- 🌊 **Conditions**: Small to medium swells, offshore in easterlies.
- ❶ **Hazards/tips**: Rips, rocks, crowds.
- 💤 **Sleeping**: Pembroke ▸▸ p221.

Best beach break in Wales with hollow, fast waves like Fistral. Picks up the most swell too and is the regular venue for the Welsh Nationals. Works on all states of tide. Although the army used to turn a blind eye to surfers jumping the fence, the firing range beach to the south is out of bounds again. Expect a big fine if you try to sneak in. Beware also of rips and rocks in the middle of the bay. The water is clean and Fresh West gets busy when it's on. Beachfront parking.

Secret spot Y Bocs

Secret spot The Pole

THE GILL

THE GILL

James Wendham

8 Broadhaven South

- **Break type**: Beach break.
- **Conditions**: Medium swells, offshore in northerly winds.
- **Hazards/tips**: Small take off zone, crowds.
- **Sleeping**: Pembroke/Manorbier ▶▶ *p221*.

Swells wrap into this bay and meet in the middle with hollow left wedges. The punchy waves and tiny take-off zone make this a wave for advanced surfers. Watch out for rips in a decent swell. National Trust parking overlooks the break. Clean water. Also known as Bosherton.

9 Freshwater East

- **Break type**: Beach break.
- **Conditions**: Big to storm swells, offshore in westerly winds.
- **Hazards/tips**: Check in westerly storms.
- **Sleeping**: Pembroke/Manorbier ▶▶ *p221*.

Needs a big southwesterly swell to turn this tranquil bay into a hollow, heavy beach break. Gets crowded when it's on and is best around mid tide. Good place to check in a westerly gale. Peaks can throw up excellent lefts and rights with fast barrels. Parking near the beach. Not for beginners when big.

10 Manorbier

- **Break type**: Beach/reef .
- **Conditions**: Medium to big swells, offshore in northeasterly wind.
- **Hazards/tips**: Crowded, easy access, rocks.
- **Sleeping**: Manorbier/Tenby ▶▶ *p221*.

Swells here are always two thirds the size of Freshwater West. There is an average, low tide beach break and a decent high tide right reef. The reef at the western edge can produce walling right-handers that are a big draw, but the wave doesn't hold a crowd. Parking overlooks the break. Beginners, stick to the beach.

11 Tenby Beaches

- **Break type**: Beach breaks.
- **Conditions**: Big swells, offshore in westerly winds.
- **Hazards/tips**: Punchy waves, polluted but improving.
- **Sleeping**: Tenby/Manorbier ▸▸ *p221*.

Tenby is the place to head for in huge westerly storms. South beach works on all tides and produces peaks which can be very hollow. Not ideal for beginners. This is a winter break that gets crowded when good. Parking above and at the beach.

12 Monkstone Point

- **Break type**: Right-hand point.
- **Conditions**: Huge swells, offshore in westerly winds.
- **Hazards/tips**: Winter break.
- **Sleeping**: Tenby/Manorbier ▸▸ *p221*.

This long, walling right-hand point is like a slow Lynmouth so proves especially popular with longboarders. Breaking in southwesterly gales from low to mid tide, this sheltered spot is a winter retreat. It's a long walk out from Saundersfoot harbour car park.

11 Tenby fort

13 Wiseman's Bridge

- **Break type**: Reef break.
- **Conditions**: Huge swells, offshore in northwesterly winds.
- **Hazards/tips**: Alternative spot in winter storms.
- **Sleeping**: Tenby/Manorbier ▸▸ *p221*.

Gentle, walling, long right-hand reef that works from mid to high tide. Watch out for the rocks on take-off. A good alternative to Tenby in big winter storms but can get crowded. Limited roadside parking.

Less experienced surfers can head east to Amroth Beach which breaks in similar conditions. However, be aware of the protruding groynes.

7 Freshwater West ▸▸ *p217*

9 Freshwater East, Dean Gough

14 Pendine Sands

- **Break type**: Beach break.
- **Conditions**: Medium to big swells, offshore in northeasterly winds.
- **Hazards/tips**: Good for beginners.
- **Sleeping**: Tenby/Manorbier ▸▸ *p221*.

Pendine sands is the nearest break for Carmarthen surfers. Long stretch of sand that produces gentle waves, good for beginners. The best surf is near the cliff at the west end of the beach in front of the village at mid to high tide. Sheltered in northwesterly winds. Needs decent swell so only check it when Freshwater is 6 ft plus. The beach is used for land speed records, so don't expect good banks. Parking on beach.

11 Tenby beaches, Glyntin

Listings

St David's

What seems like a tiny village on the A487 is actually a city (it has a cathedral) and provides easy access to Whitesands Bay as well as having good amenities.

● Sleeping
E **St David's Youth Hostel**, near the beach, T01473 720345 open Easter-Oct. **Self catering Ma Simes Surf Hut**, T01437 720433, has a cottage to let by the beach from about £275 per week. **Camping** There are plenty of campsites in the area including the large **Caerfai Bay Caravan and Tent Park**, Caerfai Rd, T01437 720274, open Mar-Nov with statics to rent, and to the south **Caerfai Farm**, T01437 720548, with an organic shop, open May-Sep. Handier for Whitesands however is **Lleithyr Farm Caravan & Tent Park**, T01437 720245, open Easter-Oct.

● Directory
Simon Noble Surfboards (SNS), Trehenlliw Farm, St Davids, T07866 737935 produce custom boards.

St Brides Bay

With **Newgale** to the north and **Broad Haven** to the south, this pretty bay is a

THE GILL

Frenchie: the search

popular draw for tourists in the summer and sits at the heart of the **Pemrokeshire Coast National Park**, stretching from Cardigan to Amroth.

Sleeping

D **Penycwm Youth Hostel**, T01437 721940, in Penycwm, has excellent facilities and is always very popular, so it is advisable to book ahead. E **Broad Haven Youth Hostel**, T01437 781688, provides an affordable place to stay in the village. **Camping** You can camp at **Newgale Campsite**, T01437 710253.

Marloes

To the southwest of Haverfordwest, Marloes has a number of accommodation options. C **The Clockhouse B&B**, T01646 636527, has a wetsuit drying area. C **Foxdale Guesthouse**, T01646 636243, is opposite the church on Glebe Lane and also offers a camping area. D-E **Marloes Sands YHA Hostel**, T01646 636667, is a cheaper option and has easy access to the beach.

Pembroke

The market town of Pembroke, with its ancient fortified walls and interesting castle, has plenty of facilities and amenities mainly centred around Main St, making it a good base, with easy access to the breaks on the south coast as well as Fresh West. **The Coastal Cruiser Surf Bus**, T01437 775227, has started a route from Pembroke dock through Pembroke, Angle, Bosherston and Stackpole running daily in the summer and 3 days a week in the winter making the car-less trek from Pembroke to Broad Haven bearable.

Sleeping

The D **Beech House B&B**, Main St, T01646 683746, is recommended, as is D **Merton Place House**, East Back, T01646 684796. **Camping** There is year-round camping available south of Pembroke at **St Petrox Caravanning and Camping site** near St Petrox village.

Eating/drinking

There are a number of eating options which provide unexceptional food at moderate prices. Check out **Brown's** on Main St and **Henry's** on Westgate Hill for basic food for around a fiver. For good fish and chips try **Rowlies** on Main St.

Directory

Surf shops There are a couple of surf shops. **The Edge**, Main St, T01646 686886; **Outer Reef**, south in Maiden Wells, T01646 680070, and **Waves 'N' Wheels**, Commons Rd, T01646 622066. **Tourist information** Pembroke Visitors Centre, Commons Rd, T01646 622388.

Manorbier/Tenby

Manorbier is a pretty village with a well-known surf break and castle overlooking the sea while the Victorian resort town of Tenby has become "the Newquay of West Wales – it's where everyone heads for their stag nights," according to Dan Harris.

Sleeping

Manorbier Youth Hostel, T01834 871803, open Mar-Oct with camping facilities. This former MOD building offers great views towards Caldey Island.

Flat spells

Castles Pembroke Castle was originally built in 1093 in wood and rebuilt in stone in 1204.
Climbing Pembrokeshire offers some excellent climbing opportunities on still days, contact **TYF**, No Limits, T01437 721611, www.tyf.com, or **Fresh Adventure**, T01646 672764, www.fresh adventure.co.uk, for further details.
Golf Get 9 holes in at **St David's City GC**, Whitesands Bay Head, T01437 721751, or head south to the Pembroke Dock and the 18-hole **South Pembrokeshire GC**, Military Rd, T01646 621453. Tenby has 2 courses –**Trefloyne GC** in Trefloyne Park, just off the A4139, T01834 842165, and **Tenby GC**, off the A478, T01834 842787, the oldest course in Wales, handicap certificate required.
Skating Off the A487, Cardigan's **Dolwerdd Playing Fields** is home to a small skatepark with bowl, 1/4 pipe and funbox. South at **Hubberston near Milford Haven** (A4076) is another small, free concrete park with ramps, rails etc.
Walking Pembrokeshire's coastline is beautiful and much of it has been designated national parkland. Walking just some of the 300 km marked coast path is a great way to see the true potential of this area and may reveal the odd secret spot.

Directory

Surf shops The Edge, Tudor Sq, T01834 842413, stocks all of the brands, as does **Underground** on Church St, T01834 844234.

Surfing South Wales

South Wales is a land of contrasts. The stunning Gower Peninsula draws tourists from around Europe to its pristine countryside and sandy bays, while further east are the mighty industrial heartlands around Port Talbot and Bridgend. Each region has a committed and talented surfing community with strong traditions going back to the earliest days of wave riding in the UK. While the Gower crew wind their way through narrow country lanes and over fields to check fickle reefs and sheltered bays, the Porthcawl and Llantwit surfers can often be found surfing the brown, industrial walls of a more urban setting at breaks such as Aberavon and the ESP. However, in fine Welsh tradition, once on foreign soil local rivalries disappear and the dragon spirit takes over. As everyone knows, the Welsh always sing with one voice.

Coastline

The westward-facing peninsula of the Gower is a designated Area of Outstanding Natural Beauty and rightly so. From the wide, open bay at Llangennith, through the rocky Gower reefs to Langland, much of this coastline is National Trust property. To the east, Porthcawl, Aberavon and Llantwit offer a mixture of good quality beach breaks with a selection of points and reefs.

Localism

Welsh line-ups are becoming more crowded as the numbers of surfers in the water increases. This is especially so at breaks like Crab Island and some of the Gower reefs. As Chris French says: "In the water, places like Langland are super competitive and down on the Gower it's ridiculously competitive. People want to get their waves after finishing their 9-5. Swansea College Uni has probably got one of

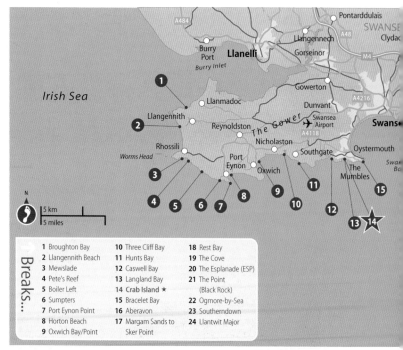

Breaks...

1 Broughton Bay	10 Three Cliff Bay	18 Rest Bay
2 Llangennith Beach	11 Hunts Bay	19 The Cove
3 Mewslade	12 Caswell Bay	20 The Esplanade (ESP)
4 Pete's Reef	13 Langland Bay	21 The Point
5 Boiler Left	14 Crab Island ★	(Black Rock)
6 Sumpters	15 Bracelet Bay	22 Ogmore-by-Sea
7 Port Eynon Point	16 Aberavon	23 Southerndown
8 Horton Beach	17 Margam Sands to	24 Llantwit Major
9 Oxwich Bay/Point	Sker Point	

the biggest surf clubs in the country so there are lots of students as well." However, incidents of localism are rare so follow the golden rules and you should have a great surf. In general the Welsh are excellent company in the water.

Top local surfers
Wales's original hellman, **Carwyn Williams**; **Pete Jones (PJ)**; king of the longboard and former three-time European champion, **Chris 'Guts' Griffiths**; rising stars **Isaac Kibblewhite** and **Beth Mason**; **Nathan Phillips**; **Mark Vaughan**; **Matt Stephens**; **Brad Hockridge**; former Welsh champion, **Frenchie**; **Swinno**; and former three-time Welsh champion, **Dan Harris**.

Getting around
The M4 runs parallel to the coast allowing access from England to the main surf areas. The Gower breaks can be more tricky with access along narrow tracks and over fields. Please show respect when parking and when on farmers' land.

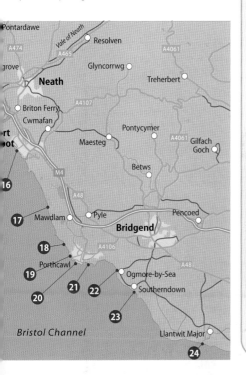

Gower reef, Crab Island ▸▸ *p227*

South Wales board guide

The '66 Dora Model
Shaper: The Gill, ODD Surfboards

▸▸ 8'4" x 22" x 2¾" for Mickey Dora.
▸▸ 9'1" x 23" x 2¾" Classic competition dimensions.
▸▸ Based on a surfboard shaped for Dora in 1982, which he kept and surfed for nearly 20 years.
▸▸ It has a wide squash tail for smaller surf, wide point in the middle and egg rails.
▸▸ It's a medium weight board with nose concave designed for gliding clean waves.
▸▸ The board has three stringers, two of them curved outer stringers in an old skool style, and a single fin with a 10 inch fin box.
▸▸ Good for summer waves at Llangennith.
▸▸ Resin tint for a true retro look.

Thruster
Shaper: The Gill, ODD Surfboards

▸▸ 6'3" x 18½" x 2¼" for Stephen Phillips.
▸▸ Narrow nose for snappy manoeuvres and squash tail.
▸▸ Performance board for good beach waves and for hollow reef breaks.
▸▸ Has slightly more tail lift and single concave for stability in hollow waves up to head high.
▸▸ Flexible enough for changeable South Wales waves.

ⓘ Boards by **ODD Boards**
Factory: Freelap Surfboards, Porthcawl, Wales. T 01656 744691
www.oddsurfboards.co.uk
gill@eurotelemail.net

Wales South Surfing

Breaks

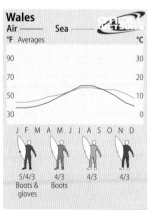

1 Broughton Bay

- 🌊 **Break type**: Point break.
- 🌥 **Conditions**: Big swells, offshore in southerly winds.
- ❗ **Hazards/tips**: Slow wave, dangerous rips.
- 💤 **Sleeping**: Llangennith ▶▶ *p231*.

Long, walling, left-hand point break that produces fairly slow waves, popular with longboarders. Worth checking when Llangennith is 6 ft. There is a strong rip, so this is not for beginners. Loads of dogfish in the shallows. Walk through caravan site and be courteous to farmer!

2 Llangennith Beach

- 🌊 **Break type**: Long beach break.
- 🌥 **Conditions**: Small to medium swells, offshore in easterly winds.
- ❗ **Hazards/tips**: Consistent, popular spot.
- 💤 **Sleeping**: Llangennith ▶▶ *p231*.

Three miles of relatively flat, featureless sand means that the waves lack punch so can be a good place for beginners. It is, however, a consistent spot that gets very busy but quieter peaks can usually be found a short walk down the beach. Works on all tides up to about 6 ft. Relatively safe beach, good for beginners. Pay parking at Hillend Campsite. Llangennith is also home to local legend and surf shop owner PJ. When the swell is too big at Llangennith, head south to Rhossili end. Best at mid to high tide and sheltered from strong southerly winds. Parking on top.

3 Mewslade (Fall Bay and Mewslade Reef)

- 🌊 **Break type**: Beach and reef.
- 🌥 **Conditions**: Medium swells, offshore in northerly winds.
- ❗ **Hazards/tips**: Powerful breaks, not for beginners.
- 💤 **Sleeping**: Llangennith/Port Eynon ▶▶ *p231/232*.

Fall Bay Wedge is a beach break that works at high tide for spongers, while **Mewslade Reef**, in the middle of the bay, is a sucky, hollow, left reef for experts only. It's a low tide break best in a northerly wind. Mewslade beach is best from low to mid tide and has powerful, semi close-outs. Park at the farmyard car park. Signed from road.

Wales

Air ——— Sea ———

°F Averages

													°C
90													30
70													20
50													10
30													0

J F M A M J J A S O N D

5/4/3 Boots & gloves   4/3 Boots   4/3   4/3

2 Llangennith beach

THE GILL

4 Pete's Reef

- 🌀 **Break type**: Reef.
- 🌊 **Conditions**: Small to medium swells, offshore in northerly winds.
- ⚠ **Hazards/tips**: Very crowded, experts only.
- 💤 **Sleeping**: Port Eynon ▶▶ *p232*.

Low tide hollow peak breaking on shallow limestone reef. Gets very crowded when it's on and holds up to 5 ft. Popular with good local surfers. Breaks like a small Porthleven. Long walk. Parking difficult.

5 Boiler Left

- 🌀 **Break type**: Left reef.
- 🌊 **Conditions**: Medium swell, offshore in northerly winds.
- ⚠ **Hazards/tips**: Long walk, difficult parking.
- 💤 **Sleeping**: Port Eynon ▶▶ *p232*.

Low tide, hollow, medium-length left breaking on limestone reef with submerged ship's boiler at the end. Has a big rip and works up to 6 to 8 ft. Small, sucking take-off zone.

6 Sumpters

- 🌀 **Break type**: Right-hand reef.
- 🌊 **Conditions**: Medium to big swells, offshore in northeasterly wind.
- ⚠ **Hazards/tips**: Popular wave, deep channel for paddle out.
- 💤 **Sleeping**: Port Eynon ▶▶ *p232*.

Quality right and another peak nearby. Easier access than Boiler. Best from low to mid tide producing long, walling rights with the occasional barrel. Not too shallow. Popular wave that holds swells up to 8 ft. Paddle out in deep channel after walking along sewer pipe.

❝ ❞

We first surfed the Gower reefs in about 1978. We heard rumours that there was a wave down there and someone just happened to know where Pete's Reef was. We thought that was it – we didn't know about the others. A car full of us would drive down, we'd surf all day and never see another soul, never meet anyone else, and we'd do it year after year. It's a lot different now.

Frenchie, former Welsh champion

1 Broughton Bay   6 Sumpters

4 Pete's Reef

7 Port Eynon Point

- 🌀 **Break type**: Right-hand reef point.
- 🌊 **Conditions**: Medium to big swells, offshore in northerly winds.
- ❶ **Hazards/tips**: Access is a walk south from Port Eynon beach car park.
- 💤 **Sleeping**: Port Eynon ›› p232.

Powerful, sucky, low tide point break which peels in front of rock ledges. Popular spot that breaks consistently. Quality wave best left to the experts.

8 Horton Beach

- 🌀 **Break type**: Beach break.
- 🌊 **Conditions**: Medium to big swells, offshore in northerly wind.
- ❶ **Hazards/tips**: Beach parking.
- 💤 **Sleeping**: Port Eynon ›› p232.

Sheltered beach that needs a good swell to work, but produces dumpy, hollow waves that can close out at high. Works on all tides but is better at low to

Worm and wreck, Rhossili ›› p224

9 Oxwich Bay

mid. An alternative to crowded Langland. Good spot for intermediates and a safe beach for beginners. Also popular with kitesurfers and windsurfers. Parking at the beach.

9 Oxwich Bay/Point

- 🌀 **Break type**: Beach break.
- 🌊 **Conditions**: Storm swell, offshore in southwesterly winds.
- ❶ **Hazards/tips**: Safe beach, Oxwich Bay Hotel for pricey refreshments .
- 💤 **Sleeping**: Oxwich ›› p232.

A hollow beach break that's best at high tide. Gets busy when breaking as it can be the only spot in storms. Breaks up to 6 ft, but is usually about 3 ft.

10 Three Cliff Bay

- 🌀 **Break type**: Beach break.
- 🌊 **Conditions**: Medium swell, offshore in northwesterly winds.
- ❶ **Hazards/tips**: Dangerous rips.
- 💤 **Sleeping**: Oxwich ›› p232.

This is a mid to high tide beach break with some good sandbanks producing lefts and rights. It's the most scenic bay on the Gower and features on many postcards. Park near Penmaen post office, on South Gower Road, and make the long walk to the beach. Usually uncrowded so an alternative to Langland.

13 Langland Bay, Mark Vaughan

11 Hunts Bay

- 🌀 **Break type**: Reef break
- 🌊 **Conditions**: Medium swell, offshore in northerly wind
- ❶ **Hazards/tips**: Difficult access
- 💤 **Sleeping**: Oxwich/Mumbles ›› p232.

A right-hand reef where there is difficult access in and out of the water due to rocks. Produces walling rights, with sections. Access long walk from Southgate, walk along cliffs. Quiet break.

12 Caswell Bay

- 🌀 **Break type**: Beach break.
- 🌊 **Conditions**: Small to medium swells, offshore in northerly winds.
- ❶ **Hazards/tips**: Popular spot near Mumbles.
- 💤 **Sleeping**: Mumbles ›› p232.

Smallish bay popular with tourists and beginners with a beachfront car park. Works from mid to high tide. Produces short peaky waves that can get crowded.

13 Langland Bay

- 🌀 **Break type**: Reefs/beach/point.
- 🌊 **Conditions**: All swells, offshore in northerly winds.
- ❶ **Hazards/tips**: Many spots for surfers of all abilities, gets crowded.
- 💤 **Sleeping**: Mumbles ›› p232.

The **Outside Point** is a reef, but not dangerous. It works at low tide only, best from 2-8 ft, and is not too challenging. A popular spot with longboarders and doesn't get too crowded.

The **Inside Point** and **Shit Pipe (Huttons)** is a mid tide reef break with long, walling right-handers. Again a popular longboard wave, nicknamed the 'Malibu of the Gower'. It has a friendly line-up, is sheltered from strong westerly winds but can be rocky and shallow.

Langland Shorebreak is a virtual close-out, popular with shortboarders on a big swell. It's really a one manoeuvre wave that works at high tide only. Crowded with locals in solid swells and generally ridden in stormy conditions.

Langland Reef (Kevs) breaks at mid tide, a crowded peak with a mixture of boards and abilities. It's a very busy, short left and long right that is shallow on the peak.

Middle of the Bay (MOTB) is a left that breaks into strong rip, opposite **The Reef** – which is actually a sandbar. Breaking from low to half tide, it produces lefts that can be hollow. Gets very crowded and can be ridden in all winds as it is quite sheltered.

Rotherslade Left is further out than MOTB, producing walling lefts with sections, over a low tide sandbank. Works best in medium swells when it can be crowded.

The **Sandbar** is a low tide, very shallow reef. It has a dangerous, dropping take-off and is best left to advanced surfers only. "This is where Carwyn used to practice for Pipeline," explains The Gill. The peak splits into a left and right, the left is the most hollow. It's a heavy wave where you don't want to get caught inside as it unloads onto the shallow reef. Breaks up to 10 ft.

Gas Chambers is a cocktail of sand, rock and air, for boogie boarders and the brave. At mid tide, **Inside Crab** produces left-hand barrels up to 5 ft.

The **Shallow Peak** is a shallow, rocky reef that works up to 5 ft. It produces lefts and rights, sucky all the way.

14 Crab Island

- ⚫ **Break type**: Right-hand reef.
- ⚫ **Conditions**: All swells.
- ⚫ **Size**: 2-10 ft.
- ⚫ **Length**: 50-100 m.
- ⚫ **Swell**: Southwesterly.
- ⚫ **Wind**: Northwesterly.
- ⚫ **Tide**: When Crab Island appears out of the water at low tide.
- ⚫ **Bottom**: Rocks.
- ⚫ **Entry/exit**: Off the rocks.
- ⚫ **Hazards/tips**: Rocks on take-off.
- ⚫ **Sleeping**: Mumbles ▸▸ *p232*.

Nestled in Langland Bay sits one of the country's best waves, the legendary Crab Island. This wave is home to a long-established and respected surf community including the likes of Guts Griffiths, Frenchie, Matt Stephens, Swinno, Tim Page and The Gill. This is a long, powerful wave that peels along a reef formed by a small island just offshore – hence the name. The peak is an elevator drop with the danger of nearby rocks always in the back of the mind. It then walls up into a fast section with barrels opening up in the right conditions. There is a strong rip pushing away from the peak in good swells, which can become quite tiring. If you are going to go and surf Crab, it's best to be respectful and try not to snag too many waves.

ⓘ *If you like Crab Island, try Thurso East in Scotland (see page 166) or Easkey Right in Ireland.*

THE GILL

14 Crab Island

Surfers' tales

Seal of disapproval

By surf photographer George Sohl

I was living and working in Llangennith and had managed to get away from the shop I ran for a much needed surf. I headed for a slightly out of the way break that not many non-locals knew about, but when I got there, although there was a 3 ft swell running, the waves were being blown out by the moderate onshore. Still, there were no other people in and I'd walked quite a way so I decided to get wet anyway.

The conditions didn't make it any easier to negotiate the minefield of rock pools and submerged reef I had to cross to get to the take-off zone. The sky was blue, the sea gulls were squawking and I was just starting to daydream when I noticed a little movement to my side. I turned to see what it was and saw a seal. A great big bull seal with a huge head, scarred from numerous fights and close shaves with boat propellers – but it was "just a seal" none the less. They're frequent visitors at local breaks, driven by a playful curiosity. So despite his appearance, I tried to ignore him and carried on waiting for the sets, which were suddenly very slow in coming.

I could feel the seal's eyes on me – things were getting a little tense. I cast a furtive glance in his direction and watched as he tilted his head back, opening his mouth wide to show me his very large, very sharp, very impressive set of canines. Simultaneously, he let out a huge, guttural roar. In response, I froze. To make matters worse he started advancing, then erupted into a full-blown charge. About a foot away from me he suddenly dived like a submarine. I was waiting for the bump or bite – I didn't know what was coming. To my surprise nothing did.

He surfaced again in the same place as before. This seal was flexing his territorial muscles. Still stunned and confused, I tried to hide my fear, keep calm and hold my ground. I thought if I tried to move or retreat somehow, I'd be in trouble – especially as I knew there was no way I was going to out-run him in the water. He tilted his head again and started another charge. All I could do was lift my feet up. Again at the last moment he dived. I just hoped that he'd miraculously go away. I think I was shouting something. He resurfaced and I knew this was the last warning I was getting. The next time he charged, I knew he was going to attack. I lay on my board and started frantically paddling just as this 3 ft mushy wave broke on me and pushed me towards the inside. I didn't look back – I just kept paddling with the white water and eventually felt the reef under me. Somehow I ended up off my board and running up the rocks and onto dry land, still not looking back. I was just running with my board still attached to my leg – dragging it and just running till I felt I was far enough away. Eventually I slowed down and had a look back for any trace of the monster. To my extreme relief I saw nothing, so I collected myself and headed back to my car and the safety of terra firma, laughing at the experience with a mixture of relief and embarrassment. Needless to say it was a long time before I surfed that spot again.

15 Bracelet Bay

- ◉ **Break type**: Right-hand reef.
- ◉ **Conditions**: Medium to big swells, offshore in northwesterly winds.
- ◉ **Hazards/tips**: Strong rips.
- ◉ **Sleeping**: Mumbles ▸▸ *p232*.

Nestled under the coastguard station is this low to mid tide right-hand reef. It produces walling rights with sections, breaking up to 8 ft. Has strong rips. Last of the Gower breaks.

16 Aberavon

- ◉ **Break type**: Breakwater.
- ◉ **Conditions**: All swells, offshore in easterly winds.
- ◉ **Hazards/tips**: Dirty water, heavy when big, access off jetty when big.
- ◉ **Sleeping**: Porthcawl ▸▸ *p233*.

Short right and long left, spoiled by new sea defence in the corner. It's difficult to get back in at high tide when it's big. This sandbar is a real industrial surf spot, breaking next to steelworks and deepwater docks. Very unscenic and crowded.

17 Margam Sands to Sker Point

- ◉ **Break type**: Beach breaks.
- ◉ **Conditions**: Small to medium swells, offshore in easterly winds.
- ◉ **Hazards/tips**: Pollution.
- ◉ **Sleeping**: Porthcawl ▸▸ *p233*.

Best at mid to high tide, this long stretch of beach break peaks are hollower at the Sker end. Park at Kenfig Pools, a long walk through the dunes. A quiet spot with better waves towards the Sker end.

> **We've got a lot of good set-ups in South Wales so that when you do get swell, there are spots that would rival anywhere in the UK, if not Europe. When it's the right swell you've got a lot of reef breaks, a lot of point breaks and more variety than a lot of the UK coastlines. Although we don't get as much swell as the rest of the southwest of Britain, what we lose in quantity, a bit like the northeast of England, we gain in quality.**
>
> *Isaac Kibblewhite, sponsored surfer*

18 Rest Bay

- ◉ **Break type**: Beach break.
- ◉ **Conditions**: Small to medium swells, offshore in easterly winds.
- ◉ **Hazards/tips**: Pollution, parking in beach car park, strong parallel rips .
- ◉ **Sleeping**: Porthcawl ▸▸ *p233*.

This popular beach produces great peaks, with some excellent waves, some of the best in the area. Works best from low to three quarter tide on the push. Can have lefts and rights up and down this long beach with the southern end, the most popular.

19 The Cove

- ◉ **Break type**: Beach break.
- ◉ **Conditions**: Small to medium swell, offshore in easterly winds.
- ◉ **Hazards/tips**: Heavy wave with rips.
- ◉ **Sleeping**: Porthcawl ▸▸ *p233*.

This spot is accessible at low tide from Rest Bay. It has heavy peaks, with lefts and rights breaking on a sand bottom. Strong rips.

THE GILL

16 Aberavon

THE GILL

23 Lloyd Cole at Southerndown ▸▸ p230

20 The Esplanade (ESP)

20 The Esplanade (ESP)

⟳ **Break type**: Reef.
🌊 **Conditions**: Medium swell. offshore in northeasterly winds.
❶ **Hazards/tips**: Crowds, shallow reef.
⬤ **Sleeping**: Porthcawl ▸▸ *p233*.

This is a shallow, hollow and fast left reef where the locals dominate. Park on seafront overlooking break. Only works at high tide.

21 The Point (Black Rock)

⟳ **Break type**: Reef point.
🌊 **Conditions**: Medium to big swell, offshore in northerly winds.
❶ **Hazards/tips**: Drive through caravan park to front.
⬤ **Sleeping**: Porthcawl ▸▸ *p233*.

This is a high tide right-hand reef point that breaks over knobbly rocks. After a shallow take-off the wave is fast and sucky, before becoming a long wall. This is a crowded spot best left to Porthcawl locals and experts.

Industrial wave, Timmy Page

22 Ogmore-by-Sea

⟳ **Break type**: Rivermouth break.
🌊 **Conditions**: Medium swells, offshore in easterly winds.
❶ **Hazards/tips**: Can be excellent, watch out for rips.
⬤ **Sleeping**: Porthcawl ▸▸ *p233*.

A fickle spot that can be a classic, right-hand rivermouth if the banks are right. Best at high tide, the spot can be quite busy, but watch out for rips out from river. Park overlooking break.

23 Southerndown

⟳ **Break type**: Beach break
🌊 **Conditions**: Small to medium swell, offshore in easterly winds
❶ **Hazards/tips**: Consistent spot
⬤ **Sleeping**: Porthcawl ▸▸ *p233*

A popular break with Bridgend/Cardiff surfers. The beach peaks can produce good, walling waves, suitable for all surfers. A consistent spot that picks up

23 Southerndown

a lot of swell, so gets quite busy.
Similar to Llangennith.

24 Llantwit Major

- 🌐 **Break type**: Selection of reefs
- 🌐 **Conditions**: All swells, offshore in a northerly wind
- ❶ **Hazards/tips**: Good quality spot, crowds, pollution
- 🌐 **Sleeping**: Porthcawl ▸▸ *p233*

A large triangular boulder reef on the Glamorgan heritage coast producing a number of waves at different states of tide. The peak works at low tide in small to medium swells. Perfect right peels off the left edge of the reef at low to mid tide and can be classic on its day. At mid to high tide there are hollow peaks on the boulders near the car park. Llantwit can handle swells between 3 ft and 8 ft. It is best on incoming tides, but beware of rips. Signposted to the beach. This break has produced a number of Britain's most talented up and coming surfers including Nathan Phillips, Mark Vaughan and the Bright brothers. A crowded spot.

Listings

THE GILL

24 Llantwit coastline

Llangennith

Llangennith is at the western edge of the Gower Peninsula, the first place in Britain designated an Area of Outstanding Natural Beauty. Llangennith sits just inland from Rhossili bay, a huge flat beach that opens out in front of a vast area of sand dunes. Popular with holidaymakers and beachgoers, this area has been at the forefront of the British surf scene since the very early days and is now home to the **Welsh Surfing Federation Surf School**.

🌐 Sleeping

C **Western House B&B**, just down the road from the King's Head pub, T01792 386620, run by a surfing family or D-C **Bremmel Cottage B&B**, T01792 386308, who are also surf friendly. **Camping** There are plenty of campsites in the area. Heading towards Broughton Bay is **Broughton Farm Caravan Park**, T01792 386213, open Apr-Oct with statics to hire. They also run **The Cross**, a year-round self-catering cottage sleeping up to 8 people from £350, within walking distance of the notorious **King's Head**. The most popular campsite is **Hillend Camping Site** overlooking the beach, T01792 386204, and housing the newly opened **Eddy's Restaurant**. Another option in Llangennith is **Kennexstone Camping and Touring Park**, T01792 391296 open Apr 30-Sep. South at Rhossili is the reasonably-priced **Pitton Cross Caravan & Camping**, T01792 390593, open Apr-Oct.

❷ Eating/drinking

The recently opened **Eddy's** at Hillend Camping Site is a good place to get a cheap bite to eat. **The King's Head** is the place to grab a pint and some pub grub and sit outside to soak up some rare Welsh sunshine.

⊕ Directory
Surf shops & resources
www.llangennithsurf.com. Excellent new resource which offers the best in swell prediction, current conditions, tide tables, wave buoy data and a webcam for Llangennith beach.
PJ's Surf Shop (PJ's), opposite the King's Head pub, T01792 386669, has been up and running since 1978 and sells and hires out surf equipment. He also runs a surf check phone line updated daily, T0901 6031603. PJ (Pete Jones) is a dedicated surfer and in his time has been the Welsh, British and European Champion. **Welsh Surfing Federation**, T01792 386426, www.wsfsurfschool.co.uk, the WSF surf school, based at Hillend Campsite, has been giving lessons since 1981.

Port Eynon

⊖ Sleeping
Camping On the A4118 from Swansea, Port Eynon has a couple of camping options. **Bank Farm Leisure Park**, T01792 390228, overlooks the Bay and is within walking distance from Horton. **Carreglwyd Camping & Caravan**, T01792 390795, is open Apr-Oct. As an alternative, **Port Eynon Youth Hostel**, T01792 390706 is right on the beachfront and open Apr-Oct.

Oxwich

⊖ Sleeping
Oxwich Bay is a nature reserve as well as a popular surf beach and has a couple of camping options including the small **Bay Holme Caravan Site**, T01792 401051, with statics to hire and **Oxwich Bay Camping Park**, T01792 390777, open Apr-Sep. Further east, overlooking the next beach is **Three Cliffs Bay Caravan and Camping Park**, T01792 371218, open Mar-Oct, who also run a self-catering cottage.

Mumbles

A general term for the village of Oystermouth, the name actually came about as a bastardization of 'mamelles' or breasts – the word French sailors used to describe the 2 off-shore islands nearby.

⊖ Sleeping
A **Langland Cove Guest House**, Rotherslade Rd, T01792 366003, gill@eurotelemail.net. Overlooking Langland Bay and within walking distance of the beach, the B&B is run by legendary shaper and surf photographer The Gill who keeps the breakfasts and stories flowing. In Mumbles try B **Coast House**, Mumbles Rd, T01792 368702.

⊘ Eating/drinking
There are some good eating options in The Mumbles as recommended by The Gill. **The Antelope** on Mumbles Rd is a lively pub with a beer garden and is just one of the many places Welsh poet Dylan Thomas is said to have frequented. **Bar Mex** on Newton Rd has something for everyone, as The Gill puts it: "There's scantily clad barmaids for the men and firemen for the ladies". **Bentley's Night Club** is popular with local surfers and comes complete with sticky carpet and

THE GILL

2 Llangennith ▶▶p224

cut-glass mirror ball. **Castellamare Pizzeria** overlooks Bracelet Bay and is a great place to spend an evening. **CJ's** on Mumbles Rd is a lively bar/restaurant where you can eat for about £5-10. For something a bit different try **The Mediterranean Restaurant** who do 2 sittings a night at 1900 and 2100. **The Rock and Fountain** at the top end of Newton Rd is a locals' pub with live music. **The Village Inn** further along the road mixes good pub grub with bad karaoke.

❶ Directory
Surf shops Big Drop Surf Shop, Tivoli Walk, T01792 368861, stocks all the essentials. **Guts Surf Boards**, Newton Rd, T01792 360555, www.gutssurfboards.com, provides longboards, shortboards and hybrids shaped by one of the world's top longboarders, Chris Griffiths. His team includes Sam Bleakley among others. JP Surfboards, Woodville Rd, Mumbles, T01792 521149. John Purton has been shaping boards since he was 13 and now shapes for some of the UK's top surfers including Carwyn Williams and Gabe Davies. **Tourist information** is on Dunn Lane, summer opening only.

Porthcawl

Accessed via junction 37 on the M4, Porthcawl is an unspectacular seaside town with a couple of camping options and plenty of amusement arcades.

● Sleeping
Camping Happy Valley Caravan **Park** is off the main A4106, T01656 782144, open Apr-Sep, and has a bar and café on site. **Trecco Bay Holiday**

Park, just east of the town, T0870 2204645, is open Mar-Nov.

❶ Directory
Surf shops There are a couple of surf shops in the town. **Black Rock** and **Porthcawl Marine**, T01656 784785, on New Rd. Just inland at Bridgend's South Cornelly Industrial Estate is **Freelap Custom Surfboards**, T01656 744691, who put out boards under the 'ODD' logo. Freelap is run by glasser Albert Harris who has been involved in the surf industry since the 1970s. ODD's Paul Gill has been shaping since 1977 and has made boards for both modern chargers such as Wales's Isaac Kibblewhite and old skool hero Mickey 'Da Cat' Dora. **No Limits Wetsuits**, based at 52-57 Fenton Pl, T01656 772202, www.nolimitswetsuits.com, was started by Greg Owen in 1994 and specializes in made-to-measure wetsuits as well as offering a speedy repair service. His team includes some of Wales's finest: Chris Sage, Jamie Bateman, Colm Garrett and Stephen Phillips to name but a few. **Simon Tucker Surf Academy**, T07815 289761, www.surfing experience.com, was started in 2000 by the former British Champion. Based in Rest Bay and open Apr-Oct, the school is BSA-approved.

Llantwit Major

❷ Eating/drinking
Colm Garrett recommends grabbing a filled baguette or a hot pie at the **Best Bite** on Poundfield for a cheap, post-surf feed. When the work is done, stop by the **New Globe** pub for a well-earned ale or even a carafe or two of wine. Check out the bar menu for reasonably priced food.

✪ Flat spells
Arthur's Stone Head to Reynoldston on the Gower just off the A4118 where this 25 tonne stone marks a Neolithic burial mound and gives awesome views right across the peninsula.
Golf There are more courses in the area than you can shake your club at. Try **Langland Bay GC**, Mumbles, just off the B4593, T01792 361721, or **Grove GC** off the A4229 at South Cornelly, T01656 788771, near Porthcawl for starters.
Horse riding Pitton Moor Trekking, T01792 390554, has treks for all abilities from Pitton Cross, Rhosilli.
Skating Head to Swansea's Cwmdu Industrial Estate on Camarthen Rd and the **Swansea Skate Park**, T01792 578478. South at Porthcawl Harbour in the **Jennings Building** is a good skate park with 1/4 pipe, street course etc. Open 1800-2100 weekdays and 1000-2100 weekends. From £2 for a half day or evening session. Just off the M4 at Newport is the pricey **Skate Extreme**, T01633 265709, with mini ramps, spines, vert ramp, bowl, grind rails and anything else you're looking for. Helmets are mandatory.

❶ Directory
Surf shops Run by Nathan Phillips's parents, **Point Break** on the Precinct, T01446 794303, is well stocked for both surfers and skaters alike.

Surfers in London

The two French men are padding silently and gracefully across the London skyline, occasional bursts of energy taking them over a wall – across a gap. The world's best Parkour, or freerunning, athletes are here to 'Jump London'. The camera draws back to reveal an image of a man doing a handstand on a handrail, three stories above the South Bank. Nice, but not as impressive as balancing a career and passion for surfing while trapped in this concrete jungle. Now that's a tough balancing act.

In many of the UK's top surfing regions jobs can be scarce and salaries correspondingly low. But hey, there's always the surf, except when you've got a four-week flat spell. The other option is head where the jobs and money are – then you can afford to travel to exotic surf locations – if you've got the vacation time. That eternal balance that surfers have faced for decades, surfing versus career. London is the extreme end of that scale. The money is there, the jobs are there, the surf… well the surf can be there, if you know where to look.

Surf shops

London is not the best place for serious surf shopping, however **Covent Garden** is home to a couple of good surf shops including **O'Neill**, T020 7836 7686, www.oneilleurope.com, on Neal St and two **Quiksilver Boardrider Stores**, North Piazza, T020 7240 5886, and Thomas Neal's Centre, T020 7836 5371. **Carnaby Street**, off Oxford St, is home to an **Animal store**, T020 7287 0557. They stock

Hop on the sleeper to Scotland

Don't be surprised by the fact that you will get waves here. Britain is an island. Don't stay in London: get to the coast, any coast.

Lee Bartlett, former British and BPSA Champion

magazines, books and videos to keep the stoke going through the dry spells and hardware to help you gear up for getting wet. Also here are **O'Neill**, 5-7 Carnaby St, W1, T020 7734 3778, and **Vans**, 47 Carnaby St, W1, T020 7287 1090, www.vans.com. Close by is **Legends Surf Shop**, 119-121 Oxford St, W1, T020 7287 6810, www.extreme.com. Further from the centre are **Low Pressure Surf Shop**, 23 Kensington Park Rd, W11, T0207 7923134; **Lizzard Surf Company**, 26 Cowley Rd, Mortlake, SW14, T0790 9921880 or T0797 1124043, F020 7488 2280; and **Urban Ocean Ltd**, 56 Liverpool St, EC2, T020 7628 8811, www.urbanocean.co.uk. If you are visiting the Home Counties try **High Life Surf Shop**, Dorking, T01306 881910, or **Better Loosen Up Surf Clothing Shop**, 33 Hermitage Rd, Hitchin, Hertfordshire, T01462 457779, betterloosenup_77@hotmail.com, which stocks Billabong, Ripcurl, Quiksilver, O'Neill, and Headworx.

Tourist information

Visit London, T0207 2345800. If you are spending any time in London, get a copy of the excellent *Time Out* magazine which has full listings of what's going on in London day and night. **Internet** There are plenty of places to get online in the city for ease and cost (from £1) – try the **easyEverything** internet cafés dotted around including Oxford St opposite Bond St Tube.

Hungry
for a
Surf?

But no time to fix a trip?

Then **Big Friday** is your answer.

Beginner or seasoned pro, on your own or in a large group, **Big Friday** creates surf weekends to suit your needs and your budget.

Let **Big Friday** sort your transport, your bed, your instructor, and your kit.

You just step onto the Surf Bus and get ready for a great weekend.

Wave Goodbye
to the City

with Big Friday

IN ASSOCIATION WITH

Davidoff Cool Water

● Getting through London with your board

If you're just passing through and using London as a gateway to the rest of the world, the following advice should help alleviate the associated headaches.

Left luggage

If you have a day or two to kill in the city and don't fancy spending it lugging your board around, leave it at one of the Excess Baggage sites, T0800 7831085, www.excess-baggage.com, handily based at the main rail stations including Victoria, Paddington, Liverpool Street, Waterloo, King's Cross and Euston. Open 0630-2330, charges around £5.50 per item.

The Underground

The **Tube** connects the corners of sprawling London – including Heathrow's four terminals to the southwest and E17's Walthamstow to the northeast. The Tube is usually the quickest and easiest way to get around, although you will miss out on some of the sights and sounds of the capital. The Underground is divided into 6 zones – zone 1 being Central. Costs are banded accordingly. Pick up a free map of the system at any tube station. If you plan to make more than two journeys in one day, buy a Travel Card to save cash. The Underground is prone to delays so always allow plenty of time (and then a bit extra) if you have a connection/ flight to make.

You are allowed to take luggage up to 2 m on the Underground – fine for most shortboarders. Longboards may be a little more tricky but the likelihood of you being stopped from travelling with your kit is pretty slim. Use common sense – head for the end carriage and get your board up against a wall, out of other passengers' way.

Avoid rush hour at all costs, this is truly an up-close and personal living hell of epic proportions – faces nestle in the armpits of strangers with nowhere else to turn, temperatures rise, tempers fray. It will be extremely difficult to get on the Tube with your board between the hours of 0800-1000 and 1700-1900.

Main Airports

Gatwick T0870 0002468, south of London, off the M23. The easiest ways to get to Gatwick is by train. Southern Railways, T0870 8306000, run a service from Victoria station, every 10-30 mins, taking around 35-40 mins. Single from £8. Gatwick Express T0845 8501530, www.gatwickexpress.co.uk, run a similar service from Victoria taking around 30 mins. Single from £12.

Heathrow T0870 0000123, www.baa.co.uk/heathrow. West of London off the M4 or M25, the airport can be reached using the Tube. Heading west, Heathrow terminals are at the end of the Piccadilly Line – around an hour from central London, with regular services every few minutes. Single around £4.50. Be warned, the Tube is prone to delay and the journey can often take a lot longer than planned. A quicker option is Heathrow Express, T0845 6001515, www.heathrowexpress.co.uk, with trains running from Paddington station every 15-30 mins. Journey time around 20 mins. Single from £13.

Stanstead T0870 0000303, www.baa.co.uk/stanstead. Just north of London off the M11, the quickest route to the airport is via the Stanstead Express, T0845 7484950, www.stansteadexpress.co.uk. Services run from Liverpool Street station every 15-30 mins.

Sleeping

London is one of the most expensive cities in the world to get a good night's sleep in. Here are a couple of hostel options that shouldn't break the bank!

B-D St Christophers Village, 165 Borough High St, Southwark, T020 7407 1856, www.st-christophers.co.uk. Smart hostel accommodation, just south of London Bridge, with easy access to centre. Offers B&B, internet access, laundry, bar, luggage storage, no curfew. Accommodation available in twins, mixed or female dorms. **C YHA St Pancras**, 79-81 Euston Rd, NW1, T020 7388 9998. Bang opposite St Pancras station, this is well placed for an evening out at Scala nightclub on Pentonville Rd and fairly swanky (as hostels go) with premium rooms available. No groups. **C YHA Oxford St**, 14 Noel St, Soho, W1, T020 7734 1618. Open every day of the year in cool Soho with kitchen facilities. Booking is essential. **C-D Dean Court Hotel**, 57 Inverness Terr, W2, T020 7229 2961. This Aussie-run pad has small dorms and doubles available with reasonable weekly rates. **C-E Ashlee House**, 261-265 Gray's Inn Rd, WC1, T020 7833 9400. Clean, bright and beautiful – this backpackers has twins and dorms available. Beds from £13. Free luggage store, internet access and a nice vibe. **D Court Hotel**, 194-196 Earl's Court Rd, SW5, T020 7373 0027, www.lgh-hotels.com. Right next to the Tube station and a firm favourite with visiting Aussies, it is small but perfectly formed with kitchen facilities. Doubles from £35.

Camping **Lea Valley Campsite**, Sewardstone Rd, E4, T020 8529 5689, open Apr-Oct.

Follow the M4 west to Wales

Free Days Out

London is expensive but it doesn't need to be as there are always planty of opportunities for saving money. Remember museums are free in the UK now. Here's how to while away a day for free!

Tate Modern, Bankside (Blackfriars Tube), T020 7887 8000, www.tate.org.uk. This gallery comprises some of the most inspiring works by contemporary and modern artists – permanent collections are free to view as are the regularly changing foyer exhibitions.

Hampstead Heath Ponds, Hampstead Heath (Hampstead/Gospel Oak Tube). If London's left you feeling a bit dry, take a dip in this free Lido open 0700-1900 May-Sep.

Speaker's Corner, Hyde Park (Marble Arch Tube). If you need to get something off your chest, feel free to say your piece on a Sunday at the oldest free speech platform in the world.

Science Museum, Exhibition Rd (South Kensington Tube), T020 7942 4454, www.sciencemuseum.org.uk. It's interactive, it's massive, it's awesome and it's certainly not like any science lesson I ever attended!

Walk You miss so much on the Tube – take a stroll around Soho and its sex shops or walk over the Millennium Bridge and take in the South Bank and the London Eye.

British Museum, Gt Russell St (Holborn Tube), T020 73238000, www.thebritishmuseum.ac.uk. Home to the Elgin Marbles, Rosetta Stone and a whole host of antiquities, one of the best bits is having a cup of tea under the canopy of the Great Court. Amazing!

London

TURTLE

London skate spots: for surfers who like to roll

Richie Hopson, www.richiehopson.com, is one of the UK's top skate photographers. Based in London Richie has travelled the length and breadth of the UK shooting the world's best skaters. Here he gives the lowdown on the best skateparks in London.

Meanwhile Gardens, Elkstone Rd, London W9. Free to skate. The original 70s concrete bowl was demolished about four years ago and the site transformed into one of London's better but quirky concrete parks. This is not a street park, it's bowls with metal coping. The shallow end is a 3-ft capsule which hips down into a circular 4/5-ft section which again drops down and hips into the 5½-ft bottom bowl with pump bump sausage waiting to claim you on the way back up. The hips are extensions and are about 7-ft high. There is also a 6-ft death box grind bar on the bottom wall of the bowl.

Great fun to carve and slash with a really friendly local scene in the middle of a park. Bring beer to make more friends and in the summer a disposable barbecue.

BaySixty6, Acklam Rd, London W11. Pay to skate. Shop. Food. Lights. Formerly known as Playstation, the park is now sponsored by XBox and has been improved upon over the years. This park sits under the Westway Flyover and is one of London's few dry spots on a wet day. On the ramp side of things you will find a 10-ft vert ramp, 3½-ft 60-ft wide mini, super fast and whippy 6½-ft mini with

Tom Crowe at BaySixty6

Neil Kirby at Meanwhile Gardens Bowls

7-ft extensions. The rest of the park hosts a huge street area with everything you would expect and a bit more – rails, blocks, driveways, kickers, hips, vert wall etc. Friendly locals and always plenty of visitors and kids at the weekend.

South Bank, under the Royal Festival Hall, Waterloo. Free to skate. Lights (sometimes). This is the original London skate/meeting spot since the 70s boom days. Slowly being redeveloped and demolished. You can still get to skate the undercover flat banks for the time being or flip down the legendary 7 set.

Stockwell Skatepark, Stockwell Rd, Brixton, SW9, www.stockwellskatepark.com. Free. Street lighting. Sometimes known as Brixton Beach, this original 70s skate park was resurfaced about six or seven years ago now and has always had a really strong local scene. No lips here, just the flowing curves of mellow bowls and hips, a home made flat bar and maybe some makeshift quarters too. Huge amounts of fun whatever your ability. Also check out Kennington Bowl on Kennington Park Rd if you are in the area.

Meanwhile 2, Royal Oak, Nr Harrow Rd, London (Royal Oak Tube). Free to skate. Street lighting. Also kept dry under the Westway Flyover. Another 70s concrete construction. Like a pre-formed concrete ditch with no flat bottom about 40-ft long but divided by the legendary Gonz gap.

Locals have also built flat banks, quarters, manual pads etc in the adjacent flat land area. Great fun but be warned junkies share this space with the skaters.

Meanwhile Gardens

Meanwhile 2

Stockwell

South Bank

Funny nights out in London

Top London comedy agent, Claire King, represents some of the hottest new talent emerging in Britain. Here she recommends some top funny nights out:

For a guaranteed fantastic bill of top stand-up you can't go wrong with one of these two established venues. **Comedy Store**, 1a Oxendon St (Piccadilly Circus/Leicester Square Tube), www.thecomedystore.co.uk, and **Comedy Café**, 66/68 Rivington St, Shoreditch, T020 7739 5706, www.comedycafe.fsnet.co.uk.

If character comedy is your thing and you are lucky enough for your trip to coincide with a comedy season at **Ealing Live!** you can't miss this unique comedy show on the sound stage at **Ealing Studios**, Stage 5, Ealing Studios, Ealing Green, T020 8758 6655. Check out www.ealinglive.com for season info. **Soho Theatre**, 21 Dean St, T020 7287 5060, www.sohotheatre.com, also runs comedy seasons where you can see top acts performing their own one-hour shows.

For up-to-date information and top recommendations buy the weekly *Time Out* magazine – their comedy reviews and listings detail comedy nights all over London.

Eating

The world is your oyster when it comes to eating in the Big Smoke – this is but the cheap tip of the iceberg of centrally based eateries. **Malletti**, Noel St, just south of Oxford St, is an excellent Italian food bar with very limited seating (5 stools), £3.25 buys you a hot slice of excellent focaccia pizza or pasta. **Italian Grafitti**, Wardour St, Soho, is a relaxed, authentic Italian restaurant with generous stone-cooked pizzas and pasta dishes. Strangely intimate. **China China**, Gerrard St, China Town – the service is fairly abrupt but the food is great – try Singapore noodles, chicken in black bean sauce and an order of pak choi for 2, around £18 with a pot of tea. **Mildred's**,

Lexington St (near Oxford St), is recommended and a whole bag of wonderful contradictions – gorgeous but no-nonsense organic and vegetarian fare is served in relaxed yet upmarket café-style surroundings. It's in London and the prices are very reasonable – massive veggie burger with chilli jam and fat chips around £6. **Food For Thought**, Neal St, Covent Garden. Eat in or take away at this relaxed vegetarian deli-style café with tasty pieces around £5.

Getting out of London

Being trapped in London when your whole being is crying out for a surf can be a soul-destroying experience. Many surfers push thoughts of waves to the back of their minds, some never return to the fold. But the irony is that surfable waves are closer than you think. You don't have to race half crazed down the A303 towards Devon for a desperate weekend before late nighting it back to the smoke on the Sunday evening. "For any surfer trapped in London, desperate to get wet, your best bet is to watch for big old lows moving across Scotland and hopefully sending swell down the North Sea," says John Isaac, owner of **Revolver Surfboards** and a London escapee. "Norfolk in particular gets some fun little waves with its various reef/beach breaks and with prevailing southwest winds there can be a lot of fun here only two hours up the M11." Two hours. A couple of mates to share the petrol costs and you could be scoring 3-4 ft peaks at Cromer.

But what if you're south of the river? "If you're stuck in the southern part of the capital you can try Brighton," says John, "which after a good blow up the Channel can get waves – if not you can always rollerblade along the prom!!! (Although watch where you get changed in Brighton in January. That

THE GILL

Chris Griffiths hits the road

men's toilet may look warm and dry, but…!) The whole of the south coast from Kent's Joss Bay and Broadstairs through Ramsgate, Hastings, Camber, Eastbourne down to Littlehampton get waves, some of which get fun even. These spots are fickle and usually only last hours rather than days but keep an eye on reliable forecasting and you can score a day trip even by train."

One of the biggest helps in being a city surfer is the company of other city-incarcerated waveriders. A couple of ways to hook up with like-minded Londoners include: **Big Friday**, T020 7793 1417, www.bigfriday.com. Big Friday's ethos is to help Londoners escape the city and make the most of their weekends. They run regular summer and autumn trips to North Devon and Cornwall for beginners through to advanced. You can opt for simple surf bus transport – return to Cornwall from £69 – through to a full 'Big Weekend' experience – transport, 2 nights dinner B&B in their surf chalet, transport to the breaks, afternoon tea plus lessons and equipment if required – around £250. They also run Surf Diva girls only trips. **Christian Surfers**, www.christiansurfers.org. This organization has chapters right across the globe, including contacts in London. **Surfers Against Sewage** Joining SAS not only helps to save the environment, it may help save your sanity too with regional contacts across the country including East Anglia and Brighton.

If you just need to get away and want to explore more of what Europe has to offer, check out Footprint *Surfing Europe*, www.footprintbooks.com, covering Ireland, Britain, France, Spain, Portugal and Morocco. From London you can be just a few hours away from scoring some epic continental surf.

MARK LUMSDEN

Jason Duffy getting away from it all

⬤ **Top 5 Music Venues**

Producer Craig Gleghill has worked on top music programmes including The Pepsi Chart Show, T4, plus music videos for top acts. Here he recommends five of London's best music venues:

Carling Brixton Academy, Stockwell Rd (Brixton Tube), T020 7771 3000. Near Stockwell skatepark, this manages to juggle being a venue large enough to stage international bands without being a huge hanger like Wembley. Regular dance, hip-hop nights as well as acts like Beastie Boys, James Brown – in fact everyone who's anyone.

Astoria, 157 Charing Cross Rd (Tottenham Court Rd Tube), T020 7344 0044. Centrally located venue with wide range of quality bands of the calibre of Nine Inch Nails, Zeppelin tribute band Whole Lotta Led and Electric Six.

Mean Fiddler, 165 Charing Cross Rd (Tottenham Court Rd Tube), T0870 150 0044. Tight venue with rock, hip-hop and dance nights as well as live acts from Suicidal Tendencies to The Beat.

The Marquee, 1 Leicester Sq (Leicester Sq Tube), T0870 4446277. Legendary nightclub and venue for live bands ranging back to the days when The Who would trash their equipment on stage.

100 Club, 100 Oxford St (Tottenham Court Rd Tube), T0207 6360933. Serving up a mix of R'n'B, Jazz and Blues in a smoky basement with a small stage used by some musical legends. Catch some of the Jazz greats before they die.

London

Surf schools

Abersoch Offaxis, Johnny Robinson, Glanafon Garage, Abersoch, Gwynedd, Wales, T 07802915424 or 01758 713407, www.offaxis.co.uk.

Adventure Sports UK, Nickie Wilkes, Carnkie Farm House, Carnkie, Redruth, Cornwall, T01209 218962 or 07790 015397, www.adventuresportsuk.com.

Animal Surf Academy operated by Wavehunters, Andy Cameron, Wavehunters Office, Port Isaac, North Cornwall, T0781 5059890, www.wavehunters.co.uk.

Atlantic Pursuits, Sam Roberts, Priestcott Park, Kilkhampton, Bude, Cornwall, T01288 321765, doc.roberts@btinternet.com.

Atlantic Surf Seekers Woolacombe, Spencer Nasey, Sticklepath Hill, Barnstaple, N Devon, T07977 924588, www.surfseekers.co.uk.

Barefoot Surf School, Nigel Brown, Davids Hill, Georgeham, Devon, T01271 891231 or 07969410854, www.barefootsurf.com.

Big Blue Surf School, Jon Price, Little Barn, Mead Barn, Cottages, Welcome, Bude, Devon, T01288 331764, www.bigbluesurfschool.co.uk.

BSA Surf school, Baz Hall, Lusty Glaze Beach, Newquay, Cornwall, T01637 851487, www.nationalsurfingcentre.com.

Blue Wings Surf School, Martin Marney, Tower Road, Newquay, Cornwall, T01637 874445, mart@bluewings.fsnet.co.uk.

Bournemouth Surf School, Andy Joyce, Southbourne Coast Rd, Southbourne, Bournemouth, Dorset, T01202419901 or 07941508531, www.bournemouthsurfschool.co.uk.

Bournemouth Surfing Centre, Paul Clarke, Belle Vue Road, Southbourne, Bournemouth, Dorset, T01202 433544, www.bournemouth-surfing.co.uk.

Bude Surfing Experience, Scott Marshall, Grenville Centre, Belle Vue, Bude, Cornwall, T0870 7775111 or 07779117746, www.budesurfingexperience.co.uk.

Clan Surf Shop, Jamie Blair, Hyndland St, Glasgow, Scotland, T0141 3396523, www.clanskates.co.uk.

Cornwall Surf Academy, Shannon Hopkins, Pendarves Street, Tuckingmill, Cambourne, Cornwall, T0870 2406693 or 07866888382, www.cornwallsurfacademy.com.

Coast 2 Coast, Sam Christopherson, Dunbar, Scotland, T07971 990361, www.c2cadventure.com.

Discovery Surf School, Martin Connolly, Newnham Road, Plympton, Plymouth, Devon, T07813 639622, www.discoverysurf.com.

Dolphin Surf School, Mark Thake, Trewinda Lodge, Eliot Gardens, Newquay, Cornwall, T01637 873707 or 07974629381, www.surfschool.co.uk.

Dreamtime Surf Sessions, Richard King, Liskey Hill, Perranporth, Cornwall, T01872 573163, www.dreamtimesurf.co.uk.

Durtz Surf School, Stuart Valentine, Strand Road, Portstewart, Co. Londonderry, Northern Ireland, T07904418865, www.benonebeach.co.uk.

Escape Surf School, Gerry Saunders, The Escape, Mount Wise, Newquay, Cornwall. T01637 874585, www.escapesurfschool.co.uk.

Falmouth Surf School, Spencer Webb, Woodlane Close, Falmouth, Cornwall, 01326 212144, webbquayboy@aol.com.

Gower Surfing Development, Simon Jayham, 6, Slade Road, Newton, Swansea, T01792 360370, www.gowersurfing.com.

Gwithian Academy of Surfing, Tyson Greenaway, Prosper Hill, Gwithian, Cornwall, T01736 755493 or 07905 630345, www.surfacademy.co.uk.

Harlyn Surf School, Chris Rea, Padstow, Cornwall, T01841 533076, www.harlynsurfschool.co.uk.

Hibiscus Surf School, Frances Carter, Farfield Place, Newquay, Cornwall, T01637 879374, www.hibiscussurfschool.co.uk.

Hunter Surf School, Pete Oram, West Road, Woolacombe, Devon, T01271 871061, www.hunter-boardwear.com.

KingSurf, Luke Farren, Mawgen Porth, Newquay, Cornwall, T01637 860091, www.kingsurf.co.uk.

Lets Go Surf, Tracey Boxall, Pennard Road, Kittle, Gower, Wales, T01792 234073.

Momentum Surf Shop, Martin McQueenie, Dunbar High Stt, Scotland, T01368 869810, www.momentumsurf.com.

National Surfing Centre, Baz Hall, International Surfing Centre, Fistral Beach, Newquay, Cornwall, TR7 1HY, T01637 850737, www.nationalsurfingcentre.com.

Nick Thorn Surf Coaching, Nick Thorn, South Street, Woolacombe, Devon, EX34 7BB, T01271 871337 or 07812768715, www.nickthorn.com.

Ocean Jack, Stuart Clarke, Garden Ave, Bexley Heath, Kent, DA7 4LH, T 07732186030 or 0208 3039223, oceanjacklimited@yahoo.co.uk, www.oceanjack.com.

Outdoor Adventure, Richard Gill, Widemouth Bay, Bude, Cornwall, T01288 361312, www.outdooradventure.co.uk.

Outer Reef Surf School, Dean Gough, Maiden Wells, Pembrokeshire, SA71 5ET, T01646680070 or 07769903653, www.outerreefsurfschool.com.

Peak Surf Academy, Andy Rodnell, Redruth, Cornwall, T01209 210271, www.peaksurfacademy.co.uk.

PGL Beam House, Mark Parnham, Beam House, Torrington, Devon, T08700 551551, www.pgl.co.uk.

Point Breaks, Simon Twitchen, The Old Aerodrome, Chivenor, Braunton, Devon, T01271 817422 or 07776 148679, www.pointbreaks.com.

Portreath Surf School, Jon Walpole, Chynance, Portreath, Redruth, Cornwall, T01209 843502 or 07792078336, porthreathsurfschool@yahoo.co.uk.

Preseli Venture, Claire Carlile, Mathry, Haverfordwest, Pembrokeshire, SA62 5HN, T01348 837709, www.preseliventure.com.

Quiksilver/ Roxy Surf School, Grishka Roberts, The Boarding House, Headlands Road, Newquay, Cornwall, T01637 873258, www.theboardinghouse.co.uk.

Raven Surf School, Mike Raven, Crabhay Barn, Stratton, Bude, Cornwall, EX23 9BN, T01288 353693, www.ravensurf.co.uk.

Reef Surf School, Antony Rowett, Agar Rd, Newquay, Cornwall, T01637 879058, www.reefsurfschool.com.

Reeflex Surfing, Mark Finch, Stones Reef, Praa Sands, Penzance, Cornwall, T01736 762991.

Saltburn Surf Hire & Shop, Gary Rogers & Nick Noble, Garnet St, Saltburn by the Sea, Cleveland, T01287 209959/625321, www.saltburnsurf.co.uk.

Sennen Surfing Centre, David Muir, Sennen, Penzance, Cornwall, T01736 871227/871156, nerdsurf@hotmail.com.

Shore Surf School, Laurence Couch, Mount Pleasant, Hayle, St Ives Bay, Cornwall, 01736 755556, www.shoresurf.com.

Simon Tucker Surfing Academy, Simon Tucker, Rest Bay, Porthcawl, South Wales, 01656 772415 or 07815 289761, www.surfingexperience.com.

St. Ives Surf School, Alex Woodward, Porthmeor Beach, St. Ives, Cornwall, T01736 793366 or 07792261278.

Sunset Surf School, Eloise Taylor, Mount Hawke, Porthtowan, Cornwall, T01209 891699 or 07799525519, www.sunsetsurfschool.co.uk.

Surf South West, Darren Burrett, Croyde, Devon, T01271 890400, www.surfsouthwest.com.

Surf's Up & Polzeath Beach Surf School, Peter & Jane Craske, Kelsing, 21 Trenant Close, Polzeath, Cornwall, T01208 862003/862002, surfsup@saqnet.co.uk.

Surfing Croyde Bay, Alistair Poll, Hobbs Hill, Croyde, Devon, T01271 891200, www.surfingcroydebay.co.uk.

The English Surfing Federation School, Rob Barber, Esplanade Road, Newquay, Cornwall, T01637 851800, www.englishsurfschool.com.

Thurso Surf , Andy Bain, Thurso, Caithness, Scotland, T01847 841300, www.thursosurf.com.

TYF Adventure, Matt O'Brien, High Street, St. Davids, Pembrokeshire, Wales, T01437 721611, www.tyf.com.

Walking on Waves, Sarah Whiteley, Saunton, Braunton, Devon, T07786034403, www.walkingonwaves.co.uk.

Welsh Surfing Federation Surf School, Mike Steadman, The Croft, Llangennith, Swansea, T01792 386426, www.wsfsurfschool.co.uk.

West Coast Surf Shop, J. Waterfeild, Lon Pew Cei, Abersoch, Gwynedd, T01758 713067, www.westcoastsurf.co.uk.

West Coast Surfari, Pat Sweeny, Trebarwith Cresent, Newquay, Cornwall, T01637 876083 or 07866508618, www.westcoastsurfari.com.

Wight Water Adventure Watersports, Scott Gardner, Orchardleigh Rd, Shanklin, I.O.W, T01983 866269/404987, www.wightwaters.com.

Wild Diamond Surf , Suds, Ballevullin, Tiree, T07793 063849, www.surfschoolscotland.com.

Winter Brothers Surf School, Dean Winter, Headland Hotel, Newquay, Cornwall, T01637 879696, www.winterbrothers.com.

Directory

Quiksilver Boardriders Plymouth

53-55 Cornwall Street, City Centre, Plymouth

Surf culture meets a high street shopping experience with one of the largest Quiksilver stores in Europe. The first floor café undoubtedly serves the best coffee and chocolate cake in Plymouth.

Surfing Life

92-94 Cornwall Street, City Centre, Plymouth

Plymouth's Original Surf Store. A full range of short boards, longboards and body boards paired with a great range of wetsuits and accessories.

… established 2002 as an alternative to the mainstream clothing brand orientated boutique style surf shops … a real surf shop with one foot in the past and looking forward using more alternative shaped boards …

England: Southeast

hi life
299-301 High Street, Dorking, Surrey RH4 1RE
☎(01306) 881910

Serving the surfers of Surrey since 1991, we continue to stock probably the best range of quality surfwear in the area, together with wetsuits, boards and accessories.

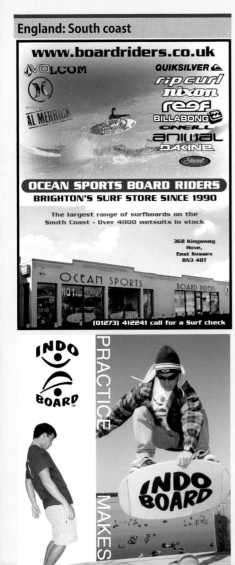

Scotland

Wild Diamond Surf School
Isle of Tiree
☎ Suds: 077930 63849
www.surfschoolscotland.co.uk

WINDSURFING
Isle of Tiree
KITESURFING

We teach surfing in the clean and sunny Hebridean Islands of Scotland. Best equipment including warm Snugg wetsuits, soft 'Bullet' boards for beginners and custom boards for advanced. BSA Qualified.

Liquid Productions
Deneside, Horncliffe Mill, Berwick-upon-Tweed, TD15 2XT ☎(07939) 194880
Email: mark@liquidproductions.co.uk
www.liquidproductions.co.uk
Liquid Productions presents Cold Rush "a Scottish surfing experience". Surfing legends and UK chargers riding Scotlands hidden gems. DVD available online and in stores now.

Wales

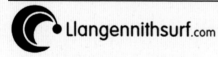

www.llangennithsurf.com
Dedicated surfing information and resources for Llangennith beach, on the Gower Peninsula, South Wales. Live surf reports, 7-day surf forecast, eyeball reports, Wave Buoy data feeds, swell & wind charts, tide times and local information. We've got this spot covered.

Langland Cove Guest House
4 Rotherslade Road, Langland
Swansea, SA3 4QN, Wales
☎(01792) 366003
gill@eurotelemail.net
We run an up market 5 bedroom (non-smoking) B&B, with two rooms that sleep 3 sharing. Next door is a self catering cottage sleeping up to 4. Situated a minutes walk down the hill from the multiple surf-breaks of Langland Bay. Best time to come for surf is Autumn, Winter and Spring. With 25 years of experience in this area I could send you to the best spots in the region on any given day. Party animals need not apply.

Tim Boal
Mentawai

Rider - Tim Boal - © Photo - Alex Laurel

Surfersvillage.com

- **Global Surf News**
- **Big Wave Events Directory**
- **Surf Reports & Surforecasts**
- **Worldwide Contests Register**

ATLANTIC · INDIAN · PACIFIC

Brochure: 0845 226 0007 online store: www.seventenths.com

Credits

Footprint credits

Editors: Laura Dixon, Patrick Dawson, Tim Jollands
Map editor: Robert Lunn
Publisher: Patrick Dawson
Editorial: Alan Murphy, Sophie Blacksell, Sarah Thorowgood, Claire Boobbyer, Felicity Laughton, Nicola Jones, Angus Dawson
Cartography: Sarah Sorensen, Robert Lunn, Claire Benison, Kevin Feeney
Design: Mytton Williams
Advertising: Debbie Wylde
Finance and administration: Sharon Hughes, Elizabeth Taylor, Lindsay Dytham

Photography credits

Front cover: Kirsten Prisk
Back cover: Demi Taylor
Inside images: Alf Alderson, Mark Baynes, Tangy Drew, Estpix, Paul Gill (The Gill), Chris Gregory, Chris Griffiths, Damon Hewlett, Chris Jeffrey, Gary Knight, Mark Lumsden, Gerrard McAuley, Al McKinnon, Stuart Norton, Roger Powley, Kirstin Prisk, Sam Robbins, Dennis Skelly, George Sohl, Turtle, Scott Wicking, Alex Williams, www.c2cadventure.com, www.sharkbait.com, www.eastcoast surf.co.uk, www.nosurfinbrighton.tk. Our thanks also go to Animal, who provided the images of Alan Stokes on pages 14 and 30 and of Josh Knowles on page 26, and to O'Neill, who provided the image of Sam Lamiroy on page 29.

Print

Manufactured in Italy by Printer Trento
Pulp from sustainable forests

 This product includes mapping data licensed from Ordnance Survey® with the permission of the Controller of Her Majesty's Stationery Office © Crown Copyright. All rights reserved. Licence number 100027877.

Footprint feedback

We try very hard to make each Footprint guide as up to date as possible but, of course, things always change. To let us know about your experiences – good, bad or ugly – go to www.footprintbooks.com and send in your comments.

Publishing information

Footprint Surfing Britain
1st edition
© Footprint Handbooks Ltd
April 2005

ISBN 1 904777 40 6
CIP DATA: A catalogue record for this book is available from the British Library

® Footprint Handbooks and the Footprint mark are a registered trademark of Footprint Handbooks Ltd

Published by Footprint

6 Riverside Court
Lower Bristol Road
Bath BA2 3DZ, UK
T +44 (0)1225 469141
F +44 (0)1225 469461
discover@footprintbooks.com
www.footprintbooks.com

Distributed in the USA by

Publishers Group West

Index